PROBLEM-BASED LEARNING FOR TEACHERS, GRADES K–8

DANIEL L. KAIN

Northern Arizona University

Boston   New York   San Francisco
Mexico City   Montreal   Toronto   London   Madrid   Munich   Paris
Hong Kong   Singapore   Tokyo   Cape Town   Sydney

Series Editor: *Traci Mueller*
Editorial Assistant: *Krista E. Price*
Marketing Manager: *Elizabeth Fogarty*
Editorial-Production Service: *Omegatype Typography, Inc.*
Manufacturing Buyer: *Andrew Turso*
Composition and Prepress Buyer: *Linda Cox*
Cover Administrator: *Kristina Mose-Libon*
Electronic Composition: *Omegatype Typography, Inc.*

For related titles and support materials, visit our online catalog at www.ablongman.com.

Between the time Website information is gathered and then published, some sites may have closed. Also, the transcription of URLs can result in unintended typographical errors. The publisher would appreciate notification where these occur so that they may be corrected in subsequent editions.

Library of Congress Cataloging-in-Publication Data

Kain, Daniel L.
    Problem-based learning for teachers, grades K–8 / Daniel L. Kain.
      p. cm.
    Includes bibliographical references and index.
    ISBN 0-205-33921-2 (alk. paper)
    1. Problem-based learning—Handbooks, manuals, etc. 2. Elementary school teaching—Handbooks, manuals, etc. 3. Middle school teaching—Handbooks, manuals, etc. I. Title.

LB1027.42 .K35 2003
371.39—dc21

2002025556

Printed in the United States of America

10 9 8 7 6 5 4 3 2 1   07 06 05 04 03 02

CONTENTS

CHAPTER ONE

Why Problem-Based Learning for Future Teachers?   1

The chapter introduces the PBL model of learning and provides a justification for using this model to educate teachers.

CHAPTER TWO

Getting Ready for the Problem-Based Learning Experience   12

Learning in a new way can be awkward and uncomfortable. This chapter provides guidance for learners as they adjust to a new approach to learning.

PART II   PROBLEMS FROM TEACHERS' WORK   27

CHAPTER THREE

What Should We Do about Andy?   27

Examines a controversial plan to develop an individualized education plan for a middle school student. Is his problem a disability or misbehavior?

CHAPTER FOUR

Whose Discipline Problem Is This?   **45**

A principal in a rural 6–12 school calls for a single classroom discipline system throughout the school. Is this something teachers can support?

CHAPTER FIVE

Math Makes Tracks   **64**

Middle school teachers, to accommodate a principal's request to reduce staff, present a plan to eliminate the gifted math classes. The parents rebel. Should the plan stand?

CHAPTER SIX

Multigrades or Migraines?   86

An elementary principal decides it's time to take her school to the next level by making all classes multigrade. Is this a defensible change for all classes?

CHAPTER SEVEN

Raise Those Scores!   106

A superintendent decides to put the school system on the map by getting superb standardized test scores. How? By using all professional development money for a commercial test-prep program. What will this mean?

CHAPTER EIGHT

Just the Facts, Please!   125

Should every class in the school be taught with constructivist methods? A principal calls for a constructive controversy procedure to investigate this question.

CHAPTER NINE

Retention or Pretension?   144

An innovative school's policy on retention in grade is unclear, but the test case is now available. Does retaining a child serve his needs?

CHAPTER TEN

Hyper Kid, Hyper Mom, Hyper Teacher— Who's Hyper?   164

The question of dealing with a child who may have attention deficit hyperactivity disorder (ADHD) comes to a group of teachers. What is the role of medication and classroom instruction?

CHAPTER ELEVEN

Bully Troubles, or "Boys will be Boys"?   182

An elementary school without a policy on bullying may have a problem. This PBL experience places teachers in the position to consider such a policy.

CHAPTER TWELVE

Who Says No to a Book?   199

A teacher's reading selection stirs up controversy in the community. Should she continue teaching this particular book?

PART III   MOVING PBL TO YOUR CLASSROOM   214

CHAPTER THIRTEEN
Reflecting on Problem-Based Learning   214

This chapter guides your reflection on PBL and your experience as a learner in this particular model.

CHAPTER FOURTEEN
Using PBL in Your Classroom   225

The final chapter takes you through the process of developing a PBL unit for use in your classroom.

PREFACE

This text may be unique among the texts you encounter in your professional education. For one thing, it's doubtful that you'll make your way through this text in the order it has been set out. It's more likely that your instructor will guide you to read part of a chapter, work with it, return to finish the chapter, and then maybe skip three chapters for your next work. That's the sort of flexibility I hope instructors will exercise and students will tolerate. But even more unusual, this is a textbook that, with a few exceptions, *doesn't have the answers in it.* I don't mean answers to practice problems, such as you find in the back of a math text. I mean **answers.** The whole purpose of this text is to provide you with a framework to learn how to raise questions about issues that are important to your work as a teacher, and then to help you learn how to go about finding those answers. If the book is successful, it will lead you to finding answers, but more importantly, to a disposition to continue learning throughout your professional life.

And one more thing. This book may lead you into some uncomfortable new territory, especially if you fit well with the way schools currently operate. It is my hope that your experience as a learner through the problems in this text will help you to see another way of organizing learning for the students with whom you work. Just as I am confident that good teachers can be trusted to seek answers, I am confident that your students, with a bit of guidance, can be trusted to seek answers. It strikes me that the essence of true learning is not only memorizing facts—which happens to us all as we use them—but learning how to raise questions and seek good answers.

HOW TO USE THIS TEXT

Several features of this text demand a bit of explanation. You will find the book divided into three parts. Part I provides introductory information about problem-based learning (PBL). The first chapter explains what is generally meant by PBL, with an eye to the recent history of the model. Chapter 2 provides coaching for you on how to get the most out of your PBL experience.

Part II of the text holds the core of what this book is about. In this section, you will encounter a series of problems that are similar to what you might face as a classroom teacher (the focus of each problem is in the table of contents). For instance, Chapter 7, "Raise Those Scores," leads you to investigate what might happen when a school district decides to devote all its energy to improving standardized test scores, regardless of the consequences to programs, personnel, or learning. You will be asked to assume the perspective of a relatively new teacher in the lowest performing school in the district. After examining what the superintendent is calling for in the schools, you will address the school board as part of a team to endorse, modify, or oppose the superintendent's test-prep plan.

Each chapter follows a similar pattern. A brief introduction sets the context for the general issue represented in the case. Although the particulars of each problem are built around unique situations, the issues at stake span across most schools. Following the introduction, each chapter lays out the particulars of the problem (for example, details about policy or the community) and the basic parameters of the solution you will be asked to come up with. These parameters will be somewhat loose, because—*and here's an asset of PBL*—you may define the problem in a manner significantly different from some of your colleagues. Where one group sees a problem with ineffective school leadership, another sees a problem with curricular organization and assessment.

A series of problem documents comes next in each chapter. These documents are modeled after the sorts of documents teachers encounter in their work. Some of the documents will look familiar to you, as in the case of a newspaper editorial having a go at educators. Other documents may seem strange, almost in need of translation. You will find, for example, a psychoeducational assessment of a student in the problem documents for Chapter 3. You may find that this assessment becomes clear after a couple of readings. You may find you need to seek some help from others to understand it. In either case, you will profit from wrestling with this sort of document in a safe learning environment rather than seeing such an assessment for the first time when you are contributing to a decision that will have a significant impact on a child's future.

My intent for you is to stop reading the chapter after you have examined the problem documents. Work through the problem, propose a solution, discuss the experience with your peers, and then return to finish the chapter. Each chapter includes guides to reflection on some of the issues that may have been raised in your solving of the problems. I know that no group will raise all the questions I have included in reflection, and I know that nearly every group will raise questions I had not anticipated. The main focus of a problem may be retaining a child in grade (Chapter 9), but homelessness emerges as a key issue for one group while another group becomes fascinated with school structures. Such is the nature of PBL.

Each chapter concludes with a set of discussion questions and an annotated list of further readings. Clearly, no such list can be exhaustive. As I've worked with these problems and my students, they always find even better readings than the ones I've collected for them. You will, too, if you look. But I've given you a starting point.

As I indicated earlier, your instructor will guide you to the problems she or he finds most productive for your learning experience. The problems in Part II are not placed in a sequence that needs to be respected. If you do Chapter 7 before Chapter 6, that's fine. In fact, this text works best when it is seen as part of a whole program of teacher education (pre-service or graduate) rather than the textbook for a single course. Some problems focus on student characteristics and needs, which suggests one course, while others focus on policy, school structures, or curriculum. Thus, using the text throughout a program reinforces the method of learning (PBL) while allowing you to explore many potential difficulties you may face in your career.

Part III concludes the book in two chapters. Although each problem chapter asks you to reflect on issues in the problem, the first chapter in Part III asks you to reflect more specifically on how you learn in this model and what you have learned about yourself. The final chapter guides you through the process of creating your own PBL unit. Some people think it is necessary to go through this process before participating in PBL activities, and they recommended that I put this chapter up front. In working with many students from middle school to graduate school, I have found that students have the greatest success when I immerse them in several problems before I ask them to try to create problems of their own. For that reason, I have left the chapter at the end of the book. However, I encourage you to glance at this chapter whenever you feel it would be of most help. The chapter reveals how I create problems as a means to encourage you to create problems of your own. Ultimately, I am hoping that your experience with PBL will lead you to create such learning experiences for your students.

PREVIEW

> *When you heard you would be teaching a third-grade class at a local elementary school, you devoted your summer to making sure you would be ready. Building on the research you were exposed to at a local university, you created a plan for a classroom characterized by cooperation and creativity. In fact, you designed a class in which cooperative learning would be the central organizing feature.*
>
> *The day before the students were to arrive, a day you were devoting to completing the final touches of an attractive classroom, the counselor came by to inform you that you would have one additional student in your class. This student is what the counselor termed a "highly-functioning" autistic boy. The only other thing the counselor mentioned was that the boy did fairly well in school as long as he was in structured, independent work, but he was a "disaster" in groups.*

What should you do? What does it mean to have a child with autism in class? And what about all those plans you had made for a cooperative learning classroom? Who might you turn to for help? What do other teachers do in such situations? What resources are there for you? Ultimately, how will you adapt your plans, your activities, your vision of the classroom to this new reality? *Or should you?*

In determining how you would adapt to this situation, you are at the beginning of a problem-based learning experience. You are also at the edges of what it means to be a teacher—where you continually confront new situations with less information than you would like, situations that demand that you consider possibilities, inquire about facts, and come to decisions about what is the best solution. Welcome.

ACKNOWLEDGMENTS

I wish to thank a number of people for their assistance with this project. Dr. Mary McLellan, Dr. Gretchen McAllister, and Russell Randall reviewed problems or portions of problems included here. Dr. Pat Hays and Dr. Peggy Raines experimented with problems to assist in their refinement. Also, I appreciate the comments of the reviewers: Marie Holbien, State University of West Georgia; Marc Mahlios, University of Kansas; Debra Pitton, Gustavus Adolphus College; and JoAnne Welch, University of Louisiana at Monroe. Traci Mueller provided helpful editorial assistance. And above all, I wish to thank Kerry Olson Kain for her assistance throughout.

CHAPTER ONE

WHY PROBLEM-BASED LEARNING FOR FUTURE TEACHERS?

Teachers work. Teachers work hard to accomplish the complex goals they have for their students. Teachers work with a variety of pressures on them from all directions, and if anyone were to enter the profession with a naive notion that teachers' work is simply standing in front of a class and explaining ideas, the system would shock them sorely.

Of course, teachers do stand in front of the class to explain important ideas, and good teachers use a host of other teaching models and techniques to help their children succeed. The process of becoming an effective teacher involves a negotiation among all the responsibilities that await you when you face those first days in an empty classroom, pondering how you'll greet the children entrusted to you. *What do I do about these classroom walls? How do I organize a curriculum? What about all those activities I have to arrange and all the materials? What's a fair way to grade these children? How about special needs and non-English speakers and dealing with parents and all the rest?* It's overwhelming at times. And that's before you consider the committee work for selecting and installing new playground equipment and another committee to decide about changing the spelling program and another to work with the PTA to establish the "grandparents in the classroom program" and another to. . . . You get the idea.

Teachers' work goes well beyond making a lesson plan—though it always also involves making lesson plans that move your students toward greater skills and understandings. This book is designed to help you at two levels on your journey to becoming the best teacher you can be. First, the book will guide you as a learner in one of the most powerful means of coming to understanding: problem-based learning (PBL). Your experience as a learner will help you to empathize with the students you face and provide you with insight about how to use the teaching/learning technique effectively. Second, the book will focus your attention on some of the other complex issues that constitute teachers' work. You will have an opportunity to address some of the problems that may await you in your job—but in the relative safety of a community of learners.

WHAT IS PBL?

Problem-based learning is not new. In a sense, informal education has always incorporated the essential elements of PBL: A person encounters a puzzling situation, formulates some understanding of what might need fixing, gathers information, and tries out a solution. I imagine early farmers did this when they noticed the eastern portion of a crop flourishing while the section west of the stream was struggling. *What could be wrong? Is it the soil? the water? the sunlight? the seed? What are other farmers doing? What if I plant this section later in the season?* At a more formal level, PBL has roots in the "project method" of William Kilpatrick (1918). Kilpatrick argued that students don't so much need to be provided with answers as with experiences in learning to pose the questions and to work out solutions. He gave a wonderful illustration in response to his critics. Someone correctly observed that Kilpatrick's method would have children rediscover what we already know well—for example, how to grow corn. He responded that if it is corn we want, then the criticism is fine. But if it is children we want to grow, not corn, then we need to let them discover how to solve the corn-growing problem themselves.

There are important differences between "project-based learning" (Wolk, 1994) and problem-based learning, which we will address later. However, it is worth knowing that the PBL approach to educating children has a long tradition in American education. Moreover, this tradition has focused on the importance of connecting students' interests with the real-world problems they encounter. John Dewey (1938/1963), a progressive educator, advocated that we organize learning around experiences, though he clarified that not all experiences are educative. He helped us understand that an experience is "educative" if it helps young people grow in positive ways. The task of the educator is to match the needs and capacities of the learner with the subject matter in meaningful experiences. The subject areas of the curriculum, he argued, should connect to "ordinary life-experience," and PBL does just that.

In a problem-based learning experience, students encounter carefully selected, but ill-structured, problems *before* they experience any instruction in the particular focus area (Bridges & Hallinger, 1992). The problem becomes the vehicle for learning. Motivation to learn is generally high because of the shift in focus: Instead of doing school work for the sake of school, the children attack real problems and the learning is embedded in solving those problems. Linda Torp and Sara Sage (1998) record an example of young students investigating the reasons why their principal's flower garden was not healthy. Students learned investigation skills (Internet, interviewing, reading), communication skills, perseverance, agricultural/botanical principles, and so on. In addition, the students were excited about what they were doing.

A basic version of PBL, which will be elaborated in the next chapter, is as follows. Students encounter a problem situation. They inquire into the problem situation using a simple three-part structure (Figure 1.1). They ask, what do we know, what do we need to know, and how will we find out (Stepien & Gallagher, 1993). As they cycle through this inquiry process, teachers coach the students on how to

FIGURE 1.1   Basic Structure of Inquiry

What do we know?

↓

What do we need to know?

↓

How can we find it out?

Source: Based on Stepien & Gallagher, 1993.

ask questions and where to seek information. Ultimately, the students present a solution to the problem in an "authentic" context—if not the real thing, then a close approximation.

Project-Based Learning versus Problem-Based Learning

How does PBL differ from project-based learning? It is a matter of focus. The project-based learning experience focuses on an outcome or product, which, though it will vary from student to student, has essentially the same characteristics. Creating a display of an insect collection would be an example of project-based learning. Each student would arrange the display differently, perhaps including different insects. But the basic projects would be similar, and the learning process from the start would focus on the product (project). In contrast, problem-based learning focuses on the process of inquiry. Instead of starting with instructions for building an insect display, a PBL experience might start with a concern that there appear to be a lot more insects in the area than there had been. Students would investigate this puzzling situation, and perhaps some would decide to collect specimens (a project) in their investigation. Some students would focus on changes in the ecosystem, while others might highlight changes in human practices nearby. Some might conclude that the problem is not insects at all, but the increasing insect population is merely a symptom of a problem with a bird migration route. In short, while both project-based learning and problem-based learning provide engaging opportunities for children to learn, the focus on what one learns in each is different.

Case Study versus Problem-Based Learning

Problem-based learning has similarities, also, to the case study method. Indeed, the teacher education program developed at the University of Colorado, Boulder, in the mid-1980s was built around a position midway between the elaborate case studies from the Harvard Business School and the brief medical problem cases from McMaster University (Kraft & Haas, 1989). Case studies have been popular in many professional education programs, including teacher education. Numerous collections of cases appear each year.

In fact, many people view PBL as a version of the case study method. Let me offer a distinction. For the most part, case studies are presented as narratives, sometimes as brief as a paragraph, sometimes as long as a book chapter. Traditionally, students read and reflect on a case study, often writing responses, before engaging in a discussion with tutors and peers. The case study authors frequently include discussion questions to focus the learner's attention, but the centerpiece of learning is the discussion itself. In contrast, the PBL approach as presented here provides the learners with a series of artifacts that are not collapsed into a narrative summary. Learners must examine the documents, determine the nature of the problem, and propose an actual solution. Following this, a discussion similar to the case study discussion ensues.

Brief History of PBL in Professional Education

Some people might contend that learning to be a teacher is too important to trust to PBL. For such critics, the popularity of PBL in other professional education programs may be worth consideration. In the late 1960s, medical education at McMaster University and Case Western Reserve (Barrows, 1996) began using PBL to educate future physicians. The technique has been applied to the education of architects, social workers, managers, economists, lawyers (Boud & Feletti, 1991), and educational administrators (Bridges & Hallinger, 1992, 1995), among others. Those charged with educating professionals have found PBL to be effective in allowing learners to assume the role of problem-solvers in areas relevant to their studies and to their future work.

How successful has this approach been? More research comes in all the time, but it seems that we do know a few things. Bridges (1991) reports that his students—school administrators—had superior attitudes and application of knowledge through PBL. Problem-based learning improves the diagnostic skills of medical students (Schmidt et al., 1995), and increases students' ability to retain and apply knowledge (Albanese & Mitchell, 1993; Norman & Schmidt, 1992). A longitudinal study of students in the professions of business, marketing, and nursing at Alverno College indicated that PBL enhanced the problem-solving skills graduates brought to their professions (O'Brien, Matlock, Loacker, & Wutzdorff, 1991). Woods (1996), who helped establish the PBL approach for a school of chemical engineering, maintains that PBL is superior to conventional instruction in every respect. Barrows (1996), in arguing that conventional instruction inhibits or destroys clinical reasoning abilities in students, suggests that PBL may avert some of the destructive tendencies of other forms of instruction. Hmelo's (1998) longitudinal comparison of PBL and non-PBL students in medical schools found evidence that PBL students used scientific concepts and effective reasoning better than non-PBL students. She concluded that the PBL curriculum moved students "along the path to novice physician" more rapidly than the non-PBL curriculum (p. 202).

The Use of PBL in Today's Schools

In recent years, problem-based learning has been promoted by a number of scholars and practitioners for use in the public schools (Arends, 1997; Delisle, 1997; Fogarty, 1997; Glasgow, 1997; Jones, Rasmussen, & Moffitt, 1997; Krynock & Robb, 1999; Savoie & Hughes, 1994; Stepien & Gallagher, 1993; Stepien, Senn, & Stepien, 2000; Torp & Sage, 1998; Wiggins & McTighe, 1998). The Illinois Math and Science Academy incorporates the technique. There is a Center for Problem-Based Learning, with a website (www.imsa.edu/center/cpbl/cpbl.html). Indeed, many schools are incorporating the practice.

The research into the effects of PBL on learning in the public schools is still emerging. However, initial results are encouraging. In his action research study of PBL in a biochemistry course, Richard Dods (1997) found that students acquired content knowledge at about an equal rate through PBL as through traditional lectures, though the students retained more of the information in the PBL approach. Also, the depth of understanding was greater in the PBL condition. This finding is similar to Gallagher and Stepien's (1996) analysis, showing that students in the PBL model did as well on multiple-choice tests as students in the traditional model, with better depth of understanding.

Increasingly, educators are realizing the benefits of PBL as a means to help students become thinkers, rather than passive recipients of information. Martin Haberman (1991) reports seeing this sign posted over a high school's main entrance: "We dispense knowledge. Bring your own container." Such a statement stands in stark contrast to what a PBL school would use for a motto. Students acquire information, yes, but in a context where they are seeing the application of that knowledge and its relevance to their own lives.

In addition, students can become better at problem-solving in general (Gallagher, Rosenthal, & Stepien, 1992) through PBL, and the demands of an information-rich world call for better problem solvers. The process of solving problems encourages a number of important dispositions in students:

- They become *collaborative learners,* capable of working together to solve problems.
- They learn *critical thinking skills,* such as problem identification.
- They *apply knowledge* and connect to prior learning.
- They realize the *relevance* of their learning experiences.
- They learn to *assume responsibility* for their own learning.
- Over time, they become more *self-directed learners.*

The idea of students becoming self-directed learners is particularly appealing. For too many students, the move through school is a bland repetition of mind-numbing sameness, with little to engage their curiosity. Seymour B. Sarason (1998) offers an inspiring notion when he describes what he would like schools to provide children: *"I would want all children to have at least the same level and quality of curiosity and motivation to learn and explore that they had when they began schooling"* (p. 69, original emphasis). Given that PBL has a record of success in sparking such curiosity and motivation, it is well worth considering as another tool to engage students.

PBL AND LEARNING TO TEACH

By experiencing PBL firsthand, you will be better prepared to become an instructional leader in your school. Working through the problems in this book will assist you in learning the features of a good problem. For example, you will see how different kinds of documents and artifacts can help make learning more relevant to the lives of students. You will witness from the inside the sorts of group considerations you will want to bear in mind as you coach (Stepien & Gallagher, 1993) your own students through the learning process. At one level, then, your experience in this process becomes a model for how you might help your own students. But there is more. . . .

PBL and Becoming a Professional

The problems you will address as you experience PBL through this book are not what most people think of as teaching issues. Yet they are the essence of becoming a professional. Beyond the teaching of reading and math and science and the rest, teachers face a host of issues that come under the umbrella of *occupational realities* of teaching (Pellegrin, 1976). All the business surrounding the job of teaching—the business of dealing with other adults and setting policies and making decisions— forms a crucial part of the occupational world of teachers, right from the start of their careers.

Richard Arends (1997) writes about the "two big jobs" of teaching. These are the interactive aspects and the leadership aspects of teaching. Interactive aspects include what most people think of as teaching: explaining ideas, guiding students in practice, showing films, and so on. The leadership aspects include planning the lessons, managing the classroom, and assessing student progress. But there's another part to this job, as any practicing teacher can attest, and it's deserving of the label the "third big job of teaching." This third job involves the broader working world of being a professional educator.

In general, teachers-in-training focus primarily on the instructional components of the teacher's work world—the interactive and leadership aspects. They are often left to discover the other parts of their work in practice. However, the "third big job" deserves attention. Consider an analogy. To prepare for a long backpacking trip, hikers train their muscles through simulations of the kind of walking they will be doing. They prepare their shoulders to be able to endure the pressure of the packs. But they also carefully plan their routes and the materials they will lug with them. Even though they will be walking, mainly, they need to be prepared for the other aspects of the experience. So, too, though teachers mainly teach, there are other aspects of the job that require careful attention in the preparation stage and systematic reflection on the job. The problems you will address in this book are designed to help prepare you to deal with the complexities of teachers' work. That said, you should know that most problems you will face in your career will bear similarities to what you face in this safe practice arena. You will want to hone the skills of collaboration, inquiry, and problem solving so that you can be a fully-rounded, effective member of the faculty of your school.

Even more important, the problems you will consider here help to move you to the position of being an architect and builder of a positive school environment. Not only will you consider issues surrounding the occupation of teaching—from the viewpoint of an active participant in conversations to make the place better— but you will also begin to develop that habit of inquiry that promises to keep the profession stimulating to you. Sarason (1998) recounts a story about trying (vainly) to beat a dead horse into action, and then he writes, "Schools are to their inhabitants uninteresting, unstimulating, impersonal places where respect for individuality is rarely found—or even possible. Contexts for productive learning do not exist for teachers. *When those contexts do not exist for teachers, teachers cannot create and sustain those contexts for students*" (p. 13, original emphasis). Perhaps a focus on teachers as learners can help to make the context of schools more stimulating for everyone.

An Alternative View of Coming to Know

In their essay on cognitive apprenticeships, Collins, Brown, and Newman (1989) focus on learning to read, write, and do mathematics. However, many of the principles they describe present a useful way of thinking about developing as a professional educator. Collins, Brown, and Newman criticize traditional education for its narrow focus on conceptual and factual knowledge, with little attention given to how experts actually *use* knowledge. By failing to place knowledge in the context of its uses, educators doom the learners to acquiring inert facts. The traditional apprenticeship, they argue, provides an excellent context for understanding; there the learner could observe a master, be coached as he or she practiced, then have the master's presence fade into the background until it was needed in another new or troubling situation.

Most of the learning that goes on in schools is not the same as a traditional apprenticeship, especially when that knowledge is not external and observable. Still, this apprenticeship model is an effective way to learn to think like experts, to solve the problems that experts solve. In preparing to become a teacher, there are many facts and concepts a person will need to master. However, learning to think like a teacher is more in line with a cognitive apprenticeship than memorizing information from a textbook. Much of the cognitive apprenticeship is carried out in the student teaching or intern relationship, especially if the mentor teacher deliberately talks through her or his thinking about actions. But more can be done for this cognitive apprenticeship even before student teaching—or after the first few years of teaching. The use of a problem-based learning approach to professional education and graduate education allows teachers to build together a "culture of expert practice" where learners articulate the elements of problem solving. Problem-based learning also helps establish "situated learning," which is a learning environment where "students carry out tasks and solve problems in an environment that reflects the multiple uses to which their knowledge will be put in the future" (Collins et al., 1989, p. 487). Interactions with your instructor allow you to see how an expert goes about solving problems. Thus, the chief elements of coming to know through a cognitive apprenticeship are in place through problem-based learning.

A WORD ON MAGIC PILLS

This text offers an immersion into a form of learning that has proven to be engaging and effective for many learners. Any given individual may find it personally challenging or frustrating. In fact, *most* learners will find it to be frustrating at first. As you will see in the next chapter, some learners have had to adjust to PBL much the same as people grieve the passing of loved ones: the loss of a comfortable means of learning is hard to handle.

This is, however, especially important for teachers to think about. Many of your learners will feel uncomfortable with one or another of the techniques you use. It never hurts to have a bit of empathy. More important, however, is the realization that this approach to learning is not offered to you as *the* solution to all teaching situations. It is not. There are places where a good demonstration or sending children off to learning centers will be far more effective for the purposes you have in mind. As educators, you must consider where your purposes and techniques match.

Indeed, PBL has its set of critics. Fenwick and Parsons (1997), for example, criticize PBL because it makes all of professional practice seem to be a matter of problem-solving. They worry that PBL creates an elite class of professionals, governed by rationality to the exclusion of other ways of knowing. Such criticism (and there are flaws in their critique, I think) reminds us that teaching is a complex act that requires openness to many means of accomplishing our goals. While PBL is not presented as a magic pill, neither is it a placebo or a poison. It is an important resource that responsible educators do well to experience.

THE PLAN FOR THIS TEXT

In the next chapter you will find a discussion of how you can best prepare for problem-based learning. One of the themes of that chapter, and this book as a whole, is that you can make much of your own education to the extent that you take responsibility to learn. You will need to be willing to pursue ideas and ask questions.

Part II of the text consists of a series of problem situations for you to experience. In each case, you will find a basic introduction to the broader issues, a few details to establish the context of the situation, a series of "problem documents," a reflection section, and some suggested further readings.

Part III of the text provides you with an opportunity to reflect on your experience (both what you've learned and how you learn) and to examine how you might create PBL experiences for your own students.

DISCUSSION QUESTIONS

Throughout this text you will find discussion questions to assist you in processing the information. Such questions are best used for discussion. That is, you ought to talk with your colleagues about these ideas so that you can experience the kind of growth in understanding that Britton (1993) and others attribute to the exchanging of ideas. In the context of discussion, you are able to articulate, adapt, and advance your ideas. Here are some starter questions.

1. Given the application of PBL to education in other professions, what does this mean for future teachers? Is it appropriate to borrow the training techniques used with future physicians, nurses, architects, and so on? What shift in focus is required of future teachers when teacher preparation moves from teaching techniques and content to issues related to professionalism? And what does this form of education offer for the continuing education of teachers?

2. Based on your emerging understanding of problem-based learning, how is PBL different from the traditional use of problems in education? Consider the problems at the end of the chapter in a math text, for example.

3. Advocates of PBL recognize that its use always involves a trade-off. Problem-based learning allows students to go into much greater depth when examining an issue, but the time required means that there is less "coverage." What do you see as the advantages and disadvantages of this trade-off for your own education or development as a teacher?

4. This chapter has hinted at a variety of non-instructional tasks teachers must face. At this point, what kinds of tasks do you think would fit in this category? Based on conversations with practicing teachers and other educators, what do you see as the surprising elements of being a teacher?

FURTHER READING

Delisle, R. (1997). *How to use problem-based learning in the classroom.* Alexandria, VA: ASCD.
> Delisle's book has a clear description of what PBL is, with a good rationale for using this approach. Such a rationale is helpful in getting parents to accept a teaching/learning technique that is not familiar to them. Delisle also includes several sample problems at the elementary level, including a third-grade social studies problem, a fifth-grade interdisciplinary problem, and a seventh-grade mathematics problem.

Stepien, W. J., Senn, P. R., & Stepien, W. C. (2000). *The Internet and problem-based learning: Developing solutions through the web.* Tucson, AZ: Zephyr.
> This book makes a link between PBL and using the Internet in the classroom. The authors provide a variety of units on interesting topics (ranging from an oil spill to fugitive slave laws), with reproducible classroom handouts. The problems are more appropriate for older children, but it is helpful to have a direct application of PBL to Internet use. Also, the model of PBL in their text provides a basis to build more locally-relevant experiences for your children.

Torp, L., & Sage, S. (1998). *Problems as possibilities: Problem-based learning for K–12 education.* Alexandria, VA: ASCD.
> Their book is an excellent, concise guide to how to do PBL in the classroom. Torp and Sage include numerous examples from the schools they have investigated, and they provide a

set of templates that will assist you in developing units. The book is a fine resource for your work in moving students to become inquirers.

WEB SITES

Center for Problem-Based Learning
www.imsa.edu/center/cpbl/cpbl.html
Features samples and relevant discussion.

Let's Get Real, Academic Competition
www.lgreal.org/index2.html
This site organizes a competition among K–12 students, giving them the opportunity to work on real problems posed by actual companies. The web site allows you to see some of the problems and solutions proposed.

Samford University School of Education, Problem-Based Learning
www.samford.edu/schools/education/pbl/pbl_index.html
Samford uses PBL prominently in its programs, and this web site provides background and samples of the procedure.

REFERENCES

Albanese, M. A., & Mitchell, S. (1993). Problem-based learning: A review of literature on its outcomes and implementation issues. *Academic Medicine, 68*(1), 52–81.

Arends, R. I. (1997). *Classroom instruction and management.* New York: McGraw-Hill.

Barrows, H. S. (1996). Problem-based learning in medicine and beyond: A brief overview. In L. Wilkerson & W. H. Gijselaers (Eds.), *Bringing problem-based learning to higher education: Theory and practice (New directions for teaching and learning No. 68)* (pp. 3–12). San Francisco: Jossey-Bass.

Boud, D., & Feletti, G. (Eds.). (1991). *The challenge of problem based learning.* New York: St. Martin's Press.

Bridges, E. (1991). *Problem-based learning in medical and managerial education.* Paper presented at the Cognition and School Conference of the National Center for Educational Leadership and the Ontario Institute for Studies in Education, September 26–27, Nashville, TN.

Bridges, E. M., & Hallinger, P. (1992). *Problem based learning for administrators.* Eugene, OR: ERIC Clearinghouse on Educational Management.

Bridges, E. M., & Hallinger, P. (1995). *Implementing problem based learning in leadership development.* Eugene, OR: ERIC Clearinghouse on Educational Management.

Britton, J. (1993). *Language and learning: The importance of speech in children's development* (2nd ed.). Portsmouth, NH: Boynton/Cook.

Collins, A., Brown, J. S., & Newman, S. E. (1989). Cognitive apprenticeship: Teaching the crafts of reading, writing, and mathematics. In L. B. Resnick (Ed.), *Knowing, learning, and instruction: Essays in honor of Robert Glaser* (pp. 453–494). Hillsdale, NJ: Lawrence Erlbaum Associates.

Delisle, R. (1997). *How to use problem-based learning in the classroom.* Alexandria, VA: Association for Supervision and Curriculum Development.

Dewey, J. (1938/1963). *Experience and education* (first published, 1938 ed.). New York: Collier Books.

Dods, R. F. (1997). An action research study of the effectiveness of problem-based learning in promoting the acquisition and retention of knowledge. *Journal for the Education of the Gifted, 20*(4), 423–437.

Fenwick, T. J., & Parsons, J. (1997). *A critical investigation of the problems with problem-based learning* (Report ED 409 272). Antigonish, Nova Scotia: St. Francis Xavier University.

Fogarty, R. (1997). *Problem-based learning and other curriculum models for the multiple intelligences classroom.* Arlington Heights, IL: IRI Skylight Training and Publishing.

Gallagher, S., Rosenthal, H., & Stepien, W. (1992). The effects of problem-based learning on problem-solving. *Gifted Child Quarterly, 36*(4), 195–200.

Gallagher, S. A., & Stepien, W. J. (1996). Content acquisition in problem-based learning: Depth versus breadth in American studies. *Journal for the Education of the Gifted, 19,* 257–275.

Glasgow, N. A. (1997). *New curriculum for new times: A guide to student-centered, problem-based learning.* Thousand Oaks, CA: Corwin.

Haberman, M. (1991). The pedagogy of poverty vs. good teaching. *Phi Delta Kappan, 73*(4), 290–294.

Hmelo, C. E. (1998). Problem-based learning: Effects on the early acquisition of cognitive skill in medicine. *The Journal of the Learning Sciences, 7*(2), 173–208.

Jones, B. F., Rasmussen, C. M., & Moffitt, M. C. (1997). *Real-life problem solving: A collaborative approach to interdisciplinary learning.* Washington, DC: American Psychological Association.

Kilpatrick, W. H. (1918). The project method. *Teachers College Record, 19*(4), 319–335.

Kraft, R. J., & Haas, J. D. (1989). PROBE: Problem-based teacher education at the University of Colorado, Boulder. In J. L. DeVitis & P. A. Sola (Eds.), *Building bridges for educational reform: New approaches to teacher education* (pp. 161–178). Ames, IA: Iowa State University.

Krynock, K., & Robb, L. (1999). Problem solved: How to coach cognition. *Educational Leadership, 57*(3), 29–32.

Norman, G. R., & Schmidt, H. G. (1992). The psychological basis of problem-based learning: A review of the evidence. *Academic Medicine, 67*(9), 557–565.

O'Brien, K., Matlock, M. G., Loacker, G., & Wutzdorff, A. (1991). Learning from the assessment of problem solving. In D. Boud & G. Feletti (Eds.), *The challenge of problem based learning* (pp. 274–284). New York: St. Martin's.

Pellegrin, R. J. (1976). Schools as work settings. In R. Dubin (Ed.), *Handbook of work, organization, and society* (pp. 343–374). Chicago: Rand McNally.

Sarason, S. B. (1998). *Political leadership and educational failure.* San Francisco: Jossey-Bass.

Savoie, J. M., & Hughes, A. S. (1994). Problem-based learning as classroom solution. *Educational Leadership, 52*(3), 54–57.

Schmidt, H., Machiels-Bongaerts, M., Hermans, H., ten Cate, O., Venekamp, R., & Boshuizen, H. (1995). *The development of diagnostic competence: A comparison between a problem-based, an integrated, and a conventional medical curriculum.* Paper presented at the Annual meeting of the American Educational Research Association, April 18–22, San Francisco, CA. (ERIC Document Reproduction Service No. 385190).

Stepien, W., & Gallagher, S. (1993). Problem-based learning: As authentic as it gets. *Educational Leadership, 50*(7), 25–28.

Stepien, W. J., Senn, P. R., & Stepien, W. C. (2000). *The Internet and problem-based learning: Developing solutions through the web.* Tucson, AZ: Zephyr.

Torp, L., & Sage, S. (1998). *Problems as possibilities: Problem-based learning for K–12 education.* Alexandria, VA: Association for Supervision and Curriculum Development.

Wiggins, G., & McTighe, J. (1998). *Understanding by design.* Alexandria, VA: Association for Supervision and Curriculum Development.

Wolk, S. (1994). Project-based learning: Pursuits with a purpose. *Educational Leadership, 52*(3), 42–45.

Woods, D. R. (1996). Problem-based learning for large classes in chemical engineering. In L. Wilkerson & W. H. Gijselaers (Eds.), *Bringing problem-based learning to higher education: Theory and practice (New directions for teaching and learning No. 68)* (pp. 91–99). San Francisco: Jossey-Bass.

CHAPTER TWO

GETTING READY FOR THE PROBLEM-BASED LEARNING EXPERIENCE

One of the mistakes we often make as teachers is to jump into learning experiences without adequate preparation for the vehicle of learning. Think about what probably seems a simple matter to you: driving a car with a manual transmission. You skim along the roads, talking with your passengers, adjusting the radio, deciding about which turns to take, slowing, shifting, speeding, deciding, talking, and so on. The actions associated with shifting gears are essentially invisible. But recall how complex the act of shifting gears seemed when you first learned it. For most people, just getting the sequence of steps and the delicate balance of footwork under control takes full concentration. Never mind all that other stuff that goes on while we drive. In the same way, learners just beginning a new means of acquiring understanding need to focus on the learning process before they can set out to use is as it is meant to be used. This chapter will help prepare you to learn in a new way.

LEARNING IN NEW WAYS

Think for a moment about the children you are currently teaching or hope to be teaching in the near future. Imagine coming into a school or classroom where the children have never been exposed to inquiry and investigation. Whatever science they have learned came to them through direct explanation. You decide that a good way to help them understand the concept of classification of plants would be to use the science workshop (Heuser, 2000), modeled after the familiar writing workshop (Atwell, 1998). Your main target for teaching is to move them to a deeper conceptual understanding of an important scientific principle, but you know that you can do that and more through this interactive workshop approach. However, before the children can succeed in understanding the concept, you must help them understand the format of learning. And it's quite likely that the first few times you use the new approach, your children will be a little confused and frustrated. You will be acutely aware that if you had used the traditional explanation method, the students would probably have caught on more quickly. Still, in the long run, you believe that their understanding will be deeper and more long-lasting if you use the workshop. In addition, you'll be able to use the workshop for a variety of other concepts once the children know how to take care of learning in this manner.

What's happening in this example is something like what Michael Fullan (1991) calls an "implementation dip" (p. 91). Whenever a school or system or teacher makes a change, things get worse before they get better. The teaching/learning technique is awkward for all parties. The immediate impulse is to abandon the new way of learning and return to the old ways, just as a tennis player wants to return to bad habits that worked rather than persevere through the difficulties of learning to serve correctly—even if that tennis player spent a bunch of money learning the right way to serve.

In fact, students themselves will sometimes pressure teachers to return to ineffective, but familiar, means of teaching if the newer models don't feel right (Haberman, 1991). A group of teachers and researchers looking into the experience of eighth-graders in a PBL format found that the shift to new forms of learning disrupted community expectations and created student anxieties (Sage, Krynock, & Robb, 2000), almost as though the teachers were changing the rules of the (school) game after the students had already figured it out. As Sage, Krynock, and Robb put it, "Students struggled with the work inherent in their new role as active learners. They were, by the eighth grade, well versed in the expectations of what they considered school to be: the teacher lectures or gives us information, we write it down and then give it back on a test" (p. 170).

Learning Styles Misapplied

There is also a myth or misconception that deserves some thoughtful attention. Ironically, in an effort to be sensitive to learners, we may do them a disservice. There has been much discussion about learning styles or preferences (Woolfolk, 1998) or multiple intelligences (Gardner, 1995; Gibson & Govendo, 1999), concepts that can help us reach more learners and generate more variety in teaching. Too often, however, this discussion becomes a means of placing limits on our students rather than a means of pushing them to greater accomplishments. Children who come to see themselves as "visual learners," for example, may develop the habit of dismissing other kinds of learning as not suited for them. David Strahan (1997) quotes one sixth-grade student who identifies her "main intelligences," but who goes on to write, "I am shy so I *can't* and hate to work in groups" (p. 80, emphasis added). It's unfortunate that a young woman not even half way through her public schooling has already decided she can't learn in certain ways. Joyce and Weil (1996) describe research that shows how students not only demonstrated they preferred different learning styles, but also managed to direct their teachers toward those styles. Children who are comfortable with group situations thrive in group learning. However, as Joyce and Weil point out, it is the children who are uncomfortable in group settings who most need to learn to succeed there. "Hence, the challenge is not to select the most comfortable models but to enable the students to develop the skills to relate to a wider variety of models, many of which appear, at least superficially, to be mismatched with their learning styles" (1996, p. 389).

Joyce and Weil (1996) acknowledge the stress of new ways of learning for *both* the students and the teachers. After providing an array of models for teachers to use, Joyce and Weil report some discouraging research to indicate that relatively few teachers (5 to 10 percent) will even try a new teaching strategy unless they are provided with a support system, such as coaching partners. "Even then," they write, "during the first half dozen trials, most teachers found the use of the new teaching strategies, whatever they were, to be extremely uncomfortable" (p. 338).

So there is a two-headed threat facing you as you prepare for becoming a teacher or as you focus on improving your teaching. First, you must consider what will push you to incorporate a variety of teaching strategies, *even when these strategies make you and your students uncomfortable.* Second, you face the prospect of being a learner in some discomfort, which, though it promises greater growth, is not exactly enticing.

Grieving or Learning?

To get less abstract and more personal, let's consider what the learning you are about to embark on will be like. People attracted to the teaching profession are generally those who found school to be a comfortable place, a place where they could succeed. In general, the traditional approaches to teaching and learning suit teachers, because that's what they have used for success. Problem-based learning, however, pushes learners to make some fairly substantial changes—and change induces anxiety.

Donald R. Woods has been a leader in the expansion of PBL for professional education. He guided the development of a PBL program for chemical engineering at McMaster University, where the medical school also uses PBL. In one of his books, Woods (1994) describes the changes his students (at the university level) experience as they begin work in PBL. He compares the impact of the changes to the typical grieving cycle a person goes through when he or she suffers a significant loss. *Grieving?* Shifting to PBL prompts the same emotions as losing a loved one? That's the comparison. Of course, the degree of emotional response is obviously different, but the nature is similar.

Woods (1994) explains that the grieving cycle moves a person through eight stages. Your school performance, which has probably become a predictable element of your life, encounters this change in instructional process, and the cycle begins. As Woods summarizes them, these eight stages are as follows: 1) shock, 2) denial, 3) strong negative emotion, 4) resistance and withdrawal, 5) surrender and acceptance, 6) struggle to affirm the new reality, 7) sense of direction and desire to make it work, 8) integration of the new approach. In recognizing that such a response to change is normal, you may be better equipped to deal with your feelings as you encounter PBL experiences. At the very least, this understanding is crucial for you to have so that you can resist the temptation to dismiss PBL or give up trying before you've had the opportunity to work through several attempts.

WORKING WITH YOUR COLLEAGUES—NOW AND LATER

The McMaster model of PBL, like most versions, involves solving problems in a group (Barrows, 1996). There is an important reason for this in medical education: often the solution to a given problem requires the integration of various professionals' expertise. Likewise, in education, the natural context in which many of the problems of our work are addressed is a group of colleagues. Committees make decisions about curricular issues; faculties join to decide on school policy; departments, teams, or grade-level cohorts collaborate to work through such issues as incorporating standards, re-evaluating resources and practices, or creating motivational plans. While little in teacher preparation addresses the collaborative elements of the profession, much of the work teachers do will require good group skills.

Researchers have found that some of the best schools are characterized by a work environment that encourages teachers to work together (Little, 1982; Rosenholtz, 1989). Ironically, the teaching profession in general is characterized by a sense of loneliness and isolation (Hargreaves, 1993; Little, 1990; Lortie, 1975; Roberts, 1992), and this isolation gets in the way of teachers' professional growth (Ashton & Webb, 1986; Maeroff, 1993). The image of the teacher privately working away in an egg-crate classroom may be accurate, but it is not hopeful for the profession. As a teacher, your capacity to work with your colleagues will do much to determine both your success and the success of your school.

Fine, you say. *In my work as a teacher, I'll be willing to work with my colleagues. But this is my work as a student, and these are my grades, and I prefer to do it myself.*

The problem with that line of thought is fairly obvious. If you practice teaching as an isolated activity, you'll learn it as an isolated activity. If you develop a habit of working through the issues of schooling alone, you'll become good at working alone. Despite the relative safety of a teacher-preparation program or a graduate course, you will have failed to learn and practice the skills of working together, skills that employers report to be most seriously lacking in new hires.

Working together goes pretty smoothly when you select people like you to work with. However, there are two major problems with doing that. First, the potential for generating the multiple perspectives that lead to excellent solutions is severely limited by making groups only of similar people. In fact, William Dyer (1995), a group researcher, argues that groups of friends worry too much about maintaining their friendships and lack the diversity that leads to innovative, creative ideas. A second problem associated with working only with the people you select is that this is simply not the way of the working world—whether in education or elsewhere. You will find, if you have anything like a typical career, that you will have to work with obnoxious people and lazy people and annoying people—in addition to creative, exciting, committed people. In short, your work world will require you to be flexible, cooperative, and somewhat thick-skinned.

Another consideration is how much you will learn through the PBL experience. Researchers examining PBL have found that when groups function effectively, attendance at group sessions goes up and achievement in terms of learning course outcomes increases (Van Berkel & Schmidt, 2000). For the sake of your own learning, it is worth your time to invest some energy in helping your PBL groups to function effectively.

Role-Playing Group Functions and Activities

One way to head off some of the potential difficulties of working with a group of colleagues is to play out some of the conflict situations *before* they arise. As part of your preparation for learning in a group for PBL experiences, join with colleagues to work through some of the following typical group snags. The best way to do this is for different groups to take on one of the situations described here, and then to perform for the rest of the larger group. Follow each role-play with a discussion about what challenge each group faced, how the group handled its particular challenge, and what might be some alternate strategies.

A note about doing role-plays: It's fine to talk through the situation briefly, but it's far more effective to move quickly into a dramatic mode, where you construct the situation together. Work through the "scene" several times, but feel free to innovate as you recreate your situation for your colleagues.

Situation One.   Construct a group meeting/discussion where one of the group members continually pulls the rest of the group off task. Your group is a committee of teachers that has been asked to come up with a solution to the over-crowded lunch room in your school. Your role-play should provide a brief demonstration of the challenging member's behavior and then focus on a productive means of dealing with this person.

Situation Two.   Create a group meeting/discussion where one member is domineering, pushing his or her ideas all the time. Assume your group is a mixture of teachers and parents who are trying to decide on a plan to acquire new playground equipment. Conduct the meeting long enough to demonstrate the problem, but focus your attention on the solution your group thinks would be most effective to the problem of a domineering member.

Situation Three.   Construct a group meeting/discussion in which one member is apparently uninterested and a nonparticipant. This member does not do anything to disrupt the meeting, but simply does not contribute. Assume the group is a committee of teachers that has been appointed to recommend a solution to the library problem at your school: the district has cut funding, so although there is a decent library, there is no money to hire a librarian. Remember, use the situation to focus on showing the problem of the nonparticipant and how your group could effectively draw this person into the group's task.

Situation Four.   Design a role-play in which two members of your group are obviously at odds. There may be some conflict between them over the ideas the group is dealing with, but it is apparent that there is also much personal animosity between the two members. Assume your group is made up of teachers who have volunteered to help the principal decide whether to distribute new computers to the various classrooms or to build a lab. Show us enough of the meeting to establish the conflict, but focus your efforts on how the group can address this problem of conflict.

For each of the role-play situations, be sure to discuss alternative ways of handling similar problems. An important point for you to consider here is that the experience of anticipating common group difficulties may help you address similar difficulties later in your own group work. Beyond that, bringing potential problems out into the open may assist all participants in recognizing their own limitations or negative tendencies as participants in group work.

Group Structure

As you have probably already discovered, effective cooperative learning requires that group members have interdependence, but also individual accountability. In your group work in PBL, you will discover that there are a number of predictable duties. To keep group members accountable, it is important that the group keep some sort of records—perhaps a log of decisions made and a list of things to do. Someone must keep such a record. It is also important that your group interact with your instructor. Someone must conduct such liaison. It is important that your group have a clear sense of direction. Someone must perform such leadership. The actual roles that group members take can change from problem to problem or even within a problem, but confusion about who is doing what will damage the effectiveness of your group's work. At a minimum, your groups should address these roles:

Leader.   This person is primarily responsible for keeping the group focused on the task at hand. Interestingly, teachers resist taking on leadership roles because of their sense of equality among colleagues (Kain, 1997). However, there is no claim of superiority by virtue of being the leader. The importance of keeping the group focused is simply too great to ignore this job.

Recorder.   You don't want to lose track of the decisions made or duties assigned. It's amazing how different each member's recollection of a group meeting can be, so to avoid this, have someone who will take minutes.

Liaison.   The leader can do this, but it is probably more effective for you to share duties. When you need to contact the instructor or another group, a liaison will be prepared to focus on that task.

Inquirer.   Peter Senge (1990) writes about the important roles of inquiry and advocacy. To get sound decisions, he argues, it is crucial that we consider options seriously. Ideally, every member of your group will be willing to question ideas instead of merely conceding. However, if you charge a group member with trying to see the other side, you will be more likely to have broad perspectives. This is not to be confused with the PBL inquiry process that every group member will conduct. The inquirer's role is simply to bring up counter positions as the group moves toward a solution.

HOW TO ATTACK A PROBLEM—A PBL PROCESS

Having examined the emotional reactions PBL might engender and the challenges of working in groups, it is now time to consider how best to attack a problem in PBL. This section will provide some guidance about what you should do as a learner in the PBL context. One note of caution: Often the pace of being a university student causes learners to want to hurry through tasks. Learners develop a checklist mentality, where their sense of accomplishment is tied to completing projects. *I finished that reading; I've turned in that lesson plan; I've completed that reflection paper. Now I get ice cream!* This checklist mentality is likely to cause you to rush to solutions prematurely in PBL. Your pace should be slow enough to allow you to experience the full range of issues and understandings embedded in each problem.

The major steps of solving the problems, which often must be repeated, are these: define the problem, seek information, generate options, select a solution, formulate and present the solution according to the parameters of the problem, debrief your experience.

Defining the Problem

Woods (1994) writes that "unsuccessful problem solvers tend to spend most of their time *doing* something whereas successful problem solvers spend most of their time deciding *what* to do" (pp. 3–6, original emphasis). That "deciding what" begins with deciding what the *real* problem is in a PBL experience. Expert problem solvers tend to spend a good deal of time in what some have called "problem finding" (Bridges & Hallinger, 1995; Gallagher, Rosenthal, & Stepien, 1992) or problem identification (Adams, 1979). Rather than assuming that the most obvious issue is the real problem, good problem solvers dig into the problem for a while, messing around with the facts and descriptions before they decide what the real problem is.

This messing about with the facts is especially important when we think about the way most problems come to us. Most problems come to us filtered through someone's perspective, and often that someone has embedded his or her view of what the solution should be in the problem description. Remember the last time you were told, "You know what *your* problem is? You . . . " In general, such statements assume a lot about "your problem." The principle of being cautious about defining a problem is illustrated well in a monologue from Robert Pirsig's (1974) novel, *Zen and the Art of Motorcycle Maintenance:*

> In Part One of formal scientific method, which is the statement of the problem, the main skill is in stating absolutely no more than you are positive you know. It is much better to enter a statement "Solve Problem: Why doesn't cycle work?" which

sounds dumb but is correct, than it is to enter a statement "Solve Problem: What is wrong with the electrical system?" when you don't absolutely *know* the trouble is *in* the electrical system. What you should state is "Solve Problem: What is wrong with cycle?" and *then* state as the first entry of Part Two: "Hypothesis Number One: The trouble is in the electrical system." You think of as many hypotheses as you can, then you design experiments to test them to see which are true and which are false. (p. 101)

Another excellent example, not from the literary world, comes to us from James Adams's (1979) book, *Conceptual Blockbusting.* Adams recounts how people spent a good deal of time and money trying to devise machinery that could pick tomatoes without damaging the skins. These people were solving a problem of the *picking technology,* when in fact the problem was broader than that. The real solution came when the problem was defined as the issue of *damaged fruit*—and the solution was in genetically creating tomatoes with tougher skins!

Once your group feels confident it has explored a number of possible problems, you should state what you think the problem is fairly concisely—a sentence or two. However, as you gather more information, you may need to revisit your problem statement and revise it to match your emerging understanding. As Larry Cuban has written, "There is, after all, no worse lie than a problem poorly stated" (1989, p. 801).

To practice identifying "real" problems, look at the following samples (Figures 2.1, 2.2). These are two practice scenarios that were used with eighth-grade students to develop the capacity to form problem statements. Notice that in the first sample, students had a multiple-choice practice, while in the second sample, the problem statement was left open-ended.

FIGURE 2.1   Scenario for Forming Problem Statements, Sample 1

The principal of a middle school expresses her frustration with the way the students in her school crowd each other, shove in the hallways, and make each other late for class. It seems as though the halls have actually become hazardous, and some of the teachers are worried that there will be a major disaster soon. The principal considers this situation to be out of hand, and she's not going to put up with it any more.

The *real* problem is
A. Children in this school are rude and do not know how to behave. They probably should have classes in proper public behavior.
B. The school is overcrowded. The school district needs to build another middle school to eliminate the problem.
C. The locker arrangement is poorly designed. The principal should remove the lockers and replace them with smaller ones.
D. The passing schedule puts all the students in the hall at the same time. A new schedule should be implemented that has kids going to their lockers at different times.

FIGURE 2.2   Scenario for Forming Problem Statements, Sample 2

The PE teachers at the middle school have approached the principal with a proposal. They say that their students continually fail to "dress out" for PE. Students refuse to put on the required outfit. Students make up excuses, such as not feeling well or that they forgot their outfits or that their mom was washing it. The teachers have proposed that students who do not have the gym uniform one time be given an hour of after-school detention and that students who do not have the uniform two times receive an F in the course. The teachers think this is the only way to get students to take this requirement seriously.

The *real* problem is

Seeking Information

In the brief introduction to PBL in the last chapter, I presented a three-part structure for seeking information. Learners gather to generate answers to these three questions: What do we know? What do we need to know? and How will we find out?

Answers to the first question come from the problem documents or artifacts and the general knowledge of the participants. Each member of the group should carefully read the problem documents to determine what facts are present. Be careful, however, not to mix up facts and conclusions drawn from those facts. For example, problem documents might make it clear that a student has a difficult time with English. That fact is not the same thing as saying the student is ESL (one *possible* explanation for the difficulties with English) or the student has a processing problem (another *possible* explanation) or the student's home life is a disaster (a *stretch*). We must also be careful about the sort of general knowledge we list as what we already know. For example, if we say that language use is an important factor in learning, we're on safe ground (though it is always helpful to back up such statements with research). On the other hand, if we say that nonnative speakers don't do as well as native speakers of English, we're probably turning what appears to be common sense into a fact when it is not.

Based on our initial hunches and questions from a careful reading of the problem documents, the next question is, "What do we need to know?" For most PBL experiences, you will find there is some information included in the problem documents that has no real bearing on the actual problem. That's the nature of real problems—the problem solver must learn to sift through material to find out what is important and what is not. But you can be certain that each problem will also have gaps in the information provided, and you will need to seek answers to questions. For example, if the problem has something to do with a teaching technique, does that teaching technique have a record of effectiveness? We need to know. If the problem addresses a new school schedule, has that schedule been implemented elsewhere? What happened where this schedule was adopted? We need to know. The group generates a list of such questions.

Armed with questions, the group then decides how to find out the answers. This probably involves two kinds of decisions. First, where are the answers available? Some questions would be appropriate to address to practicing teachers or other school personnel. Some questions might require venturing into the library or conducting an Internet search. Second, who will seek the answers? There is little point in every member of the group duplicating the efforts of every other member. It makes much more sense to consider how to divide the labor. As the group fleshes out the plan for how it will find information, make and record assignments for each group member.

At your group's next meeting, you will essentially be able to revisit the three-part structure. *What do we know?* has changed by virtue of the research conducted. Group members share what they have discovered and the list of what we know expands. At the same time, the list of things we need to know has changed. New information generates new questions. *How will we find this out?* The cycle continues.

Generating Options and Selecting a Solution

Your group has done some fact finding in a messy description, defined a problem, and conducted inquiry/research into the problem. It is now time to generate some solutions. Notice the plural there. Too many people and groups are satisfied to latch onto the first solution that comes to mind. Recall what I said about a "checklist mentality." A solution presents itself, and it is just easier to go for it. This way of thinking is not likely to lead you to the best solutions.

To avoid early closure, discipline your groups by requiring that you consider at least three possible solutions to any one problem. That way you will have some perspective, and though you may end up selecting the first solution that came to mind, at least you will do so because it is a *better* solution, not the only possible solution.

Once you have decided on the solution to a problem, you will probably need to conduct more research. Perhaps you'll only need to briefly revisit some of the resources you've already examined; perhaps new gaps will be apparent. Now you will have a refined focus for your research as you build support for your case.

Presenting the Solution

In the real-world context of problem solving, the next step would be to work for the implementation of your solution. For example, if you had decided that the solution to the overcrowded lunch room was to build a new multi-purpose room, you would start the construction. In the context of PBL, such implementation is not possible.

Instead, most problems will require you to make some sort of presentation of your solution (which, in fact, is also often the case in the real world). You might be asked to address a school board or a parent committee, for example. In this context, as in the real world, you will want to present yourself as an informed professional. If you were to address the school board in your school district, you wouldn't come to the meeting in casual attire, speaking off the cuff, and presenting unfounded opinions. You would argue your case with supporting facts and in a manner that demonstrated your careful professionalism. In the same way, your PBL presentations of solutions should demonstrate preparation and professionalism.

Pay careful attention to the parameters of the solution presentations and the context described in each problem. If, for example, a presentation can be up to fifteen minutes long, don't make yours thirty. While instructors are sometimes generous, it's rare that a board meeting that has authorized fifteen minutes will allow a presenter to go longer. As a group, rehearse your presentation. Listen to each other carefully for the effects of the presentation, as well as for the supporting evidence. It is crucial for teachers to learn to make defensible decisions that are open to public scrutiny.

Debriefing the Experience

Again, in the real world of problem solving, the final step would be to evaluate your solution and its effect on the problem. In PBL, your evaluation takes on a different form. You will undergo a debriefing of each problem in two stages.

First, after each PBL presentation, you should meet with your group to discuss your performance. What went well? What needs improvement? Ask yourselves, *If we were in the actual context, such as a school board meeting, how would people have viewed our work?* Your group should discuss its performance, and it should also share in examining any feedback your instructor or peers may provide.

Second, you should join with all the groups that have addressed this problem for a debriefing of the issues represented by the PBL experience. This does not mean you will hear from someone what the "correct" solution is for the problem. Each problem has been selected so that there are multiple solutions, each with advantages and disadvantages. Instead, the debriefing should allow you to discuss the relative merits and potential disadvantages of differing solutions. In addition, your debriefing should be a time to raise points on which you still have questions. As a teacher examining professional issues, do you see questions generated by the experience that need further clarification from your colleagues or instructor? You must take the initiative to bring these questions out for discussion.

Figure 2.3 lists some generic debriefing questions for you to consider. Not all of these questions will be appropriate for all of your PBL experiences. However, the basic pattern is sound, and the practice of reflecting on your experience is one that will help to sharpen your problem-solving skills and to make connections among the parts of your learning experience. Your instructor may ask you to respond to these prompts in writing, or your instructor may use the prompts as a discussion guide.

FIGURE 2.3   Debriefing the PBL Experience

Directions: Use these questions as a guide to assist you in reflecting on your experience. Questions can be used for personal reflection or for group debriefing of the problems.

1. What worked well in the problem-solving process? (e.g., "We changed our definition of the problem, which led to new solution ideas.") _____

    _____

2. What key issues were raised by this problem? _____

    _____

3. What did you learn about these issues? _____

    _____

4. What questions remain after working through one solution? _____

    _____

5. In terms of working with peers, what did you learn through addressing this problem? _____

    _____

6. As a teacher, what is one thing you can apply to your professional work from this problem? _____

    _____

Following each problem, you will find a section in the text that leads you to reflect on some of the issues embedded in the problem. It is important that you use these readings as a means to debrief the problem *after* you have worked through a solution. If you read the reflections while you are working out your solutions, it is likely you will be led in directions that do not match your own inquiry. This will take discipline, but the reflections will be much more valuable to you after having struggled with the problems themselves.

A Note on Learning Objectives

As educators, we tend to think in terms of objectives for each learning experience. That's a good practice, but it has limitations when students are operating in ill-defined problem solving situations. Still, keep this issue before you as you work through the problems in your program. The objective for your work is not that you solve these particular problems, but that you learn through your experience of solving these problems. Ideally, you will learn much about problem solving and working with colleagues and the substantive issues of the problems, and even the use of PBL for your classroom. The key issue, however, is learning.

DISCUSSION QUESTIONS

1. Problem-based learning can induce stress in learners, particularly those who have been successful in learning through traditional means. Are there any potential benefits to stress in a learning situation? What are some means of coping with stress that you have found to be effective? How can you use other people to assist you in dealing with stress?

2. Most manifestations of PBL involve learning in groups, yet many people complain that their group learning experiences have not been positive. What are some of the features of the best groups you've been a part of? What specific behaviors have made group membership a means for your own growth?

3. This chapter proposed several roles as a means of sharing responsibility for group performance and as a means of remaining accountable to one another. If you were helping your students lay the groundwork for successful group work, what roles would you have them take on? How can the idea of performing a specific task in the group limit a person's effectiveness? What does a group member do to make sure the role is productive for him or her?

4. Problem-based learning is obviously a version of problem solving. What are your personal strengths and weaknesses in problem solving? What approach do you find most effective? Is problem solving essentially the same whether in groups or on your own? Indeed, is problem-solving something one can teach?

5. Problem-based learning is above all a means of organizing the learning experiences for particular learners. How can you effectively keep the focus on learning? What role does the instructor assume in the context of a focus on learning? What means can a learner use to connect the disparate pieces of understanding acquired through an open-ended format, such as PBL?

FURTHER READING

Gallagher, S. R. (1997). Problem-based learning: Where did it come from, what does it do, and where is it going? *Journal for the Education of the Gifted, 20*(4), 332–362.
A brief article that provides some of the basics about PBL from the perspective of teachers in the schools. Gallagher includes information about the history of PBL, some guides for teachers to become tutors, and some information about research on PBL.

Levin, B. B. (Ed.). (2001). *Energizing teacher education and professional development with problem-based learning.* Alexandria, VA: Association for Supervision and Curriculum Development.

A short edited volume that provides a number of useful perspectives for teachers. The book includes a brief description of PBL, samples of how teachers use the technique, and a helpful chapter of questions and answers.

Woods, D. R. (1994). *Problem-based learning: How to gain the most from PBL. Waterdown, ON: Author.* The unique element of this book is that it is directed to the student in a PBL situation. Most other texts take the instructor's perspective. By focusing on what the student experiences and ways to succeed as a PBL learner, Woods provides a terrific resource for enhancing the benefits you might receive through PBL. In particular, Woods includes a great many diagrams and checklists that promise to guide reflection on the process you will be going through.

WEB SITE

Problem-Based Learning Initiative
   http://pbli.org/core.htm
   This site is available to support teachers at any level ("kindergarten through infinity") in work with problem-based learning.

REFERENCES

Adams, J. L. (1979). *Conceptual blockbusting: A guide to better ideas* (2nd ed.). New York: W. W. Norton & Company.

Ashton, P. T., & Webb, R. B. (1986). *Making a difference: Teachers' sense of efficacy and student achievement.* New York: Longman.

Atwell, N. (1998). *In the middle: New understandings about writing, reading, and learning.* Portsmouth, NH: Heinemann/Boynton-Cook.

Barrows, H. S. (1996). Problem-based learning in medicine and beyond: A brief overview. In L. Wilkerson & W. H. Gijselaers (Eds.), *Bringing problem-based learning to higher education: Theory and practice* (Vol. 68, pp. 3–12). San Francisco: Jossey-Bass.

Bridges, E. M., & Hallinger, P. (1995). *Implementing problem based learning in leadership development.* Eugene, OR: ERIC Clearinghouse on Educational Management.

Cuban, L. (1989). The "at-risk" label and the problem of urban school reform. *Phi Delta Kappan, 70*(10), 780–784, 799–801.

Dyer, W. G. (1995). *Team building: Current issues and new alternatives* (3rd ed.). Reading, MA: Addison-Wesley.

Fullan, M. G. (1991). *The new meaning of educational change* (2nd ed.). New York: Teachers College Press.

Gallagher, S., Rosenthal, H., & Stepien, W. (1992). The effects of problem-based learning on problem-solving. *Gifted Child Quarterly, 36*(4), 195–200.

Gallagher, S. A. (1997). Problem-based learning: Where did it come from, what does it do, and where is it going? *Journal for the Education of the Gifted, 20*(4), 332–362.

Gardner, H. (1995). Reflections on multiple intelligences: Myths and messages. *Phi Delta Kappan, 77*(3), 200–209.

Gibson, B. P., & Govendo, B. L. (1999). Encouraging constructive behavior in middle school classrooms: A multiple-intelligences approach. *Intervention in School & Clinic, 35*(1), 16–22.

Haberman, M. (1991). The pedagogy of poverty vs. good teaching. *Phi Delta Kappan, 73*(4), 290–294.

Hargreaves, A. (1993). Individualism and individuality: Reinterpreting the teacher culture. *International Journal of Educational Research, 19*(3), 227–246.

Heuser, D. (2000). Reworking the workshop for math and science. *Educational Leadership, 58*(1), 34–37.

Joyce, B., & Weil, M. (1996). *Models of teaching* (5th ed.). Boston: Allyn & Bacon.

Kain, D. L. (1997). Misplaced camels, crowded captains, and achieving greatness: Leadership on middle school teams. In T. S. Dickinson & T. O. Erb (Eds.), *We gain more than we give: Teaming in the middle school* (pp. 403–424). Columbus, OH: National Middle School Association.

Levin, B. B. (Ed.). (2001). *Energizing teacher education and professional development with problem-based learning.* Alexandria, VA: Association for Supervision and Curriculum Development.

Little, J. W. (1982). Norms of collegiality and experimentation: Workplace conditions of school success. *American Educational Research Journal, 19*(3), 325–340.

Little, J. W. (1990). The persistence of privacy: Autonomy and initiative in teachers' professional relations. *Teachers College Record, 91*(4), 509–536.

Lortie, D. C. (1975). *Schoolteacher: A sociological study.* Chicago: University of Chicago.

Maeroff, G. I. (1993). *Team building for school change: Equipping teachers for new roles.* New York: Teachers College Press.

Pirsig, R. M. (1974). *Zen and the art of motorcycle maintenance.* New York: Bantam.

Roberts, H. (1992). The importance of networking in the restructuring process. *NASSP Bulletin, 76*(541), 25–29.

Rosenholtz, S. J. (1989). *Teachers' workplace: The social organization of schools.* White Plains, NY: Longman.

Sage, S. M., Krynock, K. L., & Robb, L. (2000). Is there anything but a problem? A case study of problem-based learning as middle school curriculum integration. *Research in Middle Level Education Annual, 23,* 149–179.

Senge, P. M. (1990). *The fifth discipline: The art and practice of the learning organization.* New York: Doubleday.

Strahan, D., Bowles, N., Richardson, V., & Hanawald, S. (1997). Research on teaming: Insights from selected studies. In T. S. Dickinson & T. O. Erb (Eds.), *We gain more than we give: Teaming in middle schools* (pp. 359–384). Columbus, OH: National Middle School Association.

Van Berkel, H. J. M., & Schmidt, H. G. (2000). Motivation to commit oneself as a determinant of achievement in problem-based learning. *Higher Education, 40,* 231–242.

Woods, D. R. (1994). *Problem-based learning: How to gain the most from PBL.* Waterdown, ON: Author.

Woolfolk, A. E. (1998). *Educational psychology* (7th ed.). Boston: Allyn & Bacon.

■ ■ ■ ■ ■ ▬▬▬▬▬▬▬▬▬▬▬▬▬▬▬▬▬▬▬▬▬▬▬▬▬▬▬▬▬▬▬▬▬▬▬▬

CHAPTER THREE

WHAT SHOULD WE DO ABOUT ANDY?

INTRODUCTION AND PROBLEM BACKGROUND

Beginning teachers are often surprised to find out just how much the schools expect of them in relation to special education issues. Just when you feel you've mastered enough of the content areas to teach the numerous subjects required of you, you realize that you will also be expected to adapt that material to a host of different levels. If that weren't enough in itself, you will also be expected to meet with other teachers, counselors, administrators, psychologists, and parents to determine what the best possible placement and program might be for a particular child.

These placement meetings are generally called student study teams (or child study teams). Sometimes such meetings are polite discussions about how to support a particular child. But other times, such meetings are characterized by high levels of disagreement and emotion. In some cases, the various participants disagree intensely about the causes and cures for a child's behavior or performance. The psychologist may offer an explanation that supports a parent's view of the child, while the teachers may maintain that this view tries to justify a spoiled child's misbehavior. Or the parents may find themselves opposing all the school personnel. What happens then?

This problem-based learning experience asks you to examine just such a situation. While it would be convenient if there were a straightforward, single solution to every child's multiple needs, the real world offers no such simplicity. And while the players in the decision-making process struggle to make their cases, it is the child whose future is at stake. What should we do about Andy?

PROBLEM CONTEXT SOLUTION PARAMETERS

Context

King Middle School* in Paris, Arizona, is a relatively new school serving 261 students in grades six, seven, and eight. Up until two years ago, special education

*For all problem documents included in this book, the people, places, and institutions are fictional. Any resemblance to people, living or dead, is purely coincidental.

students received services in separate classrooms, isolated from other students. With the hiring of a new superintendent, all schools in the district have implemented "integration" of special needs students into the regular classroom. Initially, the professional staff strongly supported this move; after one semester, this support dissipated.

Andy P. is an eighth-grade student who has spent most of his school time in special education classes. He has a well-documented learning disability (reading comprehension and written expression), but he has most often been addressed as a behavior problem. Early in the first semester, his student study team met to review his individualized education plan (IEP), and the meeting broke up after the participants could not come to any agreements. Andy's mother refused to sign off on a new plan because she felt Andy should be treated like a regular education student; the teacher representative disagreed strongly with her. In an effort to resolve this constructively, the principal suggested an independent team review Andy's situation. For now, Andy has simply stayed in a regular class assignment with no special support.

Problem

Your group is a committee of educators working at King Middle School. You have been asked to assist in this contentious student study team. Disagreements about what is best for Andy P. have arisen among his classroom teachers, the school counseling staff, the administration, and his custodial parent. These disagreements are evident in the statements produced by each (included in the problem documents). In addition, your committee has access to the latest pyschoeducational evaluation conducted on Andy, as it is represented in his previous IEP.

Solution Parameters

You will need to make a brief presentation to the original student study team, consisting of one of Andy's teachers, a counselor, his mother, and an administrative representative. What recommendations do you make for addressing Andy's school situation? How can you persuade the student study team that your ideas are best for a child like Andy? Consider the legal and ethical obligations in this situation. The maximum time for your committee to speak is fifteen minutes; up to ten minutes discussion time will follow.

You will also need to provide the principal with a written committee report that summarizes your recommendations and the reasons for these recommendations. Be sure that you support your recommendations carefully, drawing on what is known about LD students, school delivery systems, teaching techniques, and so on.

········WORK THE PROBLEM ──➤

PROBLEM DOCUMENTS

The following documents are provided for your examination in formulating a decision about Andy's situation (but remember, you will need to go beyond these particular documents to solve the problem):

3.1 Andy's latest Individualized Education Plan (IEP), which includes information from the psychoeducational assessment completed by the school psychologist

3.2 A statement from Andy's mother about his placement

3.3 A statement from one of Andy's teachers in response to the initial student study team

3.4 A statement from Andy's school counselor

3.5 A statement from the assistant principal in charge of discipline

3.6 The progress reports filed by Andy's math and social studies teachers for consideration by the initial student study team

3.7 Andy's grade transcript from sixth and seventh grades

3.8 King Middle School daily schedule

PROBLEM DOCUMENT 3.1   *Andy's Latest IEP*

Paris School District, Special Education Programs
INDIVIDUAL EDUCATION PLAN

IEP DATES: Beginning ___8/25/03___   Valid to ___8/24/04___

IEP status: _____ Initial   _X_ Review   _____ Change of placement

Exit date: _____

Personal Information

Student name: *Andy P.* _____   Student #: *511–100–511098*   DOB: *4/12/91*

Grade: ___7___   School: *King Middle School* _____

Parent (X) or Guardian ( ) _____ *Amaldea B.* _____

Home phone: _____   Work phone: _____

Vision screening date: ___5/17/01___   P _X_ F __

Hearing screening date: ___9/22/00___   P _X_ F __

Psychological evaluation date: ___9/15/02___   Diagnostic category: *SLD*

Special Education Services

Special Education Teacher assigned: _____

Related Services

Type	Eval date	Initiate date	Duration	Frequency	Specialist
Speech					
Counseling					
OT					
PT		*None*			
VI					
HI					
OI					
Other					

TIME IN SPECIAL ED: _____ 0% _____   Time In Regular Ed: _____ 100% _____

CLASS SCHEDULE:

	S	R		S	R
Social Studies		X	Science		X
Math 8		X	Reading		X
English/Language Arts		X	Electronic music		X
P. E./Health		X			

Indicate areas in which student will participate with students who have no disabilities:

____ Recess   ____ Athletics   ____ Clubs   ____ Recreational Activities

_X_ Lunch   _X_ Assemblies   ____ Employment   _X_ Passing Periods

____ Other _____

Evaluation/Review of progress

Previous Year IEP Goals and Objectives: _____ 7 _____ *Written* and _____ 3 _____ *Met*

STATEMENT OF CURRENT LEVEL OF PERFORMANCE:

Strengths: *Andy displays average intellectual ability. Test results indicate adequate perceptual organization, visual-motor integration, and processing speed.*

Needs: *Andy exhibits weaknesses in verbal and reading comprehension and in written skills. He displays poor visual-sequential memory skills which may impact his reading and spelling skills. Andy's behavior is often marked by inattention and distractibility and some excessive motor movements. He has difficulty initiating seat work, comprehending instructions, and staying on task.*

Additional parental comments: _____

_____

_____

_____

Assessment Data (Standard Scores)

WRAT	Woodcock-Johnson		K-TEA	Other Testing:
Date: _____	Date: *9/15/02*		Date: _____	
___ Reading	*92* Letter/ Word ID	___ Broad Math	___ Read. Decod	_____
___ Math		*70* Dictation	___ Read Comp.	_____
___ Spelling	*78* Passage Comp	*75* Writing samples	___ Total Read	_____
	___ Broad Reading	___ Broad Written Lang.	___ Calculation	_____
	90 Calculation		___ Applied Prob	_____
	88 Applied Problem		___ Total Math	_____
			___ Spelling	_____
				_____

Interpretation of assessment results: *Letter/word ID, applied problems, and calculation are within the average range. Passage comprehension, writing samples, and dictation represent discrepancies between ability and achievement.*

_____

_____

Goals

Short-Term Objectives	Begin/ Master	Methods of Evaluating	Instructional Methods, Materials, Adaptations
1) Andy will obtain a daily assignment sheet for parents to check with 100% compliance.	9/25/03 12/5/03	Parent report; secretary report	Assignment sheet
2) Andy will complete all assignments with 70% accuracy.	9/25/03 12/5/03	Percent determined from log of sheets.	Longer time permitted for Andy to complete assignments and tests.
3) Andy will turn in all assignments, even if only attempted, with 85% turned in.	9/25/03 12/5/03	Percent determined.	Assignments can be completed in resource room if necessary.

Are Limited English Proficient (LEP) services needed? __X__ yes ____ no

Language of Instruction: _____

Indicate LEP modifications incorporated in student's program:

___ Use of home language   ___ Hands on activities   ___ Interactive teaching

___ Multicultural activities   ___ Simplified language   ___ Cooperative activities

___ Individualized instruction   ___ Use of visuals, graphics, audiovisuals   ___ Guarded (controlled) vocabulary

___ Other:

The above modifications will be implemented in the following settings:

___ Special Education   ___ Regular Education   ___ Other:

Least Restrictive Environment Plan

The I.E.P. Review Committee recommends:

New Placement: Category _____ IEP from _____ to _____

Student continues as _____ SLD _____ IEP from 9/25/03 to 9/24/04

Student exits from the _____ program. Date: _____

Change of placement from _____ to _____.

(Reevaluation and/or justification documentation required.)

Are related services needed to benefit this student's educational program? ___ Yes _X_ No

Continuum of Alternative Placements

Site

_X_ Regular school within district

___ Regular school outside district

___ Special school outside the district

___ Home-bound

___ Residential treatment center

___ Hospital

___ Other: _____

Instructional Setting

___ Regular education with supplementary aides and/or consultation

___ Regular education with itinerant support

_X_ Regular education with resource support

___ Special education integrated with regular classroom

___ Special education, self-contained classroom

___ Special education, individual

___ Other: _____

Explain why the site and instructional setting indicated above is **appropriate** and **least restrictive:** *Andy's ability levels warrant his inclusion in the regular classroom. Andy can profit from learning to comply with basic academic and behavioral standards in the context of peer interaction.*

_____

If less restrictive options were determined to be inappropriate, explain why: *Andy's self-esteem could be injured if he were placed outside the regular classroom.*

_____

_____

Describe any potential negative effects of this placement on the student: *Andy may have difficulty keeping up with normal classroom demands and customary classroom behavioral expectations.*

_____

SITE AND SETTING DETERMINATION

1. The site selected is the school the student would attend if he/she did not have a disability. _X_ Yes ___ No

2. The site selected is as close as possible to the student's home. _X_ Yes ___ No

3. The instructional setting selected is based on the student's IEP. _X_ Yes ___ No

4. To the maximum extent appropriate and feasible, the student will be educated among nondisabled students. _X_ Yes ___ No

Explain any "no" responses:

_____

_____

Test exemption: ___ Yes _X_ No   Tests: _____

Behavior plan needed: ___ Yes _X_ No

Extended school year needed: ___ Yes _X_ No

Parents' rights explained: _____ (Parent's initials)

(Signature page filed with district office)

PROBLEM DOCUMENT 3.2   *Statement from Guardian (Andy's mother)*

Andy has never done very well in his classes because the teachers don't seem to understand him. He was pretty good as a student when he was younger. Maybe teachers were more patient. He didn't spend half his time in the office for trouble-making. He's basically a good kid, but he needs lots of attention. And that obviously isn't his fault. If his father had been any kind of father he would have helped the kid, even after the divorce. But it seems like now even visiting his dad makes Andy crazy. You should see the pictures he draws after that. And he's always talking about guns and stuff. In class, Andy just doesn't get interested if the teachers don't notice him and give him some time. I don't expect college work or anything like that. We all know Andy is no genius and he will have to learn some kind of trade. He just needs to know enough to get some kind of job, and he's never gonna learn that if he keeps getting kicked out. But you can't put him in with the special ed classes. What's a kid gonna learn there? He's not a little kid anymore and we need to get him ready for a real world where there aren't special ed classes.

PROBLEM DOCUMENT 3.3   *Statement from Ms. R (Andy's teacher)*

Andy is a difficult case. He's been identified as a special needs student, and I understand he's received services in the past. It's really hard to say what his needs are in that sense, because he is so needy in so many other ways. I understand he's from a broken home, and it's probably not his fault. That's not the issue anyway; we all just want whatever is best for Andy. His placement in my class is probably a mistake, because Andy is so unmotivated that he's getting nothing out of the time he spends in class. I hear from other teachers that they have the same problem with him. If the goal has been to give Andy some lessons on social adaptability, it's been a terrific failure. The one area he cannot handle is social. He speaks out of turn; he interrupts his classmates; he says "off the wall" things all the time. In fact, I've sent him to the time-out room five times just for inappropriate language. What I have not seen from this kid is <u>any efforts whatsoever</u>. I suspect he needs the full-time surveillance of a paid aide, but he hasn't got that in my class. I have 27 normal kids in that class who all need my help; I also have three other special education kids who don't have Andy's potential, but who don't disrupt class continually. At least they try when I give them work; Andy finds any excuse to get all eyes on him. I've simply exhausted all possibilities for Andy and I don't see why the class as a whole should pay for the ignorance of some short-sighted law! He will not make it in class.

| PROBLEM DOCUMENT 3.4 | *Statement from Mr. C (Andy's counselor)* |

Andy is exactly the sort of kid who can make inclusion work. If there was a case for 94-142 to prove, Andy is it. I'm sure that patient, caring professionals could find a way to bring out this kid's abilities. He's not dumb. I think his I.Q. score was around 90, and that's probably higher than some of our teachers! He just has what Dr. T, the visiting school psychologist, calls a disability in written expression and reading. So why can't teachers allow him to talk, maybe find some alternative assignments? Isn't that flexible professional behavior? In all my dealings with this kid, I find him to be courteous, reasonable, intelligent. It would be a mistake to place him in a special ed classroom when he can make it elsewhere.

| PROBLEM DOCUMENT 3.5 | *Statement from Ms. H (assistant principal in charge of discipline)* |

Andy P. has managed to offend just about every teacher in this school, except for a couple that he seems to run to when he's about to get hammered. And too often they cover for him. What I guess bothers me most about this kid is that he has been covered for throughout his life. His mother likes to blame all his problems on Dad; the counselors are quick to blame his teachers; the teachers won't face it either. Who is there to blame Andy? The kid has had enough chances, now it's time to live out some choices. I think Andy will never make it in a regular classroom because he sees it as an audience for him. I would like to be able to support my teachers, who complain about a lot of frustrations with this kid. And I think that we'll have too many other kids suffering from Andy's obnoxious behavior. Andy ought to go into a holding pattern: another year and a half in special education classrooms, and Andy could move on to some vo-tech training, where he belongs. I guess that's the ideal world. The real world is there are laws that maybe don't know what's best for kids. And there are parents, who are the bottom-line clients in a school. Unless we can work out something else, I've got to go with Mom's decision here.

Progress Reports Completed by Mr. Rios and Ms. Ostrum

Student Study Team: Progress Report

Teacher: __Mr. Rios__   Student: __Andy P.__

Date: __9/19/03__   Subject: __Math__

Please address the indicated concerns to the best of your ability. Attach extra sheets or documentation as necessary.

The things I see as this student's greatest strengths:

Andy is able to complete straightforward assignments involving basic calculation skills. Working with numerical symbols seems easier than dealing with word problems. Andy can be a lively, fun student. He seems bright, but he's not working up to his ability.

The things I see as this student's greatest weaknesses:

Andy seems confused when working on word problems. He appears unable to understand the material and thus can't work toward any solutions. He then gives up quickly and begins to talk to nearby classmates. He can be very distracting to others, as well as easily distracted himself. He turns in assignments that are done in class, but rarely completes homework. Tests reflect his difficulty with word problems and an apparent lack of studying.

Current grade: C

Attendance: Generally good.

Other concerns:

I wonder if Andy's English proficiency is impacting his performance.

Student Study Team: Progress Report

Teacher: _Ms. Ostrum_ Student: _Andy P._

Date: _9/19/03_ Subject: _Social Studies_

Please address the indicated concerns to the best of your ability. Attach extra sheets or documentation as necessary.

The things I see as this student's greatest strengths:

Andy has a good sense of humor and can be very enjoyable in one-on-one conversation. He seems most interested in special activities like creating topical maps or other hands-on projects.

The things I see as this student's greatest weaknesses

Andy doesn't seems to put much effort into any assignments involving reading or writing. Much of his work is either incomplete or not turned in. On written tasks, he fails to develop or organize ideas and lacks mechanical skills. It seems that he never reads the textbook. Andy rarely enters into classroom discussions. He does tend to get into noisy conversations with friends and can seem restless and distracted.

Current grade: _F_

Attendance: _poor_

Other concerns:

I honestly doubt that Andy has the capabilities or motivation to pass this class.

Grade 6

Course	Grades				Course	Grades			
English/Language Arts	D	D	F	D	Math	C	D	F	D
PE/Health	C	C	D+	C	Science	D	D	F	D-
Geography	F	D-	F	F	Vocational Elective Experiences	B	C	D	B

Grade 7

Course	Grades				Course	Grades			
Reading	D	F	F	F	Math	C-	D	D	D
PE/Health	B	D+	C	C	Science	D	F	F	D-
Social studies	F	D-	F	D-	Art	B	C	-	-
English	D	F	F	F	Computers	-	-	D	D

Period	Times	Period	Times
1	7:40–8:24	5	11:49–12:33
2	8:28–9:12	6	12:37–1:21
3	9:16–10:00	7	1:25–2:09
4	10:04–10:49		
Lunch	10:49–11:19		
Advisory*	11:19–11:45		

Note: 6th-grade double periods (English/Language Arts) may use the passing time for breaks if the teachers elect to do so.

*Advisory period may be used as study hall at the teacher's discretion. Teachers are discouraged from using the advisory period for resource room support.

•••••PROPOSE A SOLUTION ➡

SOLUTION SUMMARY

Before proceeding to the reflection section of this chapter, write a brief summary of your team's solution here:

Our team defined the "real" problem here as _____

_____

_____

_____

_____

_____

_____

_____

_____

The key features of our solution were _____

_____

_____

_____

_____

_____

_____

_____

My personal view of the problem and solution is _____

_____

_____

_____

_____

_____

_____

TIME FOR REFLECTION

As you considered Andy's case, you probably found a variety of issues you needed to think about and discuss. This reflection section is designed to add to your deliberation, by focusing on the nature of inclusion, the complicated role of teachers, and the importance of learning about the network of colleagues available to assist you in your work.

The Nature of Inclusion

An unhappy reality in too many schools is the half-hearted compliance with inclusion laws. Teachers, generally under-prepared for the demands of inclusive teaching, are told this is something they must do. So new children are assigned to their classes, without help for the teachers or the students. And as Rogan and his colleagues put it, "Inclusion without support is abandonment" (Rogan, LaJeuness, McCann, McFarland, & Miller, 1995, p. 35).

One of the tasks all teachers face, in the midst of the complex and demanding world of teaching, is acquiring a child's perspective on the issue of inclusion. Inclusion isn't a matter of doing yet another chore demanded by the bureaucracy or an interruption to the smooth flow of neatly planned lessons. This is a question of a child's learning. And more, it's a question of a child's developing successful approaches to learning, successful attitudes about school, and a sense of efficacy about his or her own abilities. From the perspective of the included child, it's not a matter of inconvenience, but of opportunities.

There is some evidence that providing students who have learning disabilities with support in the form of learning strategies can help them catch up with their peers, but far too often the included children find themselves simply dumped into lower track classes with no support at all (Rogan et al., 1995). Yet there are many options available for schools to create more inclusion-friendly environments (Fisher, Sax, & Pumpian, 1999; Sage, 1997).

The starting point is coming to an understanding of inclusion as helping children, as opposed to inconveniencing teachers. The task then becomes, in part, gaining a balanced perspective—what Virginia Roach (in Fisher, Sax, & Pumpian, 1999) calls the three legs of the achievement stool: curriculum, instruction, and placement. Fortunately, it turns out that much of what we do to help special needs children is helpful to all children. For example, using groups for learning, using hands-on activities, and providing organizational supports are all solid recommendations for teaching most learners. Becoming a good inclusion teacher builds on becoming a good teacher (Capper, Frattura, & Keyes, 2000; Tomlinson, 1999).

You don't need to know all about inclusion and inclusive teaching techniques to start teaching, *as long as you are willing to be a learner throughout your career*. Tomlinson (1999) suggests a gradual approach, where each year you expand your capacity to differentiate curriculum in order to address the varied needs of the learners. If you are growing year by year, you will find yourself increasingly able to help all learners succeed.

Teachers or Counselors?

As you worked through the details of Andy's case, considering the stresses placed on him from home and school, it may have occurred to you that this situation calls on the teacher to be a lot more than a teacher. To what extent, you fairly ask, is a teacher also a counselor or surrogate parent? It may be worse than that question. DeCicco and Allison (1999) worry that the teaching profession is suffering from "mission clutter," an inability to focus on a specific purpose. They describe a third-grade teacher as having to wear these occupational hats: social worker, psychologist, baby sitter, paramedic, recreation director, maitre d', fundraiser/telemarketer, miracle worker, and teacher. It's a lot to expect from one person, and these expectations bring stress.

While the tradition of a caring parental figure has a long history in elementary schools, the idea that "caring" is important has recently found more acceptance even in upper levels of schooling. The National Middle School Association, for example, has argued that each child should come into contact daily with an adult who knows and cares for him or her (1995). Nel Noddings (1995a; 1995b) makes the case that schools are obligated to make themes of care a part of every day. Deborah Meier (1996) sees the kindergarten model as an ideal for all levels of schooling to aim at. In short, there are increasing calls for teachers to be more than technicians of instruction, but also to be role models and confidantes.

There are, of course, limits. You should become familiar with the counseling resources at your school and the legal issues surrounding teacher-student interactions. You are not expected to be a trained counselor, and you should be certain to refer children to the appropriate resources as you see the need. For example, your response as an educator to the possibility that Andy's time with his father is unproductive is completely different from your response to evidence that Andy may be experiencing abuse. The first situation calls on you to be empathetic and supportive; the second calls on you to report through official channels.

Consider how you can be an empathetic, caring person who connects to students. Your success in teaching most students will be enhanced when they sense your caring perspective.

The Network of Colleagues

One of the potential frustrations in this problem is the need to deal with so many people: a parent, an administrator, regular teachers, special educators, a psychologist, and a student. However, by seeing these forces as frustrating, we may be losing sight of one of the most important aspects of helping special needs students—the network of professionals that can assist teachers.

As you begin to uncover the complexities of working with included children, you should also be uncovering all those resources that are there to help. You may find that there is a classroom aide, and with clear expectations for how you will work together (Giangreco, 1997), this aide can become a powerful tool. You may encounter a speech therapist, a physical therapist, an occupational therapist, a counselor, a psychologist, and more. What is essential is that you enlarge your view of the resources that you can draw on—without passing off the child to other "experts" to handle. Early in your teaching assignment, it's a good idea to find out just what resources—human and material—are available for you. For the most part, don't view your place in this as an independent contractor. Instead, learn to see yourself as a part of a team that is sincerely concerned about the child's welfare. Success is much more likely in the context of a supportive instruction team (Bauer & Shea, 1999). You may be surprised how much you can improve life for your students by making a quick visit to a special education teacher and asking what is working for various students. A simple adjustment, such as providing your notes for a child rather than asking her to write them, can make dramatic improvements. The specialists in your school will not only have generic suggestions like providing notes, but they may also know particular techniques that work for the particular students you have in class.

This awareness of the "team" you have to work with should expand your thinking to reflect on the whole school context. Whenever you enter a school, you gradually become aware that there is a culture to this school. That culture is made up of the beliefs and practices and traditions and hero stories of the school. Some cultures are positive; some are negative. However, it is important for you to realize that the cultures will have an effect on your efforts and your ability to work with the support team for inclusion of special needs children. Anne Wheelock writes, "The rhetoric of *all students achieving* is little more than empty promise without a school culture, including the norms, values, routines, and beliefs about learning that define school practices, that nurtures that vision" (1998, p. 27). Given this, consider how you might contribute to creating a school culture that honors positive, motivating relationships between adults and the children.

DISCUSSION QUESTIONS

1. The perspectives of Andy's mother and the teachers were clearly at odds in this situation. How does the beginning teacher balance the focused concern of a parent with the accumulated wisdom of other teachers? When is it reasonable for the beginning teacher to oppose what a parent thinks is best? And how do you weigh varying perspectives of parents, particularly in a case where the child's time is split between parents who do not live together?

2. A student's behavior and a student's disability may have the same effect in a classroom, but these issues are quite different when thinking about what serves that student. How can you keep the behavior and disability separate, and still create the classroom atmosphere you wish to promote?

3. In the teams that address needs of students, teachers are in an interesting position. They generally know the students better than anyone else, but they may be in a position of lower status than their colleagues. How can a teacher establish and maintain credibility and a spirit of cooperation with the specialists in the school?

4. Just how much should a teacher be expected to adjust his or her lessons or teaching style to meet the needs of individual students?

5. Considering the PBL process, what did you notice about your own frustrations with this particular approach to learning?

FURTHER READING

Fitzgerald, M. A., Staurm, M., McGinnity, T., Houghton, L., Toshner, J., and Ford, A. (1997). The Grand Avenue Middle School story. In D. D. Sage (Ed.), *Inclusion in secondary schools: Bold initiatives challenging change* (pp. 75–102). Port Chester, NY: National Professional Resources, Inc.

This account of one middle school's work with inclusion provides a number of features worth thinking about. The school has been creative in deploying staff and organizing students into a "family" structure, where students and staff work in smaller groups. The curriculum that is offered builds on the ideas of multiple intelligences and integrated studies, making it a more natural process to create appropriate IEPs for included children. The account includes sample assessment approaches, schedules, and stories about inclusion.

Giangreco, M. F. (Ed.). (1997).*Quick-guides to inclusion: Ideas for educating students with disabilities.* Baltimore: Paul H. Brookes.

This book is a collection of ideas to help teachers succeed with inclusion students. Written as a series of "quick," reproducible recommendations, the book is user-friendly. You can easily find sections that will assist your work. The five major categories the guide addresses are these: including students with disabilities in the classroom, building partnerships with parents, creating partnerships with paraprofessionals, getting the most out of support services, and creating positive behavioral support. The book has many practical, promising suggestions.

Jarrett, D. (1999). *The inclusive classroom: Mathematics and science instruction for students with learning disabilities: It's just good teaching.* Eugene, OR: Northwest Regional Educational Laboratory.

This brief publication focuses on math and science, but it provides a number of practical ideas for how to make a classroom friendly to students with learning disabilities. For example, Jarrett points out the importance of cooperative learning and peer tutoring for students with learning disabilities. She also explains how to use inquiry-based science instruction with these students and how to enhance the students' problem-solving abilities in mathematics. Jarrett gives a number of general strategies for making textbooks more accessible to students who have trouble with the written word. The subtitle of this monograph, *It's Just Good Teaching,* is an important reminder that much of what we do for students identified as having special needs is simply effective instruction that all students could benefit from.

Tomlinson, C. A. (1999). *The differentiated classroom: Responding to the needs of all learners.* Alexandria, VA: Association for Supervision and Curriculum Development.

In her short book, Tomlinson builds a compelling case for teachers to create learning environments and experiences that help students grow and succeed. Her book has numerous examples of teachers adapting the curriculum (differentiating) to students of varying ability levels. The examples run the full range of public schools. In addition, she provides a list of many specific ways to adapt the learning environment and experiences for students. Lest the reader be overwhelmed by the demands of such a list, Tomlinson provides practical suggestions for how to ease into differentiation and continue to grow as a learner. This is a book well worth reading for inspiration and guidance on the issue of adapting the curriculum.

WEB SITES

Disability Rights Education and Defense Fund, Inc.
www.dredf.org/index.html
This site focuses on issues of the law as it pertains to questions of disabilities. The site includes a summary of IDEA changes for 1997 and 1999: www.dredf.org/idea10.html.

IDEA Practices
www.ideapractices.org
This site includes an index of resources and practical ideas for addressing inclusion of special needs students.

Internet Resources on Disabilities
http://busboy.sped.ukans.edu/disabilities
From the University of Kansas.

REFERENCES

Bauer, A. M., & Shea, T. M. (1999). *Inclusion 101: How to teach all learners.* Baltimore: Paul H. Brookes.
Capper, C. A., Frattura, E., & Keyes, M. W. (2000). *Meeting the needs of students of ALL abilities: How leaders go beyond inclusion.* Thousand Oaks, CA: Corwin.
DeCicco, E. K., & Allison, J. (1999). Ockham's razor applied: It's mission clutter. *Childhood Education, 75*(5), 273–275.
Fisher, D., Sax, C., & Pumpian, I. (1999). *Inclusive high schools: Learning from contemporary classrooms.* Baltimore: Paul H. Brookes.
Giangreco, M. F. (Ed.). (1997). *Quick-guides to inclusion: Ideas for educating students with disabilities.* Baltimore: Paul H. Brookes.
Jarrett, D. (1999). *The inclusive classroom: Mathematics and science instruction for students with learning disabilities: It's just good teaching.* Eugene, OR: Northwest Regional Educational Laboratory.
Meier, D. (1996). Supposing that. . . . *Phi Delta Kappan, 78*(4), 271–276.
National Middle School Association. (1995). *This we believe: Developmentally responsive middle level schools.* Columbus, OH: National Middle School Association.
Noddings, N. (1995a). A morally defensible mission for schools in the 21st century. *Phi Delta Kappan, 76*(5), 365–368.
Noddings, N. (1995b). Teaching themes of care. *Phi Delta Kappan, 76*(9), 675–679.
Rogan, J., LaJeuness, C., McCann, P., McFarland, G., & Miller, C. (1995). Facilitating inclusion: The role of learning strategies to support secondary students with special needs. *Preventing School Failure, 39*(3), 35–39.
Sage, D. D. (Ed.). (1997). *Inclusion in secondary schools: Bold initiatives challenging change.* Port Chester, NY: National Professional Resources, Inc.
Tomlinson, C. A. (1999). *The differentiated classroom: Responding to the needs of all learners.* Alexandria, VA: Association for Supervision and Curriculum Development.
Wheelock, A. (1998). *Safe to be smart: Building a culture for standards-based reform in the middle grades.* Columbus, OH: National Middle School Association.

CHAPTER FOUR

WHOSE DISCIPLINE PROBLEM IS THIS?

INTRODUCTION AND PROBLEM BACKGROUND

"Don't smile until Christmas." How many beginning teachers have received this bit of advice in starting off their school years? How many students may have suffered under artificial hostility as a result? The serious business of maintaining a safe, orderly environment in schools spawns an industry of systems and packages that promises help for the dedicated teacher. But the array of options can be paralyzing—and too often the advocates of any one approach to discipline come across as hawkers for the one true answer to a multifaceted challenge.

It's hard to overplay the importance of the discipline/management issue, either from the perspective of teachers facing unruly students or from the perspective of a concerned public. Surveys regularly discover that the biggest concern of the general public about education is discipline and safety in the schools (Rose & Gallup, 1999). At the same time, researchers document the importance of a well-managed classroom in promoting student learning (Wang, Haertel, & Walberg, 1993). In short, we often hear it said of a teacher that she or he "has a discipline problem," and this is a strong indictment of a teacher's abilities. An alternative reality may be that *schooling* has a discipline problem.

Perhaps it's worth looking at some of the extreme examples. A few teachers seem to manage classes effortlessly. They may not be able to articulate any "system" that they use, claiming instead that it's just a matter of relating well to the children. Some teachers will say they have no discipline problems, as though this were simply an innate quality. More often, teachers make deliberate and sustained efforts to run their classes well—and sometimes with quite mixed results. Consider the teacher who wants to create the supportive, nonconfrontational classroom. Students learn quite early that anything goes. The teacher may plead with students, play on their sense of guilt, and occasionally express profound disappointment. But the environment created here is not terribly supportive, maybe not even safe. Boundaries for behavior are fuzzy, and the guiding principle for the teacher's actions—a feel-good ethic—does not match the crowded and contrived gathering that constitutes a classroom. At the other extreme, a teacher may replace feel-good passivity with domineering aggression. Such teachers will brook no contradiction, no challenges to their authority. The primary weapon of such teachers becomes the harsh tone of voice, fueled by an array of put-downs ever at the ready. Students know they will incur the wrath of their teacher in any moves away from quiet compliance. Yet there is some mysterious attraction to sending that teacher over the edge of control. Whole schools can become sites of conflict and coercion. Here's the way one teacher–student interaction in the hallway of such a junior high school occurred:

> "You! Yes you! Come here!"
> "Yeah?"
> "Let me see your pass."
> "Pass?"
> "Come on, come on. Your pass."
> "Here."
> "This thing isn't any good!"
> "Huh?"
> "It isn't signed."
> "No?"
> "Let me see your program card."
> "I'm in Mister Brown's class."
> "I don't remember seeing you around. You better come with me."
> "But why?"
> "Because! Because you don't have a pass. YOU DON'T HAVE A PASS!"
> (Rothstein, 1987, p. 59)

There are intermediate positions as well. Some teachers work for democratic environments with clear expectations. Some create well-oiled classroom machines. In the 1984 movie *Teachers,* one educator, known to his students and peers as "Ditto," had created such a routinized classroom that it ran well for several periods even after he had died in the back of the room!

The nature of public schooling guarantees that classroom management and discipline will always be an issue. Public schools draw together people who would not normally associate. Schools crowd these forced companions into small spaces and give them tasks to do which too often seem unpleasant to students (Jackson, 1968/1990). These crowded companions—the students—then find they need somehow to assert themselves and establish some sort of status in the group. It is, of course, a formula for challenges. So whether we talk about an invitational school (Purkey & Novak, 1984), a quality school (Glasser, 1990, 1993), a community of learners (Kohn, 1996), a positive school (Jones, 1987), or any other sort of school, discipline issues will be awaiting us.

This chapter invites you to think about the issue of discipline at a level that may not have occurred to you yet. Of course each teacher needs to form policies and practices and routines for the classroom he or she inhabits. However, discipline may be an issue that spills out the individual classroom door and into the school more generally. In fact, there are schools where every teacher must use the same discipline approach, just as there are schools where every classroom is distinct from its neighboring room in this regard. One text on classroom management (Froyen & Iverson, 1999), for example, argues that the real starting place for good discipline is at the schoolwide level: "Professional educators need to think about management at a systems level (e.g., ecological systems theory). This means fitting classroom management plans into the schoolwide discipline policy, the culture of the school, and the culture of the community" (p. 31).

The problem you will investigate invites you to think about the bigger picture of discipline. When there is a discipline problem at a school, whose problem is it? Do we see each teacher as a maverick who will either make it or not in the rough world of classroom discipline? Or do we view a school as a community where all participants are called on to work together in order to create a positive place where learning is central? Is the teacher who "has a discipline problem" suffering, in part, because of the whole system of discipline in the school, as opposed to being personally weak or incompetent?

A reminder is in order. As with all problem-based learning experiences, don't forget to spend some time messing around with the problem before jumping at solutions. What seems enticingly simple at a quick glance may be more complex under the surface.

PROBLEM CONTEXT AND SOLUTION PARAMETERS

Context

You are a third-year teacher at Reston Junior-Senior High School, the only upper-level school in a rural community. You have worked exclusively in the junior division of the school, grade seven. You know all staff members fairly well, and you have a reputation for running an effective classroom. In fact, you've been called upon to serve as the only elementary-certified member of the peer coaching* committee, which was mandated by the superintendent. In that role, you allow teachers to visit your classroom in order to observe how you manage students.

The school houses 437 students in six grades. The largest set of students is the seventh grade, with ninety-two; the smallest class is grade twelve, with forty-seven. School demographics indicate a majority of white children, with 15 percent Hispanic and 12 percent Native American. More than 70 percent of the students qualify for free or reduced lunch.

The school uses teachers flexibly. Four teachers work exclusively with the lower grades, teaching the "solid" subjects; four teachers work with mixed junior/senior groups (art, music, physical education, special education). The remaining ten teachers work only with senior-division students. A copy of the daily schedule is included in the problem documents.

---

*Peer coaching is a form of ongoing professional development that usually involves observing a colleague teach and then offering neutral or clinical feedback to this person.

Problem

Your principal, Ms. Westlund, recently completed her second round of state-mandated teacher observations and evaluations. In addition to observing all nontenured teachers for the second time this school year, she managed to get into all tenured teachers' classrooms briefly. The rumor around school was that she did not like what she saw. This rumor has been confirmed by the memo received by every teacher today (see the copy of her memo in the problem documents). Clearly, Ms. Westlund plans to shake up the school.

Are things that bad at RJSHS? You have been content with your own classroom discipline. You don't recall any serious problems beyond what anyone would expect of seventh graders. Also, you had not heard of any widespread concerns about discipline at the school.

The memo was disturbing to you, and since you were already on the peer coaching committee, you arranged for the committee to get together to determine how you might respond to Ms. Westlund.

Solution Parameters

As indicated in the memo, your group will have an opportunity to present its ideas and recommendations to Ms. Westlund or her assistant principal, Mr. Oesterman. You should understand that there may or may not be questions about your ideas. You may choose to present the ideas in the form of a panel discussion or a presentation by one representative of your group (supported by colleagues) or in some other form. You may include visual aids or handouts in your presentation. The administrators will give you no more than twenty-five minutes of their time—and that includes time for asking questions. Essentially, you will need to decide what you will recommend for your school to do. Also as indicated in Ms. Westlund's memo, each individual will need to write a memo to Ms. Westlund, addressing her requests.

•••••••WORK THE PROBLEM ——▶

PROBLEM DOCUMENTS

A number of documents are included with this packet for your group to examine. You will find information about the context here, but remember the importance of going beyond the documents provided. Here are the documents:

4.1 Ms. Westlund's original memo

4.2 Section of a newspaper article on disorder in local schools. This section was a sidebar to a larger piece titled "Standards Move Education in the Right Direction." This sidebar generated more letters to the editor than any other issue in the previous year of publication. Members of the school board reported receiving numerous telephone calls as a result of the piece

4.3 RJSHS daily bell schedule

4.4 RJSHS school code of discipline

4.5 Comparative data on discipline referrals

4.6 Synopsis of several major management systems. These samples provide some indication of the range of options among management systems. There are many other approaches to management, so be careful about limiting your exploration to systems on this chart. Several books provide excellent, concise descriptions of various management systems (Cangelosi, 1993; Edwards, 1997; Queen, Blackwelder, & Mallen, 1997)

4.7 A sample evaluation form for presentations

PROBLEM DOCUMENT 4.1   *Ms. Westlund's Original Memo*

RESTON JUNIOR-SENIOR HIGH SCHOOL

Memorandum

Date: February 27, 2003

To: Faculty

From: Ms. Westlund, Principal

RE: RJSHS classroom discipline

I have completed all required observations and evaluations for our current schedule of mandated visitations. While I see a number of excellent things happening in our classes, I am more concerned than ever about the tone of the building and how this faculty is contributing to a problem perceived by the community at large.

As you know from recent news coverage, this community is concerned about the discipline of students in our secondary program. Kids are said to be running wild. Those of you who know me well are aware that I have supported the staff and defended our school publicly and privately. I have not wavered in my support.

However, I was surprised at the number of classrooms that seemed to lack basic control and respect. Students in the classrooms of novice and veteran teachers are not treating the learning situation seriously and they are not treating other persons with the respect they deserve. This is, simply put, unacceptable. I am not interested in blame. I know as well as the rest of you that "the times, they are a changin'." We have to deal with it.

So, here is the plan. Two weeks from today, we will meet as a faculty to determine a course of action. I will no longer tolerate the haphazard and fragmented approach to discipline at this school. We need to commit our whole school to one consistent, workable discipline program. I know that some of you don't think you need this, but our school does! It's a problem we all own.

I am asking two things of you in advance of that meeting. First, if any of you wishes to express an opinion about a schoolwide discipline plan, I would like to hear from you one week from today. We can meet and discuss the issue. This will give me a chance to weigh ideas before our faculty meeting. Second, I want a memo from each faculty member describing how you intend to manage your classroom. I need to know what "system" you use, or what system you think is best for you. Don't tell me you don't need a system or you don't have problems. I will consider these ideas in devising a proposal for our school.

PROBLEM DOCUMENT 4.2   *Excerpt from a* **Reston Weekly** *Article on Standards in Education*

Are Standards *Enough* at Reston?

EDITORIAL STAFF

While the rest of the state is leaping forward with the help of rigorous standards, Reston Junior-Senior High School may be left behind due to the oldest problem in the books: kids' not behavin'. How can any serious learning go on if there is not order in the school? Is it possible for even the brightest, most motivated scholar to master tough standards in an environment where more kids act out than push on?

Visitors to RJSHS in recent months have reported witnessing behaviors that were not part of schools in their experience. "Kids wear hats," reported one mother, who asked not to be identified. "When we were in school, hats were forbidden. There used to be an atmosphere of respect for authority." Another parent, who visited RJSHS as a guest speaker, added this comment: "I won't be going back there. I came as a guest, prepared my lecture carefully. The stu-

dents not only didn't listen, but they literally harassed me. Kids were wearing walkman stereos in class; everybody had gum. I actually had to tell the students to be quiet so I could be heard, and I was a guest! What are those kids learning?"

Ms. Olivia Westlund, principal at RJSHS, conceded that discipline can be a problem at the school. "There's a huge mix of kids here, as you know," Ms. Westlund commented, "and it's a challenge to get them all focused on learning. We realize the unique challenges of rural education, and we are working on climate improvements even now."

Who knows what "climate improvements" might mean? From this writer's desk, it looks as if more educationese is preventing our local school from taking charge, setting up some reasonable discipline and getting on with the business of educating our kids. Does anybody else care?

Junior Division		Senior Division	
Period 1:	7:45–9:15	Period 1:	7:45–8:35
Block SS/LA or M/SCI			
9:15–9:30		Period 2:	8:40–9:30
Advisory and Break			
Period 2:	9:35–11:05	Period 3:	9:35–10:25
Block SS/LA or M/SCI			
Lunch:	11:05–11:25	Period 4:	10:25–11:25
Period 3:	11:25–12:05	Lunch:	11:25–12:05
Mini-course elective			
Period 4:	12:10–1:00	Period 5:	12:10–1:00
Period 5:	1:05–1:55	Period 6:	1:05–1:55
Period 6:	2:00–2:55	Period 7:	2:00–2:55

Student Discipline

RJSHS is a community of learners. As with all communities, there are expectations for how we can make the community function well. Our theme at RJSHS is SMART. Stay SMART!

Supportive—we are all supportive of every learner

Mature—we must be mature in dealing with each other

Academic—there is one main reason why we are together: academics

Responsibility—take responsibility for your actions

Trust—we can only build community if we trust one another

Certain essentials are needed in a SMART school. These rules are listed below.

1. There is zero tolerance for use or distribution of controlled substances.

2. There is zero tolerance for vandalism, fighting, or harassment.

3. There is zero tolerance for excessive absences or tardies.

4. There is zero tolerance for disrespect, abuse, or insubordination toward faculty and staff.

5. There is zero tolerance for gang activity.

RJSHS will use out-of-school suspension for initial violations, followed by an expulsion hearing with the school board when warranted.

PROBLEM DOCUMENT 4.5 *RJSHS Summary Table on Discipline Referrals*

DIVISION	ATTENDANCE-RELATED	FIGHTING	INSUBORDINATION	OTHER	TOTAL
Jr, Fall 2001	87	12	16	44	115
Sr, Fall 2001	143	13	27	50	183
Jr, Sprg 2002	112	17	25	61	154
Sr, Sprg 2002	168	10	43	77	221
Jr, Fall 2002	114	14	18	61	146
Sr, Fall 2002	181	9	41	72	231

PROBLEM DOCUMENT 4.6 *Brief Comparison of Features of Sample Management Systems*

AUTHOR(S)	ASSUMPTIONS	TEACHER'S ROLE	STUDENT'S ROLE	SAMPLE TECHNIQUES
Canter and Canter (1992)	Everyone can control behavior, if expectations, rewards, and consequences are made clear.	Assert control by setting clear expectations and following through on rewards and consequences.	Focus on learning and self-control.	Clearly articulated rules, rewards, and consequences. No excuses for misbehavior.
Emmer et al. (1998)	Misbehavior results when children are not kept engaged and challenged.	Organize an academic, business-like atmosphere.	Focus on academic tasks.	Make organizational decisions well before meeting students; plan activities to keep all learners busy.

AUTHOR(S)	ASSUMPTIONS	TEACHER'S ROLE	STUDENT'S ROLE	SAMPLE TECHNIQUES
Glasser (1990, 1993)	People need to learn to control their own behavior and to become more logical. Misbehavior results from unmet needs.	Leader, not a boss. Facilitate problem-solving among students, helping them to make value judgments.	Learn to accept responsibility and act rationally.	Confront misbehavior with clear description; use of logical consequences, the classroom meeting.
Jones (1987)	Most discipline problems will disappear if there is a more efficient management of time.	Learn to communicate calm control Build positive relationships with students.	Respond to teacher's direction to stay on task.	Set limits with awareness, body position, eye contact, "praise, prompt, and leave."
Kohn (1996)	Behavior does not need to be controlled, but community must be built.	Do not dispense rewards or punishments; instead, assist students in learning to become good citizens.	Participate in creating community by making real decisions.	Actively construct a community of learners.

PROBLEM DOCUMENT 4.7   *Sample Evaluation Form for Presentations*

1. The team demonstrates *consideration of the audience.*   Lo   Med   Hi

- Acknowledges principal's concerns
- Links ideas to memo
- Builds presentation appropriate to purpose

2. The team demonstrates *sensitivity to the context.*   Lo   Med   Hi

- Proposes ideas that do not violate teacher norms
- Makes suggestions that address the range (7–12) and setting (rural) of the students
- Addresses (directly or through questions) implementation

3. The team demonstrates *understanding of management issues.*   Lo   Med   Hi

- Utilizes research in proposal
- Builds an internally consistent (philosophy) proposal
- Applies principles and strategies in defensible ways
- Acknowledges proactive nature of management (as opposed to merely reacting to misbehavior)

····PROPOSE A SOLUTION ⟶

SOLUTION SUMMARY

Before proceeding to the reflection section of this chapter, write a brief summary of your team's solution here:

Our team defined the "real" problem here as _____

_____

_____

_____

_____

_____

_____

The key features of our solution were _____

_____

_____

_____

_____

_____

_____

My personal view of the problem and solution is _____

_____

_____

_____

_____

_____

_____

TIME FOR REFLECTION

A great many issues arise in contemplating how to address the principal's request for a single classroom management system throughout the school. This reflection section attempts to guide you through some of these issues. Beginning with a general framework, the reflections invite you to think about several categories of management, including the difference between management in a specific classroom and an entire system. We will also examine questions about teacher independence, building a classroom environment, the relationship between discipline and development, and theories and principles of classroom management. Of course, you will find it important to continue your inquiry on this topic well beyond the reflections included here.

Three Components of Classroom Management

Froyen and Iverson (1999) offer an interesting way of conceiving of the task of establishing classroom management. They picture a triangle, the vertices of which represent these three components of management: *content* management, which focuses on organizing activities, space, and instruction; *conduct* management, which focuses on rules and consequences; and *covenant* management, which invites teachers to focus on relationships between the school and home, teacher and student, and students and students. Whatever management system we may be attracted to, this conceptualization of management broadens our thinking so that we don't reduce classroom management to one facet only. The triple focus reminds teachers that management is a part of a complex system of interactions, not a formula with precise and simplistic steps.

Theories, Techniques, and Stategies

Another distintion to keep in mind as we reflect on management issues is among theories, techniques, and strategies. A *theory*, in relation to classroom management, is a broadly-based explanation of how people act. For example, one theory of human interaction says that humans do that which is reinforced by rewards. This is a simplified view of behaviorism, of course, but it gives a certain power to explanations. A different theory might say that humans act to achieve self-fulfillment. Management ideas can be traced back to basic theories about how people function.

In contrast to the idea of a theory of human behavior, we can speak of management techniques. A *technique* is a relatively neutral means of performing an action. For example, some teachers' technique for getting a class to quiet down is to stand at the front of the room and shout, "All right, let's quiet down!" Another teacher's technique to achieve this goal might be to flip the light switch off and on, or to hold up one hand and begin the dreaded one-two-three count with fingers. There is often a relationship between a technique and a theory, but techniques have the capacity to cross over among theories, too.

At a different level, we can speak of *strategies.* Think of how we understand the notion of a "military strategy." In this case, a set of plans come together to achieve a certain goal. The strategy might be to isolate an area by cutting off supplies (a blockade), to patrol the back roads, and to squeeze the enemy with random bombardment. Essentially, the strategy pulls together a set of techniques (blockading, patrolling, bombing) based on a theory. In the same way, classroom management involves building a strategy (or system) that pulls together techniques in a way that fits a theory.

The confusion of many novice teachers comes about because of a narrow focus on only one of these levels—techniques. Too often beginning teachers have gathered techniques from their mentors, their reading, and their experiences, and attempted to bring them together like the shiny collections of packrats plundering the neighborhood. While most of the techniques are worthwhile and potentially effective, what is missing is the notion of strategy: a system of techniques that work together consistently because they draw on the same theory.

Given that broader perspective of the content–conduct–covenant management and the need to align techniques in a strategic way, there are several areas worth reflecting on to bring closure to this experience in understanding the question of who owns a discipline problem.

System Issues: The Broad View of All Components

The Total School.   Fullan and Hargreaves (1991) speak of the "total school" as a way of describing how various factors interact to create an environment that is worth fighting for. They contrast a culture of individualism with a culture of collaboration, arguing that the latter can help to create a school that is not "negative by default," but "positive by design" (p. 37).

Fullan and Hargreaves (1991) are concerned with getting teachers to work together to improve schools. But their notion of complexity and the need for time and careful attention to building a culture also applies to the "total school" from the students' perspective. What if the total school is teaching children that they are not responsible for making good decisions, because there is someone there to decide for them at every turn? What if the total school, as in the Rothstein (1987) example that opened this chapter, is moving children to the place where they begin to "see themselves through the eyes of their caretakers: They were lazy, incompetent, ungrateful, unreliable, ignorant, untalented, untrustworthy persons" (p. 70)?

This is too significant to pass over quickly. Imagine if you were placed in a job where your boss reminds you daily that you aren't very good at what you do. She restricts all your actions by insisting that you get permission for the most routine decisions; she publicly belittles you for your mistakes. After a time, you are elated to learn that you are being transferred to another division of the company. Unfortunately, your next boss is just about as bad. He doesn't belittle you on purpose, but it is clear from his actions that he doesn't think you are very competent. He creates an elaborate set of rules for you to follow and he watches for opportunities to catch you when you make mistakes. He believes that you can learn from your mistakes. So it goes year after year. An occasional supervisor reinforces your intelligence and independence, but most follow the lead of your first boss. After five or six years of this treatment, if you last that long, it's likely you will come to see yourself as incompetent and incapable of making important decisions. The cumulative effect of your bosses will have marked you. Even if you encounter a more trusting boss in your seventh year, it's unlikely that you would be able to shake off your patterns of belief and behavior.

Just so, the cumulative effect of years of control from the outside may limit our students' abilities to take on serious self-control. This illustrates the importance of teachers becoming active in the conversations about what a school system should be like. The system sits like a weight on the noblest of our goals. We need to care for the system.

Teacher Autonomy.   An argument can be made that discipline is a schoolwide issue. Any discipline problem, so this reasoning goes, quickly affects the entire community. A student whose tardiness is tolerated in one classroom will carry the effects into the next classroom; the emotional strain in one place will ooze through to the playground or the hallways or other classrooms in the same building. In contrast, some would argue that discipline is, at its most basic level, always a classroom issue. A given teacher faces a specific group of children in a particular context. That teacher must make decisions that are consistent with her beliefs, decisions that fit her style. Thus, it would seem, the decisions made about management are individual and independent.

Although the main focus of this problem is classroom management, one of the issues raised by the problem is the occupational community in which teachers function. Novices are generally not well equipped for the autonomous and isolated world of teaching. Indeed, you may have been teaching for years and still be bothered by such isolation. There's a certain irony that such a social occupation— you are always around lots of people—should feel so isolated. This situation has been well documented by numerous researchers (Ashton & Webb, 1986; Doyle & Ponder, 1977–1978; Hargreaves, 1993; Kainan, 1994; Rosenholtz, 1989). Teachers generally operate on their own, decide how to run their classes alone, choose and implement instructional plans by themselves.

While some work is being done to correct this isolation, it is an "occupational reality" that most teachers face. And this autonomy raises two questions that deserve some reflection. First, when is it appropriate to violate the "hands-off" norm of teaching and to offer help, advice, or intervention to a colleague? Second, how can a new teacher continue to grow professionally in such isolation?

Let's consider the first question. Suppose you are working next door to a teacher whose classroom is clearly out of control. The "hands-off" norm says that you leave the situation alone. When I was a beginning teacher, I heard noises coming from a nearby classroom, and I saw a stapler fly across the back of the room. With impressive panache, I marched into the classroom to tell the students to behave while they waited for their teacher to return from wherever she had gone.

Before I could utter my threats, I noticed the teacher—she was there! And she apparently was aware of what was going on. I quickly turned and left the room, embarrassed by my gaffe. I did not talk to the teacher. Should I have done so? The "hands-off" norm is a pattern of interaction that says teachers are professionals who handle their classrooms as they choose. Trust them. The teacher whose room I visited so rashly later left the profession, but not before hundreds of students had suffered through her class, with at least one receiving a stab wound during class. And the teacher, herself, experienced years of frustration. Is this really what's best?

From the other side, what about the teacher who wants to grow professionally, but worries about this "hands-off" norm? Fortunately, for beginning teachers, there is a tolerance for seeking assistance. You should be cautious about who you seek help from and about how you seek that help. Imagine the effect of going to your principal with this statement: "My class is out of control and I need help getting it fixed!" Even if that is true, it's not a productive opening. It betrays a lack of competence and self-confidence, hardly the message you want to deliver to your supervisors. Instead, first consider who to talk to. Most teachers can find colleagues who can create productive environments and who are eager to help novices. After discovering a willing colleague, start off with a better opening line: "I've noticed that your kids always seem to get right to work without your having to yell at them. Can you share some of your ideas with me?" You will find that most of your colleagues will respond positively to that sort of request.

Development?   The school described in this chapter's problem serves a wide range of students. What implications does this breadth have for answering a question about discipline or classroom management? Is it appropriate to build a management system that gains consistency by sacrificing appropriate treatment?

Children in the early adolescent period face unique issues of development (National Middle School Association, 1995; Stevenson, 1992). Among other things, the young adolescent is likely to be experiencing a radical shift of identification from the family to peer groups. At the same time, this young person is probably wrestling with understanding his or her identity, dealing with what David Elkind (1984) calls a persistent "imaginary audience." These issues are difficult, and they lead to different sorts of behavior, to forms of acting out that are potentially disruptive.

While all children differ, the students who are finishing their public school years are likely to be much more mature and confident than their middle school counterparts. The question, then, becomes this: Is it possible or desirable to create a management system that "fits" students across such a wide rage of development? And what if this system were to extend to the elementary schools as well? One might argue that if a management system taps into the way people work— that is, if the *theory* of behavior is universal—this system will work with all children. The other side would argue that the differences among developmental stages are so significant that no one system can possibly be an appropriate fit. What do you think?

In the Classroom—Content and Conduct Management

Classroom Environment.   While the problem for this chapter focuses our attention on schoolwide management, we need to devote some attention to the classroom level as well. In particular, it is crucial that new teachers recognize the importance of building a positive classroom environment for students, as opposed to simply orchestrating a quiet room.

The connection between the management and instruction aspects of teaching is well documented. Kauchak and Eggen (1998) state this quite forcefully: *"It is virtually impossible to manage a classroom without simultaneous effective instruction, and it is virtually impossible to have effective instruction without effective management"* (p. 332, original emphasis). In other words, a big chunk of the management issues can be taken care of by making sure the class is engaged in some worthwhile task. Does this mean class has to be "fun"? Can a professional make a distinction between time spent in *diverting* activities and time spent in *engaging* activities?

One way to address this question is to consider the outcome of activities. If students are merely filling time in entertaining ways, this is probably mere diversion. Admittedly, a teacher is likely to encounter fewer discipline problems in that situation than when kids are bored. However, it is more defensible for teachers to create activities that are both engaging and worthwhile. The positive classroom environment has at its base a strong instructional focus (Tomlinson, 1999).

Some writers have even seen management as an appropriate realm for incorporating the theory of multiple intelligences (MI) to assist with creating a positive classroom environment (Gibson & Govendo, 1999). Having thought through the use of space and collected varied and engaging activities, the teacher will be able to promote among the students a sense of autonomy and empowerment. Of course, there may be a danger here, in that the theory of multiple intelligences may have to be stretched to make it fit classroom management. For example, Gibson and Govendo (1999) cite the example of the teacher who stands at the door to greet students with a smile and handshake as a case of employing "bodily-kinesthetic" intelligence. Is this a case of taking a sensible means of establishing relationships with students and attempting to "dignify" it by tagging it with MI labels? Perhaps the more important point is that the environment can be made a positive experience by providing comfortable space and a warm tone.

Theories and Principles of Classroom Management

At this point, you should have investigated a variety of systems for managing a classroom. Clearly, there are too many for any one teacher to learn them all. Moreover, there is no point in learning them all. You may have decided that the theory that a given system relies on just doesn't match your beliefs about good education. For example, you may have seen virtues in a system like Assertive Discipline (Canter & Canter, 1992), which lays out a clear plan for establishing control. But the basic assumptions of this perspective, including the idea of rewarding and punishing, may not match your views. If you are not convinced of the basis, it's probably a good idea not to adopt the approach. Likewise, you may have seen the Glasser (1990) or Kohn (1996) approaches as naively optimistic about human interaction. One surely does not want to institute Glasser's classroom meetings as a technique in a context governed by a reward-and-punish view of human action.

Sometimes people express scorn for the diversity of theories. "That's all theoretical stuff," you might hear. "We want what works! Who cares about the theories?" This paraphrased complaint dismisses important differences, and it assumes that "what works" is readily apparent. It is not.

The conscientious teacher must be prepared to look beneath the techniques of management in order to assess the effects of management. Orderly classrooms where no one learns are no better, from an instructional point of view, than disorderly classrooms where no one learns. We need to ask ourselves whether the theories and principles we are bringing to life in our classrooms are having the desired effect. That is, are kids learning?

"Being" Issues—Covenant Management

Playing Roles.   Beginning teachers face a puzzling situation in learning to relate to their students initially. The idealism teachers typically bring to their first job is a wonderful asset. Too often, it is a short-lived asset. One factor in the demise of idealism is the pressure to fit the teacher role.

In terms of covenant management—the idea of relating well to students—the teacher faces a difficult balancing act. How can a teacher learn to build positive relationships in the context of responsibility for the classroom? How can the teacher be supportive and friendly without having to be a friend?

Froyen and Iverson (1999) offer some guidance through the idea of roles. Teachers must come to understand the expectations placed on them by virtue of their participation in the public institution of schooling. That is, the role a teacher plays in the system is not simply an expression of the teacher's personality. There is an established view of what is appropriate in the adult–child relationship in the culture that created the school. However, there is also a personal dimension to this relating. Teachers and classes build a history together, and each group differs. The teacher can express a caring attitude toward students, even while keeping the class focused on competent learning (Noddings, 1995). Noddings calls for us to relax the impulse to control others, to allow more autonomy for both students and teachers in decision making.

A Caution about Judging that First Year.   Whether you are facing a first year of teaching or in a position to help someone else who is, a caution is in order. The most anxiety-producing dimension of teaching, at least at the beginning of a career, is keeping control of a class. You want to make sure that your learning environment is positive and safe. However, be careful about adopting the perspective that all judgments about your effectiveness are rooted in this question of discipline. If you become too obsessed with this question, you might lose sight of that far more important issue: student learning. There will be many challenges in your first year of teaching. Give yourself some space to learn.

DISCUSSION QUESTIONS

1. How does a school decide on large system-wide issues? Are any voices lost in such decision making?

2. What are some distinctly different management systems? What fundamentally different views of education do they draw on?

3. What are the implications and consequences of adopting particular systems or approaches to classroom management across the school?

4. What makes for effective rules and procedures in a classroom? Does this vary by the type of classroom (e.g., elementary versus secondary; math versus music)? How does one remain sensitive to individual differences and still maintain "fairness"?

5. What is the extent of the power of a school administrator in determining classroom practices?

6. What "blame" does a school as an institution deserve for the way students behave?

7. What difference does it make for discipline matters that this school is a rural school?

8. Considering the PBL process, what did you learn about working in groups through this experience?

FURTHER READING

Cangelosi, J. S. (1993). *Classroom management strategies: Gaining and maintaining students' cooperation* (2nd ed.). New York: Longman.
   Of the many general management texts, Cangelosi's is one of the most readable. He includes a wealth of examples and scenarios for the reader to consider, and he gives fair play to many different approaches to discipline.

Koenig, L. (2000). *Smart discipline for the classroom: Respect and cooperation restored* (3rd ed.). Thousand Oaks, CA: Corwin.
   Koenig's book provides an interesting perspective in light of the discussion above about theories, techniques, and strategies. He starts by providing reasons why teachers should reconsider disciplining the way they were treated as young people. Then he provides a progression of strategies, from those that don't work through general strategies and on to strategies for managing specialized and difficult cases. Koenig's book is reader friendly, providing the beginning teacher with a rich pool of ideas at the level of techniques.

Kohn, A. (1996). *Beyond discipline: From compliance to community*. Alexandria, VA: Association for Supervision and Curriculum Development.
   A powerful book to contemplate what teachers should do in order to motivate students and manage classrooms. In particular, Kohn raises questions about the role of rewards in the sort of teaching and management systems we create. He makes us ponder whether treating our students the way you treat pets is a good idea. In a statement that has double meaning for the kinds of classrooms we create, Kohn writes, "Rewards usually improve performance only at extremely simple—indeed, mindless—tasks, and even then they improve only quantitative performance" (p. 46).

MacDonald, R. E. (1991). *A handbook of basic skills and strategies for beginning teachers: Facing the challenge of teaching in today's schools.* New York: Longman.

MacDonald's handbook has a chapter in it on a special form of teacher survival: "Learning to Work Creatively within the System" (pp. 23–38). This chapter does not provide a manual for management (though he does have a chapter on that, too). However, it is an excellent examination of what it means for teachers to participate in the larger system. Beginning teachers focus on a form of survival that is typically centered on just making it through each day with their classes. They have little time to look elsewhere, and as a result, they may find their creativity stifled by the organization of schooling. MacDonald helps teachers see the big picture, to "see the system for what it is and have the personal strength to resist being overpowered by it" (p. 27).

Tomlinson, C. A. (1999). Mapping a route toward differentiated instruction. *Educational Leadership, 57*(1), 12–16.

In her brief article, Carol Tomlinson says very little about classroom management. However, her description of three different teachers' work is well worth reflecting on from the perspective of seeing management as connected with instruction. Tomlinson describes three teachers. One is teaching important material, but in a way that is devastatingly boring. The second creates an exciting, action-packed classroom, but without any sense of purpose. And the third combines the best of both predecessors: a classroom that is engaging, but directed toward learning. Reading the article helps keep the focus on the learning environment we create for our students.

WEB SITES

MiddleWeb: Exploring Middle School Reform
www.middleweb.com/index.html
A terrific resource for middle school issues. The site is searchable, so entering the phrase "classroom management" will get you a host of up-to-date ideas.

Teachnet.com: Smart Tools for Busy Teachers
www.teachnet.com/how-to/manage
This particular section looks at a variety of ideas for how to handle the classroom management question.

National Middle School Association
www.nmsa.org
This site has links to research, resources, and practice issues.

REFERENCES

Ashton, P. T., & Webb, R. B. (1986). *Making a difference: Teachers' sense of efficacy and student achievement.* New York: Longman.

Cangelosi, J. S. (1993). *Classroom management strategies: Gaining and maintaining students' cooperation* (2nd ed.). New York: Longman.

Canter, L., & Canter, M. (1992). *Assertive discipline: Positive behavior management for today's classroom.* Santa Monica, CA: Lee Canter & Associates.

Doyle, W., & Ponder, G. A. (1977–1978). The practicality ethic in teacher decision-making. *Interchange, 8*(3), 1–12.

Edwards, C. H. (1997). *Classroom discipline & management* (2nd ed.). Upper Saddle River, NJ: Merrill.

Elkind, D. (1984). *All grown up and no place to go: Teenagers in crisis.* Reading, MA: Addison-Wesley.

Emmer, E. T., Evertson, C. M., Clements, B. S., & Worsham, M. E. (1998). *Classroom management for secondary teachers* (4th ed.). Boston: Allyn & Bacon.

Froyen, L. A., & Iverson, A. M. (1999). *Schoolwide and classroom management: The reflective educator-leader* (3rd ed.). Upper Saddle River, NJ: Merrill.

Fullan, M. G., & Hargreaves, A. (1991). *What's worth fighting for? Working together for your school.* Andover, MA: Regional Laboratory for Educational Improvement of the Northeast and Islands.

Gibson, B. P., & Govendo, B. L. (1999). Encouraging constructive behavior in middle school classrooms: A multiple-intelligences approach. *Intervention in School & Clinic, 35*(1), 16–22.

Glasser, W. (1990). *The quality school: Managing students without coercion.* New York: Harper & Row.

Glasser, W. (1993). *The quality school teacher: A companion volume to The Quality School.* New York: Harper Collins.

Hargreaves, A. (1993). Individualism and individuality: Reinterpreting the teacher culture. *International Journal of Educational Research, 19*(3), 227–246.

Jackson, P. W. (1968/1990). *Life in classrooms.* New York: Teachers College Press.

Jones, F. H. (1987). *Positive classroom discipline.* New York: McGraw-Hill.

Kainan, A. (1994). *The staffroom: Observing the professional culture.* Brookfield, VT: Avebury Ashgate.

Kauchak, D. P., & Eggen, P. D. (1998). *Learning & teaching: Research-based methods* (3rd ed.). Boston: Allyn & Bacon.

Koenig, L. (2000). *Smart discipline for the classroom: Respect and cooperation restored* (3rd ed.). Thousand Oaks, CA: Corwin.

Kohn, A. (1996). *Beyond discipline: From compliance to community.* Alexandria, VA: Association for Supervision and Curriculum Development.

National Middle School Association. (1995). *This we believe: Developmentally responsive middle level schools.* Columbus, OH: National Middle School Association.

Noddings, N. (1995). A morally defensible mission for schools in the 21st century. *Phi Delta Kappan, 76*(5), 365–368.

Purkey, W. W., & Novak, J. M. (1984). *Inviting school success: A self-concept approach to teaching and learning* (2nd ed.). Belmont, CA: Wadsworth.

Queen, J. A., Blackwelder, B. B., & Mallen, L. P. (1997). *Responsible classroom management for teachers and students.* Upper Saddle River, NJ: Merrill.

Rose, L. C., & Gallup, A. M. (1999). The 31st annual Phi Delta Kappa/Gallup poll of the public's attitudes toward the public schools. *Phi Delta Kappan, 81*(1), 41–56.

Rosenholtz, S. J. (1989). *Teachers' workplace: The social organization of schools.* White Plains, NY: Longman.

Rothstein, W. S. (1987). The ethics of coercion: Social control practices in an urban junior high school. *Urban Education, 22*(1), 53–72.

Stevenson, C. (1992). *Teaching ten to fourteen year olds.* New York: Longman.

Tomlinson, C. A. (1999). *The differentiated classroom: Responding to the needs of all learners.* Alexandria, VA: Association for Supervision and Curriculum Development.

Wang, M. C., Haertel, G. D., & Walberg, H. J. (1993). Toward a knowledge base for school learning. *Review of Educational Research, 63*, 249–294.

CHAPTER FIVE

MATH MAKES TRACKS

INTRODUCTION AND PROBLEM BACKGROUND

A fairly common distinction between the levels of teachers can be characterized by the response to this question: What do you teach? Stereotypically, the secondary teacher will answer math or English or chemistry; the elementary teacher will answer "kids." And it is generally somewhere in the middle school years that the distinction begins to be made with some regularity. Increasingly, the middle school is the level where the teacher's identity becomes tied closely to subject specialization, even if that teacher has an elementary background. At the same time, strong notions emerge about what the subject area requires of its adherents. In short, it is not just that one teaches math, but that one teaches math *the way it should be taught.*

Just how a thing should be taught seems to be a combination of some understanding of psychology, some practical considerations (such as available texts), some influence from other teachers in the school, and some powerful traditions. We often associate a certain logical sequence or natural categorization with subjects. For example, consider the reading group in a primary classroom. What possible sense would there be in grouping together a nonreader with someone who has mastered books several grade levels ahead of that child? To group them together, logic would tell us, would be to doom one to failure and the other to boredom. Likewise, the tradition of placing children into a math class or sequence based on their abilities seems to be the most logical response to differences among the learners.

Rarely do we question such givens in education. With such a long-standing tradition, surely there is good cause for the way things are. Surely the "integrity" of a subject like math requires that we bring students along in a systematic and logical manner, and the best way to do so is to group students according to proven ability. Beyond that, what other organization makes sense for busy, overworked teachers who don't really have the opportunity to interact with each child for very long?

This PBL experience invites you to look into that assumption. While the vehicle here is math, it is important for you (as a learner) to consider several other implications. Consider, for example, how the organization of math classes by ability levels affects the mix of students in other classes (since middle school is where students typically leave the self-contained classroom). That is, do the effects of the way we organize a single subject area reach into other areas of the school? Consider also how the logic of organizing a math class applies to other subjects. After all, are there not music students who are well ahead of their peers? Are there not gifted science students? talented writers? budding historians? actors? Is the logic of sequence unique to mathematics? Finally, consider what it is that gives a teacher the conceptual basis for such decisions. In terms of the organization of schooling, what do teachers who begin to specialize by a subject area share with practitioners at their level and subject?

PROBLEM CONTEXT AND SOLUTION PARAMETERS

Context

Burton Middle School, one of two 7/8 middle schools in this community of about 60,000 people, has proposed a major change in the curriculum. Due to reductions in student population, the school is restructuring its staffing, which spills over to the curriculum. Whereas the school previously offered an honors math section and a "basic" math section, they are proposing a program that mixes all levels of math students together. Teachers are to gear their instruction to meet the individual needs of the students in this mixed context.

The change in math instruction is part of a larger effort to mix all the "gifted" students in with their peers. The school has seen the development of a curricular system that separates children according to abilities. And some critics have pointed out that this separation is merely a smokescreen for the true separations in the school: separating ethnic groups and social classes. The proposal to make all classes heterogeneous, in addition to solving the staffing problem, will reduce the segregation of student groups.

The teachers proposed a solution to the staffing/tracking problem, and they presented their ideas to a school site council, which indicated its support of the plan. However, when the ideas were presented to a larger audience (all "interested" parents were invited, but the audience consisted exclusively of "gifted" parents), it became clear that there was widespread discontent with the plan. The teachers argued that a good school will meet the needs of all children, and that math could be taught in heterogeneous classes. Furthermore, they argued that the benefits of mixing the classes were well established, and consistent with the National Council of Teachers of Mathematics (NCTM) standards. However, parents were generally not convinced. Indeed, a number of parents made it clear at the initial meeting that they would be looking for other schools for their children. Another group of parents formally protested this plan (memo enclosed).

Problem and Solution Parameters

Your team has been appointed by the Burton school superintendent to investigate this problem. You are to make a recommendation in writing to the school board regarding the changes in the middle school curriculum structure. The team has educators, parents, and an administrator represented. You will present a team memo and an oral presentation lasting no more than ten minutes to the school board that addresses the following issues:

1. A statement of a curriculum perspective (some explanation about your team's view of the purpose of curriculum)
2. A recommendation regarding the program for honors students in math
3. Curricular and/or teaching recommendations you see as appropriate to the situation

On the day your memo is expected, the various teams will hold a discussion of the principles raised and solutions suggested.

PROBLEM DOCUMENTS

In order to assist you in your exploration of this problem, a number of documents have been included. These documents include the following:

5.1 Principal Wellington's memo to the curriculum committee, asking them to recommend a solution to problems created by staff reduction

5.2 Document created by teachers for the parent meeting at which the changes to the curriculum were announced

5.3 Memo from a concerned parent group to Superintendent Farley, complaining of the proposed changes at BMS

5.4 Letter of support from a parent, Margarita Delgado

5.5 Letter of protest from a parent, Dr. J. D. Stromberg

5.6 An alternate plan, proposed by a collection of teachers from the feeder elementary schools

5.7 An open letter from members of the three high school math departments

---

PROBLEM DOCUMENT 5.1 *Memo from Principal Wellington*

MEMO

To: BMS Curriculum Committee
From: Mr. Wellington
Date: 2/15/03
RE: Curriculum changes

As you know, I'm not one to do a lot of memo writing. I just want to remind each of you of our conversations. We have some changes for next year, as you know. We need to figure out how we're going to deal with a couple of problems, mostly caused by reduced teacher numbers.

BMS **current** staffing:

Grade 7:
23 FTE (3.5 math, 3 English, 3 reading, 3 social studies, 3 science, 1 technology, .5 library, 1.5 special ed., 2.5 P.E., 1 art, 1 music)

Grade 8:
25 FTE (4 math, 3 English, 3 reading, 3 social studies, 3 science, 1 technology, .5 library, 1.5 special ed., 2.5 P.E., .5 art, 1.5 Spanish, 1.5 music)

BMS reductions for next year:

Grade 7:
1.5 FTE (.5 math, 1 reading)

Grade 8:
1 FTE (.5 math, .5 reading)

For next year, we want to operate completely in teams. There will be no more "singleton" classes in the core areas (math, science, English, reading, social studies) that have students coming from a variety of teams. You must figure out a way to deal with this problem.

PROBLEM DOCUMENT 5.2 *Document Created by Teachers for the Parent Meeting*

BMS Moves Forward

Times change. Techniques change. What we understand about learning changes. And it is time that BMS made some changes in order to provide our students with the best possible educational opportunities.

In a move forward, Burton Middle School is making a number of changes for next year that will serve *all* our students better. The centerpiece of this change is in the math curriculum, which has traditionally been the sticking point for most reform at this level. To help our parents and students understand the changes, we have provided you with two resources in one. First, we provide a summary of the changes that we are proposing. Second, we list a series of questions and answers we anticipate to be important for the members of our community. We wish to stress that the teachers of BMS are fully supportive of this plan and what it can mean for *all* students.

Summary of Changes
In the past, the math curriculum at BMS has been organized into three separate programs for the regular student. (Our special education program offers individualized support to students in that category.) Most students have entered the main math program, which consists primarily of advanced arithmetic and some pre-algebra work at the seventh grade level, with focused pre-algebra at the eighth grade. Roughly 10 percent of our students have been in a more basic arithmetic plan, with "basics" in the seventh grade and "applications" in the eighth grade. Roughly 10 percent of our students have worked in an advanced program, with a rigorous pre-algebra course in seventh grade and high school algebra in eighth grade.

Next year, there will be only math classes, with no separation into the previous groups. All students will receive instruction together. However, through a process called "curriculum differentiation," we will address children's needs individually in each math class. This means that every class will have a broad range of abilities and interests (as is the case in almost every other subject now), and the teachers must differentiate the *activities* so that each child can progress.

Can it be done? The answer is an emphatic yes! Programs throughout the nation are able to provide adequate instruction for children in mixed groups. And many of the negatives associated with fixed math groups can be eliminated through this plan. But we know you have more questions. Read on!

Questions and Answers

Q: What does this mean for my child in pursuing high-level math in the high school?

A: We have analyzed the programs for all three high schools BMS children typically attend. For West High and Burton High School, there is no problem pursuing the full gamut of math courses. The use of "block scheduling" at those schools means that students can take far more math courses than are normally available. The freshman student who does not yet have a designated "algebra" credit can easily work through the highest math possible. For Rio de Colorado High, students face a little more challenge, but they can still easily reach the highest math with only one summer school course.

Q: Will my child learn as much math?

A: More. We have a tradition of hurrying through complex concepts in order to "cover" a textbook. The differentiation model means that students will explore concepts at their own pace long enough to develop deep understanding.

Q: What will class look like?

A: The traditional math class consists of a fixed routine: grade yesterday's homework, introduce a new skill, practice together for a while, begin homework. The differentiated model puts math in applied contexts. Students will face complicated problems, work on these alone and in groups, and meet with the teacher to examine their processes. At the end of each unit, students summarize their own learning.

Q: Is it fair to grade good math students against students who have math anxiety?

A: It's not fair to grade students against students in any case. We believe students should be graded "against" what those students' abilities suggest. As we come to know the students and their strengths and weaknesses, we believe the fairest possible grades will result.

Q: What about the state math test?

A: All students should improve on this. If there is good, solid instruction, then the students will learn.

Q: How does this change fit the school's mission?

A: Well. The mission of BMS is to build learners whose success makes them believe in themselves. The restructured math program will be the most positive step toward fulfilling the mission that we have taken to date.

Q: What about Sylvan Heights Middle School? Will they follow suit?

A: That's hard to say. We expect our example to push a lot of middle schools—well beyond the city limits—to improve math instruction. But we control only BMS.

Q: What about the students who were scheduled to start algebra next year?

A: Differentiation will work for them, too. We won't have any algebra sections.

Q: Does this mean an end to gifted education at BMS?

A: No. We know that we have an obligation to our "gifted" students, and we won't fail to meet that obligation. We simply believe that we can do so better under this system. Opportunities for expressing one's giftedness continue throughout the school— in extracurricular activities, differentiated activities, after school clubs, music, and so on. Each child, whether gifted or delayed, will find a full range of options available. But the best thing is that the children won't have as many doors closed on them as the current system allows.

We believe that what we are doing will be the best thing that has happened at this building since we changed from a junior high school to a middle school. This change lets us put action behind the words of being a developmentally appropriate school that puts the success of its children first!

PROBLEM DOCUMENT 5.3   *Memo from a Concerned Parent Group*

<u>MEMO</u>

Date: 3/10/03

To: Dr. Farley, superintendent

From: Burton Middle School Concerned Parents

RE: Curriculum changes at BMS

We, the undersigned parents, attended a meeting at Burton Middle School this week. While we were impressed with the care and thoughtfulness of the teachers, we were horrified at a number of things. We are requesting that you put an immediate stop to the proposed curricular changes at BMS. In particular, we wish to point out the following issues:

1) No serious consultation with parents occurred in making the decision to incorporate all math students into mixed-ability classes. The teachers indicated that parents could give input to the site council, but it is readily apparent that this site council does not represent our views. For one thing, most of these concerned parents do not currently have children enrolled in BMS—our kids are scheduled to enroll next year, and we were therefore unable to participate. Even if we had been members of the BMS community, we seriously doubt that our input would have been heard by the council.

2) What evidence is there that this change in curriculum will serve our kids? The whole reason behind gifted programs and advanced courses is that some kids are bored with school and the pace of instruction. Special classes provide that extra bit of motivation that allows our kids to stay connected. What assurance do we have that our kids will get any extra attention? This will probably become another instance of teaching to the middle in overcrowded classrooms, so neither end of the extremes is dealt with fairly.

3) Where is the administration on this? We heard from a group of teachers, particularly Ms. Southwerk, but where were the administrators? We don't understand why something this important does not come from the superintendent or at least the school principal. Where were the experts from State College? We feel as though this plan came from well-intentioned and overworked teachers, but without the necessary grounding in current research.

4) The whole process seems rushed, shaky, and indefensible. Why the need to act so quickly? We are asking for one thing only: that you delay the implementation of this misguided policy until we have a chance—as a community—to fully investigate what the consequences of such a policy might be.

PROBLEM DOCUMENT 5.4   *Letter of Support from a Parent*

3/9/03

Dear Mr. Wellington:

I know I speak for many parents in our community when I applaud the recent changes described in the BMS curriculum. For far too long this system has created the most insidious form of institutional racism: tracking!

As you are well aware, the honors courses at BMS and throughout Burton are hardly representative of the student population. While our schools are roughly 60 percent majority and 40 percent minority, the "honors" programs across the city are about 90 percent students of the dominant culture. Something's wrong! And it's even worse at BMS. The upper track math courses have a makeup of 95 percent Caucasian students, with only 3 percent Native American and 2 percent Hispanic. With a school made up of nearly 20 percent Hispanic children, is it possible that we can only get a 2 percent representation in the gifted programs? And I understand this is perfectly typical of such programs all across the country.

I have heard that the methodology for teaching math--and other subjects--has advanced to the degree that tracking is really no longer serving its original purpose. This is good news for all of us, and I only hope that the teachers at BMS take advantage of this opportunity to infuse their courses with relevant, top-notch learning experiences. But I congratulate you and the school on this important first step!

Sincerely,

Margarita S. Delgado

Margarita S. Delgado

Letter of Protest from a Parent

J. D. Stromberg, M.D., 101 Lakeside Circle

3/15/03

Mr. Wellington,

I won't waste your time on niceties. I'm pulling my daughter out of your school. While I have found the school to be generally effective (there are always exceptions), this move seems to take away the opportunity for excellence.

Now, in the service of some misguided political correctness—an attempt to include every-body—we will see a lowering of standards all around. No longer will children with natural abilities and inclinations be allowed to pursue excellence. We now have a ceiling set, and we will make darn sure no one moves any farther than the crowd.

It's a sad day for Burton when our schools hop on some PC bandwagon to the detriment of the few talented and motivated children. Fortunately, I'll be able to find other options for my daughter. Unfortunately, there are people who won't have that luxury. I think the whole community will suffer.

J.D. Stromberg

Open Letter to BMS Teachers from Elementary School Teachers

As your professional colleagues, we, the undersigned teachers from Burton, have heard of your intention to alter the math curriculum. We don't pretend to have any special mathematical expertise to help you in your decision, but our knowledge of children and their needs leads us to offer an alternate plan for solving the real problems at BMS.

We are all aware of the fact that enrollments are dipping throughout the city. This seems the perfect time for us to reconsider the role of the middle school in our entire system. Clearly there are first-rate teachers at both of the city's middle schools—there is no challenge to their qualifications. Yet, consistent with what has emerged across the country, the middle school may not be the best way for us to meet the needs of the children at this age. The greater specialization in math is not, perhaps, so much a response to the real needs of our learners as it is a concession to the conditions of schooling: large, anonymous schools to warehouse too many children.

Our proposal is to eliminate the middle schools completely. The students could continue to learn in the more friendly setting of a neighborhood school, where each child can be known by caring adults. By spending eight or more years in such an environment, the child has a true and powerful opportunity to be known well. The math program, or any other program, can be built around intimate knowledge of each child rather than building such a program around faceless conditions that apply in large schools in *which every child is either just arriving or about to leave.*

We ask that our ideas be given serious consideration in your attempt to solve a very real problem in our community.

(Letter signed by fifty-eight elementary teachers from all fourteen elementary schools in the city.)

Open Letter to BMS Teachers from High School Teachers

As members of the mathematics departments at the three high schools in Burton, we are calling on our colleagues at BMS to reconsider their position relative to the elimination of honors math at the middle school. We have several reasons for our position, which we outline below.

- Careful groundwork must be laid in order for a math program to have the integrity and depth that life in the 21st century calls for. Students need *more,* not *less,* math than ever before. Unless we push students to achieve at the middle level, they will not have opportunities to get that math.

- A leading group of mathematicians and scientists out of Berkeley has called for a moratorium on unfounded math practices that do not permit students to achieve at their highest level.
- From a practical perspective, students arriving at the high school from BMS will be seriously disadvantaged in comparison with students from other schools in the city or from transfer sites. The simple fact is that BMS students will have nowhere to go. They will be forced to the lowest track of math at our high schools, and their aspirations will be frustrated.
- The decision to make such radical changes in the math curriculum is unwise, given the isolated conditions of the decision making. Surely this is a slap in the face of the expertise of high school instructors, who, it should be noted, have far more advanced mathematical training than the middle school teachers, many of whom teach math without even a college major in the subject!

A more thoughtful, deliberate process for your change would be to bring together key players in the math curriculum throughout the city. Let us open the discussion from a perspective that will honor the goals we have as a system.

(Signed by the chairs of the math departments of the three public high schools in Burton, and twenty-two other high-school math teachers.)

SOLUTION SUMMARY

Before proceeding to the reflection section of this chapter, write a brief summary of your team's solution here:

Our team defined the "real" problem here as _____

_____

_____

_____

_____

_____

_____

_____

The key features of our solution were _____

_____

_____

_____

_____

_____

_____

My personal view of the problem and solution is _____

_____

_____

_____

_____

_____

_____

_____

TIME FOR REFLECTION

As you reflect on your experience with this PBL activity, you should draw up a list of the issues that need further exploration. This section will guide you to think about a number of such issues, though you may discover that topics you found important are not anticipated here. We will consider some of the needs of gifted students and their parents. This leads to an examination of the grouping of students more generally. Thinking about how to organize a course in mathematics may raise questions about the assumptions of subject areas—math and others. The reflections also invite you to think about the differences among models of educating children at this level. Finally, the problem suggests a number of questions about how teachers should relate to the leadership in their schools.

Gifted Students

Much of the controversy in this particular PBL activity arises from the school structures that surround the idea of the "gifted" student. What do teachers need to know about gifted students? Does any such client really exist?

A somewhat underrated part of special education, gifted education builds on the theory that each child should receive an education that is a best fit for that child. Students with disabilities receive the sort of assistance that allows them to compensate for those disabilities; students who are gifted receive assistance and opportunities that allow them to stay engaged in the learning process. Surprisingly, gifted students have unusually high levels of attrition from schools, perhaps due to the boredom they encounter.

Traditionally, giftedness has been defined in terms of exceptional verbal and quantitative abilities. That is, people who performed well on standardized tests were the ones who were identified as gifted. In recent decades, giftedness has been thought of more broadly than just a narrow range of abilities. A student might be gifted in ways that don't show up on standardized tests—gifted as a creative thinker or as a problem solver or as an artist. So, a first point to raise in reflecting on the "gifted" students represented in this PBL experience is that the students in the advanced math classes may have some "giftedness," but they will certainly not be the entire population of gifted students at a school. If the school officials or the parents have somehow managed to reduce *giftedness* to the children who make up the advanced math class, the definition of giftedness is in serious need of revision at that school. (It may interest you to know that such notions as "gifted" or even "intelligence" are what we call *constructs,* human inventions that are heavily dependent on context and culture. For example, intelligence in Australian aboriginal society is often associated with the spatial ability to find one's way in the wilderness. That ability does not generally enter the American view of intelligence.)

On the other hand, there is almost no question that some of the children in an advanced math class are "gifted," and that fact deserves consideration. To neglect such children's needs would be indefensible. How, then, can teachers help gifted children without setting up special sections or classes that separate these children from their peers? The answer, addressed in part below, may have to do with the notion that the best teaching for gifted children is the best teaching for all children. Provide all children with opportunities to face interesting, relevant challenges in their work; provide all children with chances to deal with big ideas and to solve important problems. Gifted children as well as low-achieving children can benefit from rich curriculum (Haycock, 2001).

"Gifted" Parents and Parent Relations in General

Learning to work with parents is an important part of the job of a teacher. And this is true beyond the elementary level. In fact, one of the most crucial ages to focus on effective parent relations is at the middle school level, when children typically begin to assert more independence and realign themselves with peers more than family members (Stevenson, 1992). If for no other reason than public relations, teachers at the middle level do well to consider how they can succeed with parents. Just imagine how the world looks to a parent of a seventh-grader: "I gave you teachers my delightful child, and you gave me back a moody, unpredictable, difficult adolescent." Of course, we all know that it's not the teachers' fault, but in the turbid times that families face at adolescence, it's nice to have allies among the teachers.

Ironically, many times the parents that provide the most challenges to teachers who wish to change the system are the parents of "gifted" children (Wheelock, 1992). In their work with middle schools engaged in reform, Oakes, Vasudeva, and Jones (1996) found that parents from lower income groups were most likely to trust teachers with change, while parents from upper income groups (and most often in the "gifted" category) resisted change. The "advantaged" students were doing fine, so there was no reason to change the system.

This suggests that dealing with the parents of gifted children is a delicate matter. Traditional schools have worked well for them and their children, and altering the system now may seem unnecessary and unfair. In the problem documents for this PBL experience, you may have noticed that the parents of gifted students felt excluded from the decision-making process. Do you think there might have been a better way to include them? Would some other mechanism for sharing information provide some comfort? Or does it seem that the very nature of the change will provoke opposition? Like virtually all parents, the parents of gifted students want what is best for their children. If a school is to be successful with all children, alienating any group of parents is foolish—but alienating the group most likely to support your school is exceptionally foolish.

As a member of the professional community in your school, beware of any tendency among educators to view parents as obstacles to change. Keep the notion before your colleagues that the parents want what is best, and your task is both to make sure you seek what is best and to communicate this effectively. Relating to the parents who take an interest in the larger life of your school is another of the crucial, but generally unexplored, skills a teacher must develop.

Wheelock (1992) provides several suggestions for working effectively with parents. The key element, however, appears to be communication. Parents should be offered opportunities early in the process of change to participate and express concerns and questions (which teachers should address). Parents should be informed continually as the process goes forward. Parents are far less likely to oppose a change that is committed to providing benefits for all children than they are to oppose changes they perceive to be withdrawing benefits from their own children.

Heterogeneous versus Homogenous Classes

What seems on the surface to be an organizational issue very quickly transforms into an issue of curriculum and instruction. That is, the demands on a teacher to employ a wide variety of teaching techniques increase dramatically when the learners have diverse abilities. Unfortunately, research isn't very encouraging about varied teaching techniques. Goodlad's (1984) massive study of schools revealed that the range of teaching options tends to get smaller as the children get older, with increasingly passive models of teaching used by teachers and increasingly bored students. Oakes, Vasudeva, and Jones (1996) hoped to find tremendous variety in the reformed middle schools they examined. Instead, they write, "the most salient finding from our interviews and observations is that traditional, teacher-directed instruction remains firmly in place in the vast majority of middle grades classes. Upon close inspection, we found that innovative-looking curriculum and learning activities often turned out to be conventional teacher-led, coverage-driven lessons" (p. 18).

What has that to do with the makeup of classes? A great deal. The uniform teacher-dominated lesson, whether in math or language arts or social studies or any other subject, doesn't work well when the students represent a wide range of abilities. Thus, to contemplate changing the composition of the classes demands contemplating changes in instruction. Clearly it makes no sense to simply install a sequence of teacher-dominated lessons that have students alternate between passive listening, practice, and waiting their turn while kids of another ability level receive similar instruction. Relying on the lecture, which Kauchak and Eggen (1998) call the "least effective but most popular mode of instruction" (p. 288), will not lead to much success.

But the prior question is perhaps the one that most products of a traditional educational system would ask: Why change at all? What's wrong with the homogeneous classes? Much of the investigation you have conducted with this problem will help you to formulate a response to that issue. However, for the sake of reflection, here are some questions to guide your thinking about the implications of organizing students in similar or different groups:

- What does this mean for instructional practices?
- What does this mean for the interactions among students?
- What does this mean for the opportunities students have for further study?
- How does such a decision influence high standards of achievement?
- How will community members respond to such changes?
- Who might benefit and who might lose from such reorganization?
- What new demands for beginning teachers are created in such changes?

In her book on tracking, Wheelock (1992) makes a powerful point. The key to changing from homogeneous to heterogeneous classrooms is "a shift from an emphasis on teaching to an emphasis on learning" (p. 191). She also reminds us of the dominance of homogeneous grouping in math, with 94 percent of students in homogeneously grouped math classes by ninth grade.

Challenging the Assumptions of a Subject Area

This PBL experience focused on the issue of mathematics instruction, but it really raises a broader question. Is there a place to challenge the assumptions of a subject area? For years, math has been sequenced in a certain manner, even when prestigious groups such as the National Council of Teachers of Mathematics have recommended changes. We find, in math, that although society has changed dramatically and our understanding of pedagogy has changed, math instruction has not. It remains "numbingly predictable" (National Commission on Mathematics and Science Teaching for the 21st Century, 2000, p. 20).

But math is not alone here. Each of the areas taught in public schools carries with it assumptions about what good teaching looks like or what the order of learning events must be. For example, must one master the sentence before writing a paragraph? Are phonics the key to reading? Is the right way to teach the history of a country to proceed through key events in chronological order? Each question pushes at the basic assumptions of the subject area.

Clearly, at the beginning of a teaching career, novices are probably more concerned with getting down the names of Civil War figures than with questioning how the Civil War fits reasonably in an innovative re-ordering of the topics of history. So why bother with such questions now? The fact is that the habits you develop and the structures you endorse early in your career (all influenced by the mentors you find) will have a powerful, long-lasting mark on how you teach. While it is true that beginning teachers worry mostly about "survival" issues and need time to develop practitioner's expertise (Reynolds, 1992), unless you begin the practice of reflecting on the assumptions of your area, it will be very difficult to learn this practice later. For those who have been teaching for some time, you will recognize the two-fold difficulties of such reflections. First, the habits and assumptions of the subject area may have come to seem like "common sense."

Second, the lessons and plans a teacher has created become a template for future work, and the difficulties of changing that template often don't seem worth the effort.

Middle Schools, Mini-High Schools, or Extended Elementary Schools?

A group of elementary teachers and a group of high school teachers both offered suggestions for how best to organize Burton Middle School. Not surprisingly, the high school teachers urged a structure on the middle school that would make it look much like a mini-high school. And the elementary teachers urged a structure that would bring the middle school students back into the elementary fold. Both groups argue, as do many others, that the middle school is simply not an effective institution. Ruth Mitchell of the Education Trust went so far as to call the middle school a "disaster" (Norton, 2000). Thomas Dickinson (2001) points out that the middle school has fallen far short of its high goals (though he advocates its "reinvention" rather than its elimination).

The issue raised is a concern that the structure does not attend to the needs of children as well as it might. Part of your consideration for this PBL experience should have placed you in a position to consider whether middle schools are, in fact, effective. While such schools arise from a mandate to be developmentally appropriate (National Middle School Association, 1995), their effectiveness in this goal is less evident. There is good evidence that thoughtful implementation of the *Turning Points* (Carnegie Council on Adolescent Development, 1989) reforms will lead to effective middle schools (Felner et al., 1997). Among other things, these documents advocate the end of tracking students according to academic ability, and they further call for interdisciplinary team teaching so that students can become part of smaller teams where teachers can create instruction that fits their levels.

Still, the alternative of extending the elementary structure deserves thoughtful consideration. What trade-offs would be made in such a structure? For example, would there be greater sensitivity to learners, as the elementary teachers claim? Would there be a loss of disciplinary knowledge? And what of the arguments that make a case for the middle school as the most appropriate structure for the developmental needs of young adolescents? Are children in this stage different enough from their younger counterparts to warrant a separate school?

All this suggests that the way schools are put together into a system has some basis in what best serves children and young people. Reflecting on the question of how to organize the math classes invites us to contemplate why schools are structured as they are. Is there some value to the interdisciplinary team structure so widely advocated for middle schools?

Perhaps a side issue here is school size. Many districts combine multiple elementary schools into a feeder system whereby one middle school serves them all, resulting in a large, "efficient," and impersonal structure. Would a smaller middle school avoid the problems generated at BMS without altering the curriculum?

Relating to Administrative Leadership

The principal of a school is sometimes seen as the instructional leader, the lead teacher. In this role, the principal serves to model sound teaching practices for the staff, to set a direction for the interactions among learners and teachers in the school. That may or may not be the case. You may find yourself in a school with an instructional leader, a facilities manager, a clerk, a bureaucrat, or some other model. Given this range of leaders, it is crucial that teachers learn how best to relate to the administration, whatever perspective on leadership that person exhibits.

A first step in gaining this understanding is to realize that leadership is not restricted to the positions sanctioned by an organizational chart. Leadership has been widely studied in educational and business settings, making it what Bennis and Nanus (1985) call the "most studied and least understood topic of any in the social sciences" (p. 20). These authors indicate there are over 450 definitions of leaders! They draw on interviews of ninety business leaders to conclude that everyone has some capacity for leadership, and it's a matter of learning how best to exercise it. As a teacher, you will be called on many times to exercise leadership, and not just with students in your class. To relate successfully to your administrative leaders, begin by recognizing you have both the capacity and obligation to exercise leadership, too.

Still, there generally is an occupant in the principal's office, and that occupant has much to say about the quality of life you will lead and the quality of the school you will be a part of. Desperate for that first job, teachers rarely research thoroughly the person they will be working for. Consider the following possibilities as you think about different types of school leadership.

Let's assume you've found yourself in a school with a leader like Mr. Wellington. How do you assess him? He apparently has seen that something must be done, but he hasn't taken it upon himself to do anything. He appears to be comfortable letting his teachers take the initiative—and whatever heat may result from that. What does the conscientious teacher do? On the one hand, you can become an active, informed participant in the conversations about the curriculum. If you are beginning a career, recognize that your experience level will be less than most of your colleagues, and often with teachers, "experience counts, theory doesn't" (Hargreaves, 1984). This may mean that your participation in the dialogue should be thoughtful, but quiet. In general, the new teacher can bring much to improve a school, but primarily through the process of asking questions and building rapport, an important leadership dimension (Wellins, Byham, & Wilson, 1991). Even good ideas may not be well received from the newest staff member, unless that member establishes some credibility both as a teacher and as a person who can interact effectively with other adults.

Another possibility, however, is that the principal is at the opposite end of the spectrum from Mr. Wellington. Principals are often sure of themselves, confident in their decisions, and not at all hesitant to push their staff in a particular direction. It would not be unrealistic for a principal to communicate to the teachers that certain changes would be in effect the next year, and if the teachers don't like it, they are welcome to move on. Of course, there are limits to what even principals *may* do, even if they feel they *can* do anything. How does a teacher work effectively with this sort of administrator? As in all human interactions, sensitivity to the particular context will help you succeed. Consider these general questions as you reflect on how you might respond to such a leader:

- Is it likely you would change this person's mind with direct opposition?
- Which is more important to such a leader—the *appearance* of knowledge and authority or the *substantive support* for knowledge and authority?
- What other leadership do you see in the school, and how can you connect to this leadership without jeopardizing your position?

As in most areas or occupations, it is quite possible that someone will occupy a position of authority over you without being the sort of leader who will inspire you to good work. If you find yourself in this situation, you have some choices to consider. Leaving is an option. When your ethical position is endangered, leaving may be the only legitimate option. Generally, there are some other choices. Exercise leadership yourself, look to mentors and colleagues for leadership, become a learner. What is least likely to support you for a successful life as a teacher is to develop and dwell on the cynicism that far too many teachers have opted for in the face of mediocre or poor leadership in the schools.

DISCUSSION QUESTIONS

1. What assumptions do you have about the way your subject matter should be taught? Are there alternative ways of seeing various subjects? What gives credibility to a particular view of the organization of a subject ?

2. What can you learn from the BMS approach to curriculum change? Were the teachers placed in a position that demonstrated trust in their professionalism, or were they exploited? Were parents properly involved in the decisions?

3. What do you see as some of the unintended consequences of creating advanced or gifted classes of students? Do these consequences reach to teachers, also?

4. What sort of leadership do you expect in a school? How can teachers be effective leaders, even when the "authority" rests in the principal's office?

5. How has your exploration of the issues embedded in this problem influenced your view of the basic structure of schooling (elementary, middle, high school)? What reasons are you aware of for the structure of schools in your area? Do factors such

as efficiency or available space dictate arrangements despite what we know about good practices? Are schools allowed to get too large?

6. Considering the PBL process, what did you learn about your ability to look at issues from a new and unfamiliar perspective? How does perspective-taking help you gain insight?

FURTHER READING

Harrison, J. (1993). Strategies for the heterogeneous math class. *Middle School Journal, 24*(4), 10–16.
Harrison recounts how a Florida middle school team restructured their math groupings so that all children could experience the subject together, with an emphasis on reducing barriers between races and socioeconomic groups. Her account provides a living example of what one school was able to do in the name of reform and math.

Kladder, R., Peitz, J., & Faulkner, J. (1998). On the right track: Connected Mathematics Project seeks to eliminate the disparities of academic tracking. *Middle Ground, 1*(4), 32–34.
A very brief introduction to a sample math curriculum that attempts to draw all students— whatever their abilities—together in order to focus on the conceptual understanding that lies beneath the math procedures children typically learn.

Ma, L. (1999). *Knowing and teaching elementary mathematics: Teachers' understanding of fundamental mathematics in China and the United States.* Mahwah, NJ: Lawrence Erlbaum Associates.
This descriptive account of teaching mathematics may be too specialized for most readers, but it is interesting to note Ma's observations on how the subject knowledge is built among teachers. Despite having an average of four years less education than their American counterparts (and far fewer math courses), Chinese teachers manage to develop and impart a greater understanding of mathematics. The key difference appears to be that Chinese teachers continue to see themselves as learners in their teaching careers, and they work with their colleagues to develop their understanding over time.

National Middle School Association. (1995). *This we believe: Developmentally responsive middle level schools.* Columbus, OH: Author.
This position paper from NMSA helps establish what is generally meant by the notion of a "middle school." The document establishes some of the characteristics of young adolescents, a list of characteristics of "developmentally responsive" schools, and specific recommendations about curriculum, instruction, assessment, organizational structures, support programs, and guidance services. Among other things, the document expresses opposition to tracking.
The NMSA web site (www.nmsa.org) also provides some useful information for thinking about this particular situation. At this site you can find a link to resources, including fax sheets that provide concise information on issues such as organizing schools and heterogeneous classrooms.

U.S. Department of Education, National Center for Education Statistics, Third International Mathematics and Science Study, Videotape Classroom Study, 1994–95. Available: http://nces.ed.gov/pubs99/timssvid/index.html
The Third International Mathematics and Science Study provides a wealth of information about how mathematics might be taught. This portion of the TIMSS work highlighted differences among the methods of instruction in U.S., Japanese, and German classrooms during an eighth-grade lesson. The contrast between U.S. and Japanese math lessons is interesting, and not just for math teachers (since it highlights a general approach to pedagogy). The U.S. lessons followed this pattern: teachers explain a skill, teachers demonstrate,

then students practice. The Japanese lessons followed this pattern: teachers pose a complex problem, students struggle with the problem, some students present ideas or solutions, the teacher summarizes the conclusions of the class, and then students practice similar problems. (See http://nces.ed.gov/pubs99/timssvid/chap7.htm#86 for a comparison chart.) The result was a different emphasis, with the U.S. lessons focusing on skills and the Japanese lessons focusing on concepts.

The TIMSS data figure heavily in another important document, *Before It's Too Late: A Report to the Nation from The National Commission on Mathematics and Science Teaching for the 21st Century*. In this report, the commission contrasts the virtually unchanged instructional practices of math classes over the past fifty years with "high quality teaching." Among such ideas as inquiry, high standards, and using information, the commission calls for teaching that "allows for, recognizes, and builds on differences in the learning styles and abilities of students" (2000, p. 22).

Wheelock, A. (1992). *Crossing the tracks: How "untracking" can save America's schools.* New York: The New Press.

This book provides an extended argument for eliminating tracking, with numerous examples from schools and comments from the teachers and principals in those schools. Two chapters in Part II of the book are particularly relevant to the work on this PBL experience. Chapter 5 addresses instruction and assessment in heterogeneous classes. Chapter 6 looks at math classes in particular. Wheelock acknowledges that math classes are the least likely to be untracked, pointing out that by ninth grade, 94 percent of students are in homogeneous math classes. However, Wheelock stresses the benefits to all children of simply providing better instruction and assessment in math, with more interaction among peers and better focus on the thinking behind problem solving.

WEB SITE

The Middle Web
www.middleweb.com
This web site gathers together links and resources that will assist you in thinking about the complexities of teaching at the middle level. Of particular interest to this PBL experience is the section of list serve conversations (on such topics as math and literacy or teaching math). You can access this at www.middleweb.com/MWLISTCONT/MSLstringsINDEX.html

REFERENCES

Bennis, W., & Nanus, B. (1985). *Leaders: The strategies for taking charge.* New York: Harper & Row.

Carnegie Council on Adolescent Development. (1989). *Turning points: Preparing American youth for the 21st century.* New York: Carnegie Corporation.

Dickinson, T. S. (Ed.). (2001). *Reinventing the middle school.* New York: RoutledgeFalmer.

Felner, R. D., Jackson, A. W., Kasak, D., Mulhall, P., Brand, S., & Flowers, N. (1997). The impact of school reform for the middle years: Longitudinal study of a network engaged in Turning Points-based comprehensive school transformation. *Phi Delta Kappan, 78*(7), 528–532, 541–550.

Goodlad, J. I. (1984). *A place called school: Prospects for the future.* New York: McGraw-Hill.

Hargreaves, A. (1984). Experience counts, theory doesn't: How teachers talk about their work. *Sociology of Education, 57*(4), 244–254.

Harrison, J. S. (1993). Strategies for the heterogeneous math class. *Middle School Journal, 24*(4), 10–16.

Haycock, K. (2001). Closing the achievement gap. *Educational Leadership, 58*(6), 6–11.

Kauchak, D. P., & Eggen, P. D. (1998). *Learning & teaching: Research-based methods* (3rd ed.). Boston: Allyn & Bacon.

Ma, L. (1999). *Knowing and teaching elementary mathematics: Teachers' understanding of fundamental mathematics in China and the United States.* Mahwah, NJ: Lawrence Erlbaum Associates.

National Commission on Mathematics and Science Teaching for the 21st Century. (2000). *Before it's too late.* Washington, DC: U.S. Department of Education.

National Middle School Association. (1995). *This we believe: Developmentally responsive middle level schools.* Columbus, OH: Author.

Norton, J. (2000). Important developments in middle-grades reform. *Phi Delta Kappan, 81*(10), K2–K4.

Oakes, J., Vasudeva, A., & Jones, M. (1996). Becoming educative: Reforming curriculum and teaching in the middle grades. *Research in Middle Level Education Quarterly, 20*(1), 11–40.

Reynolds, A. (1992). What is competent beginning teaching? A review of the literature. *Review of Educational Research, 62*(1), 1–35.

Stevenson, C. (1992). *Teaching ten to fourteen year olds.* New York: Longman.

Wellins, R. S., Byham, W. C., & Wilson, J. M. (1991). *Empowered teams: Creating self-directed work groups that improve quality, productivity, and participation.* San Francisco: Jossey-Bass.

Wheelock, A. (1992). *Crossing the tracks: How "untracking" can save America's schools.* New York: The New Press.

CHAPTER SIX

MULTIGRADES OR MIGRAINES?

INTRODUCTION AND PROBLEM BACKGROUND

My grandmother studied to take the Montana Teachers Examination in 1921. She saved the test questions from the exam, offered over the course of two days in June and again in December. These questions asked for some interesting bits of knowledge. Here are a few of the many questions she faced:

> "Name five of the most important taxes by which the Federal Government obtains the funds necessary to operate. Discuss the good and bad points of each tax you have mentioned." (Civics)
>
> "How much profit will a farmer make in a year from a cow which milks 12 quarts a day testing 4%, if butter fat is worth 50¢ a pound? For six months pasture costs $3.00 a month, for the remainder of the year feed costs $9.00 a month." (Arithmetic)
>
> "Tell what each of the following is: (1) tide, (2) tundras, (3) pampas, (4) latitude, (5) standard time, (6) steppes, (7) savannas." (Geography)
>
> "Discuss the new problems which the American people were and are called upon to solve as a result of the Spanish-American war." (American History)
>
> "Why does a good teacher have her pupils think through a poem to be memorized rather than have them start by memorizing the first two lines?" (Theory and Practice)
>
> "Is it profitable to feed the same balanced ration to a beef cow as to a dairy cow? Explain your answer." (Agriculture)

Assuming the test taker passed the hurdle of this collection of knowledge (there were eight required questions in each of the categories above, as well as physiology and hygiene, reading, spelling, and language and grammar), there were other hurdles still to face. For many teachers at this time, the classroom awaiting them was a combination of numerous grade levels, ability levels, and surprises. The teacher fresh from this examination could easily face two beginners who knew nothing about reading, three youngsters who learned (sort of) how to read the previous year, a mix of third-, fourth-, and fifth-grade boys and girls who varied in talents and abilities (though they probably knew how to get the right balance for a dairy cow), and a handful of older children in grades six, seven, and eight. This new teacher, like a conductor of a symphony, must bring together all these diverse capabilities and developmental stages with the score of a curriculum represented by the teachers' examination. It would have been a monumental chore. My grandmother became an accountant.

So it must have come as a tremendous relief to teachers this century as class-rooms shifted from the rural one-room schoolhouse model to the divisions by age and grade level. The wide-ranging demands on a teacher's knowledge and the nearly impossible demands on the teacher's ability to manage all ages of children suddenly scaled back. A teacher could focus on the curriculum for a particular age group; a teacher could sharpen the skills of relating to and managing children at a specific grade level. A type of specialization allowed the teachers some breathing space.

I suspect that teachers who lived through the transition from the one-room school experience to a school of specialization would be shocked to learn that there is currently a strong movement away from strictly graded elementary schools. Advocates of this movement, which dates back to at least 1932 (Cuban, 1989), argue that the graded school structure doesn't allow students to develop at an appropriate pace. Graded schools, they contend, especially damage children from poor and minority backgrounds. Graded schools are focused on what Cuban calls the "DNA of the graded school" (p. 784): putting students into categories, separat-ing them into groups, and eliminating children who don't fit with the others. In the end, Cuban adds, the "graded school has trapped both staff members and at-risk students in a web of shared failure" (p. 801).

As you might expect, however, the story is more complicated than that. This problem invites you to think about the implications of organizing schools by grade levels and what changing that particular feature of schooling might mean.

PROBLEM CONTEXT AND SOLUTION PARAMETERS

Context

Montrose Heights Elementary School lies in the heart of the Midwest. Schools like MHES pride themselves on high family involvement, caring and committed teach-ers, safe environments, and stability. Housing some 470 students, including a group of tuition-paying preschoolers, MHES has not been notorious for bad per-formance or famous for good. While most parents are content with the school, it is almost nondescript in its typicality.

In recent years, a new principal has decided to move MHES out of the "malaise of mediocrity." Ms. Justine Watson has high hopes that her school will become an exemplar of excellence, but she has been disturbed by two features of the school. First, it strikes her as, in virtually every respect, a plain school. Second, she is bothered that this doesn't bother anyone. She believes there ought to be some striving for improvement, and she wonders how to light a fire under her apathetic staff.

Problem

After a year of patient observing, Ms. Watson decided in her second year as principal that there simply had to be some changes made. She submitted a proposal to the superintendent of schools to alter the grade structure at MHES so that all classes would become multiage classrooms. While she has maintained that this could not possibly be a surprise to her teachers, given that she talked about it continually during her first year, many teachers disagree. A group of teachers has submitted a signed petition to the superintendent, calling not only for an end to the proposed changes at MHES, but also for the firing of Ms. Watson.

The superintendent has never liked controversy in his district, and as one of the few superintendents anywhere to last more than a decade, he feels justified in his approach to conflict management. He has indicated that he would like to hear more before going to the school board with the proposed changes. He has invited various parties—Ms. Watson, teachers, and parents—to speak to him about "what's wrong at MHES." Your group is a collection of teachers from the school. While you did not sign the original petition, you understand that your colleagues are upset, and you have a commitment to help determine what will best serve this particular school.

Solution Parameters

Your group will present a case to Superintendent Williams. You will be given fifteen minutes to explain what should be done at MHES. The superintendent has indicated that he is not particularly interested in a "basketful of opinions" or "a lot of stories." He wants to make a decision to go to the board with "rock-solid information" to support whatever course of action he sees as appropriate.

········WORK THE PROBLEM ⟶

PROBLEM DOCUMENTS

To assist you in resolving this situation, the following documents have been provided:

6.1 The principal's position paper, outlining her proposed changes for the next school year

6.2 The executive summaries from three evaluations of classrooms at Montrose Heights Elementary School. These evaluations were provided by the principal as "typical of the instruction at MHES." The actual teachers' names or other identifying features have been deleted.

6.3 A copy of the most recent "school report card" as required by the state

6.4 A map of Montrose Heights Elementary School

6.5 Current enrollment figures for Montrose Heights Elementary School

6.6 The petition signed by a majority of teachers at MHES protesting the principal's plan

6.7 Unsolicited parent letter supporting the change to multiage classes at MHES

6.8 Unsolicited parent letter opposing the change to multiage classes

---

PROBLEM DOCUMENT 6.1   *The Principal's Position Paper*

Grade Configuration at Montrose Heights Elementary School

A Position Paper

Justine Watson

Walk down any hall in any typical elementary school in this country, and you'll see essentially the same scene played over and over. Children are contained in row upon row, and they are constrained to fit and conform. Cookie-cutter activities in art and worksheet drills in everything else help to mold all the different lives into a paste of uniformity.

Much of the explanation for this tragic suppression of children lies in that organizational feature of American schools called "grades." I do not refer to letter grades, though that practice deserves attention also. I refer to the idea of placing all children of about the same age in a group called "grade three" or "kindergarten." Where in society does one find such an arbitrary link as age? How often does a company hire candidates because they are of the same age? Who selects friends because they were born on or before September 1 in 1995? The whole idea is ridiculous in any context but schools, where it has become "reasonable" only because we no longer challenge it.

The idea of grouping children by age, however, deserves to be challenged. Besides the absurdity of forcing children to relate only to their age mates, it is likely that grouping children by age only disguises and excuses a host of bad teaching practices. Montrose Elementary is no different from most schools in this respect. The use of a graded organization pushes textbooks to the center stage and calls on teachers to teach to the middle of groups that are so diverse that there is no meaning in the idea of a middle ground. All children are expected to progress roughly at the same pace through the same material for the same reasons. The conformity, as evidenced in my observations, is appalling. Teachers are not at fault for this; it is a system of schooling that pushes teachers and students toward a mindless conformity and deliberate ignorance of the differences among children.

Clearly, Montrose Elementary is not much different—better or worse—than most schools in this country. Just as clearly, things could be substantially better both for the children and their teachers. In this spirit of innovation and improvement, I am proposing a dramatic change in the organization of the school for the next academic year.

There is one pocket of innovation in this building, and it is found in the only multiage classroom the school boasts of. Whereas other classrooms are characterized by continuous drills and passivity, the multiage classroom is characterized by a continuous buzz of learning activities. In this multiage classroom, an observer can readily find examples of children asking questions and helping one another to find answers. In this multiage classroom, an observer can readily find examples of children caring for one another rather than seeking whatever means possible to escape the tedium of school.

What one might observe in the MHES multiage classroom comes as no surprise. Schools around the country have proven over and over again that shifting the structure of our elementary schools can release the students from the bonds of sameness. Students can learn more; professional educators do not have to burn out in routines.

All classrooms have the potential to become places of learning, just like the Montrose multiage primary classroom. Therefore, I am proposing that beginning next year, the entire school be reorganized into multiage classrooms. Given our current enrollment, current building facility, and projections for next year, I propose this arrangement:

GRADES	STUDENT COUNT	LOCATION
Pre-school (paid, no multi)	20	209
P–K	20	103
P–2	32	105
P–2	34	109
P–1	30	115
1–3	25	201
2–3	27	203
2–4	23	205
3–4	28	207
3–5	30	302
4–5	25	304
4–6	28	306
4–6	30	409
5–6	28	401
Special education	34	403
TOTAL	414	

Clearly our current staff and facilities can sustain this change. Our students need this change. I am asking that the district consider this as a means to make MHES a model school among our elementary buildings.

PROBLEM DOCUMENT 6.2   *Executive Summaries from Three Evaluations*

Executive Summary for the Evaluation of ▊▊▊▊▊▊▊▊▊

Year: 2

The strengths I saw in ▊▊▊▊▊▊▊▊▊'s classroom were evident. She is a teacher who clearly enjoys children and treats them with the respect they are due. She works hard to group and re-group her students in meaningful ways, providing them with the support they need to learn in an atmosphere of respect. Her love of literature is evident in the stories she chooses and reads aloud to her pupils.

The weaknesses evident in ████████'s class are also important to consider. First, there is a lack of balance in her curriculum. I have observed three times and have yet to see any evidence of attention to science. Second, there is a tedium in the routine of worksheets in this classroom. While ████████ justifies this as a means of "preparing these kids for middle school," I do not support this. It appears to be drudgery of the worst sort, and I believe students will lose interest in schooling through such routines. I would urge ████████ to connect the two conflicting features of her teaching life: the care she has for children and a commitment to meaningful learning.

Executive Summary for the Evaluation of ████████

Year: 15

As a school, MHES does well to build on the expertise and experience of such teachers as ████████. Her classroom is probably the best behaved group of youngsters you could find anywhere. This clearly speaks to ████████'s capabilities as a classroom manager, considering the normal energy level of second graders. The strength of ████████ in managing children is so obvious, that it is imperative we allow other teachers to watch and learn from her example.

At the same time, the orderliness of ████████'s classroom may disguise a learning environment that is somewhat impoverished. Students rarely ask questions; students learn early on to fill in blanks without any vision of what filling in such blanks can mean. In this classroom, students behave with respect toward people, but it seems unlikely they will develop any respect of ideas. Where there could be habits of thinking, we find habits of conforming. Indeed, it seems the main pressure in this classroom is for each child to emerge looking like every other child. In short, ████████ has perfected the management of children to be an efficient move through an unchanging factory line of drills.

Executive Summary for the Evaluation of ████████

Year: 5

As the only male teacher at MHES, ████ forms a vital component of the effectiveness of this school. Indeed, his importance as a role model and as a mentor to our boys cannot be overstated. Children obviously respect and enjoy ████. Whether in the classroom or the hallways or the playground, one can always find a mass of children eagerly seeking ████'s attention and approval. At the same time, his presence is obviously a force for order in the school, for while children are eager to play with ████, they are equally eager not to cross him or disappoint him. I would gladly have three or four more of this teacher in the building.

's weakness relates also to his strengths. He is fair and equitable in his treatment of children (though there is an obvious preference for the active, sporting child), and this equality of treatment leads to a sameness in the work of his classroom. There is a sense of anticipation in his classroom, a waiting for an end to the school work that so obviously interrupts the fun he enjoys. This is evident in statements ▇▇ makes in class. "I know this stuff is boring, gang, but we've got to get through it before we can do the fun stuff." "Just fill in the right answers and we can be through with this, guys." The learning, as presented to his students, is something to get through in order to deserve the reward of enjoyment. And the students trudge through the work, often looking over the shoulders of their peers for right answers, in order to please this enormously appealing adult. Take away the magnetic personality of ▇▇▇▇▇▇▇, and you have the most dismal collection of worksheet drills and students who have found that learning is the worst sort of drudgery, but that it's worth it to please someone else. I worry about that in the long run.

PROBLEM DOCUMENT 6.3   *"School Report Card"*

Montrose Heights Elementary School
School Report Card

Principal: Justine Watson, Ed. S.   Grades: Preschool to 6
Schedule: 8:00 a.m. to 3:30 p.m.   Enrollment: 475
Web address: Phone:

Principal's Overview of the School

Montrose Heights Elementary School brings together committed professional educators and a community characterized by involvement to create a place of learning. The mission of Montrose Heights Elementary School is to bring out the best in *all* students through an academic curriculum focused on the state standards in an environment that honors diversity. The faculty and staff of Montrose Heights Elementary School strive to support the intellectual, academic, emotional, aesthetic, and social growth of all children.

Organizational Features

Multiage classroom

Inclusion model of special education

Professional growth program

Reading for Success

Movement education

Multiple Intelligences

School Goals

Reading scores at each grade level will increase by 2 percent per year.

Self-esteem of students, as measured by standardized self-reports, will increase from previous year's results.

Acceptance of special needs children will increase, as evidenced by a 10 percent reduction in complaints from parents and children.

Staff Profile

Position	Number	Position	Number
Administrator	1	Teacher	20
Professional staff	3	Teacher aide	5

Stanford Achievement Test Scores

Percentile Ranks	2001	2002	2003	*Percentile Ranks*	2001	2002	2003
Grade 3				**Grade 5**			
Reading	48	52	50	Reading	51	48	53
Language	50	49	51	Language	52	49	54
Math	46	48	49	Math	51	47	50
Grade 4				**Grade 6**			
Reading	48	46	51	Reading	47	45	51
Language	42	47	47	Language	48	52	54
Math	45	48	51	Math	47	47	53

PROBLEM DOCUMENT 6.4   *A Map of Montrose Heights Elementary School*

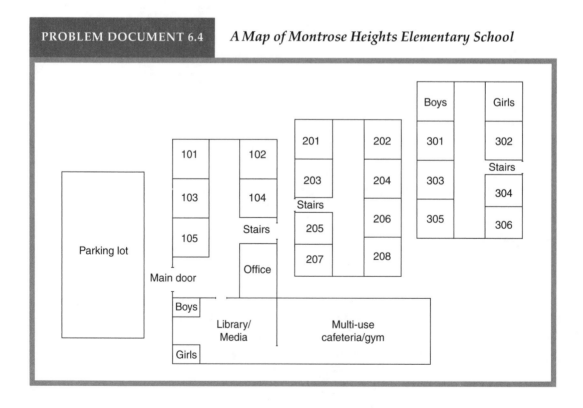

Current Enrollment Figures for
Montrose Heights Elementary School

CLASSROOM	FEMALE	MALE	TOTAL
Preschool A*	7	8	15
Preschool B*	6	7	13
Preschool C*	8	5	13
Preschool D*	7	7	14
Kindergarten A	11	9	20
Kindergarten B	12	10	22
Kindergarten multi	4	5	9
First grade A	13	11	24
First grade B	12	13	25
First grade multi	3	4	7
Second grade A	14	10	24
Second grade B	13	12	25
Second grade multi	5	4	9
Third grade A	15	13	28
Third grade B	15	15	30
Fourth grade A	14	16	30
Fourth grade B	16	11	27
Fifth grade A	13	13	26
Fifth grade B	12	14	26
Sixth grade A	11	15	26
Sixth grade B	13	14	27
Special ed	14	27	31
TOTAL			471

*Indicates tuition-paying students.

Petition Protesting the Principal's Plan

We, the undersigned teachers at Montrose Heights Elementary School, respectfully request that recent changes in our school's structure, as advocated by the Principal, be overruled by Superintendent Williams, as representing the Board of Education and this community.

Whereas the change in structure has not been initiated or approved by the long-term staff of MHES, and

Whereas the change in structure is not supported by evidence that a new structure will enhance the achievement of the students, and

Whereas the performance of MHES has been above state averages for the last decade,

We call upon the Superintendent to intervene and preserve the excellence of this school by canceling the proposed shift to all multiage classrooms.

Furthermore,

Whereas the Principal has consistently refused to include teachers appropriately in decision-making, and

Whereas the Principal has failed to create a supportive environment for teacher professionalism, and

Whereas the Principal has demonstrated a lack of understanding as an instructional leader,

Therefore we call upon the Board to replace this person with a committed leader who can better address the needs of our children.

(Petition signed by eleven MHES faculty members.)

PROBLEM DOCUMENT 6.7 *Unsolicited Parent Letter Supporting the Change*

Dear Ms. Watson,

I write to express my enthusiastic support for your proposed changes at MHES. How exciting for all children to have the same opportunities that only a very few have had in the recent past. How exciting to extend what we've seen as excellent teaching to all grades in the school. I doubt that there is a more significant move that we could make to improve this school.

As you know, my daughter, Leticia, has participated in the one multiage classroom at MHES for the past two years. Her experience in that class has been outstanding. Not only has Ms. Cline provided Leticia with countless journeys into learning, but her classmates have also helped Leticia to learn. I've had older children go through the primaries without multiage classes, and I can tell you that there is simply no comparison. Leticia's experience has been much more powerful than her sisters'. Leticia has learned what it means to become independent as a learner, while at the same time being a contributing member of a community. Not many school experiences can offer that!

So when I heard that Leticia will not have to end her wonderful learning experience, but will instead move to another great situation, I was thrilled! Bravo to you for doing what's so clearly the best for our children. I know I speak for all the other parents when I say that this is truly education for the whole child. Our support for your work is absolute.

Mary Ellen Barrows

Dear Ms. Watson,

I was distressed to hear of your decision to transform all of MHES into a multiage school, and I'm asking you to reconsider this plan. I have several reasons for my views, which I would like to explain to you.

First, a little background. My oldest son, Ronald, was a student in the multiage primary classroom three years ago. My middle child, Cheryl, has been a student in the multiage room this year. I don't have any real complaints about what they experienced under Ms. Cline's leadership. Both children have learned the essentials—how to read, how to write, some math—and both children have been generally favorable about their experiences. Ronald, who I see as a fairly average child, has even indicated that he misses the warmth of the multiage class, though that strikes me as missing a kind teacher more than anything else.

My real concern comes with Cheryl, who, as I said, has done fine in the multiage classroom. I believe Cheryl is truly a gifted child, and I think her test results support this. She is an outstanding thinker and potentially a gifted mathematician. I fear that Cheryl has not been adequately challenged in the multiage setting, particularly this past year, when she has been at the top of the heap, so to speak. In fact, Cheryl has probably been held back from achieving her full potential because of multiage schooling. Whereas Cheryl should be pushed to take on harder work, she has spent much of her valuable learning time dragging along less capable and younger learners. I think Cheryl has learned from helping younger students, but I suspect she might have learned much more in a different arrangement.

Perhaps you can already see my direction here. I do not see multiage schooling as a bad idea, but as an idea with *limited application*. Multiage grouping was wonderful for Ronald, and perhaps it would suit him now, though I think he will grow up more readily in the traditional graded classroom. Multiage grouping was a pressure toward mediocrity for Cheryl, and I think to continue in this mode would be the worst possible plan for this girl. Therein lies my concern. While multiage classrooms serve some students well, they do not serve all students well. While multiage grouping may be efficacious for the beginning scholar, it probably stunts the growth of older children. In short, Ms. Watson, why should we turn the school into a one-size-fits-all model that offers only mediums?

Surely there is a better way to bring out the best in our children and our teachers.

Sincerely,

Anne Rockwell Smithers

Anne Rockwell Smithers, M.D.

····**PROPOSE A SOLUTION** ➞

SOLUTION SUMMARY

Before proceeding to the reflection section of this chapter, write a brief summary of your team's solution here:

Our team defined the "real" problem here as _____

_____

_____

_____

_____

_____

_____

_____

The key features of our solution were _____

_____

_____

_____

_____

_____

_____

_____

My personal view of the problem and solution is _____

_____

_____

_____

_____

_____

_____

_____

TIME FOR REFLECTION

To bring some closure to the issues raised by this problem, this section guides your reflection on questions that may have been raised by your inquiry. First, we will explore the patterns of grouping students by age. Developmentally appropriate practice and continuous progress, two key ideas involved in the debates about how to organize elementary schools, focus the next portions of the reflection. The reflections conclude with an exploration of good teaching in general and work-place harmony among teachers.

Age Grouping

For most of us, if we were to conceive of the way schools could be, it would be fairly difficult to imagine most of schooling organized in any way other than by age groupings. This notion is deeply embedded in our experience of schooling. Most people, and certainly most teachers, take our system to be the natural order of things. You reach the age of kindergarten and begin the process of working through the grades one year at a time. Any divergence from this pattern is most likely because you are a failure.

But as professionals working in the schools, it is worth thinking about the "naturalness" of this system. Does it have to be this way? Is this really the only way to organize schooling? Connell (1987) ties the development of graded schools to the system's inability to deal with massive numbers of immigrant children in any way other than the date on a birth certificate. The connections between the organization of schooling and workplace models of efficiency are well known (Kliebard, 1975). Yet Shepard and Smith (1989) remind us that "As the basis for organizing pupils and learning opportunities within schools, the grade is neither universal nor historically inevitable, though we are apt to take it for granted as such" (p. 220). What is missing in the development of the system, of course, is a focused concern about what is best for the learners.

Still, are there advantages in organizing children by age groups? Certainly we can generalize to a certain degree. Third-graders are more like fourth-graders than seventh-graders. Doesn't that imply that grouping similar ages together is a *response* to developmental similarities rather than an *ignoring* of such issues of development?

Another angle on this subject might be to question just how broadly the idea of multiage grouping might apply. Sure, it may make sense to group the widely-diverse abilities of children between the ages of five and seven, but what about older children? Hasn't that diversity diminished by the time children reach eleven? Apparently not. In fact, the kinds of differences we see in primary children actually widen over the course of years of schooling, becoming most pronounced in high school (especially if the low-ability children do not drop out). The argument that multiage grouping belongs only at the primary level cannot be made on the basis of some sort of unique diversity of abilities, though there may be other justifications for this.

While I am not proposing an answer to the question here, I do think teachers owe it to their profession to reflect on the basic organizational patterns found in schools. To say that grouping by ages is "the way we've always done it" is hardly a defensible attitude for the thinking professional. The tradition of organizing children into grades is one of several reasons why there has been resistance to the notion of multiage schooling (Yarborough & Johnson, 2000). Instead of merely accepting traditions, we ought to seek solid reasons for our positions, and in the absence of such reasons, perhaps we need to rethink those positions.

In fact, the grouping of students by age into graded schools may be a convenience to teachers due to the instructional demands of any other options. As discussed below, it may be that we need to reconsider how instructional techniques have placed limits on what we do with children.

Developmentally Appropriate Practice

We find certain phrases in education that nearly demand we stand and salute them or at least get a little teary-eyed when they are uttered. "Integrated curriculum" is one. Who, after all, could possibly support a disintegrated curriculum? Another such phrase is "brain-based learning," a notion that implies any other approach to learning works only with lobotomized pupils. So, too, the phrase "developmentally appropriate practices" invites allegiance and defies opposition. What self-respecting educator would stand up and proclaim, "No more! Let us have some good old developmentally inappropriate practices!"

Of course, in the slogan-like appeal of such phrases, we sometimes lose sight of the obligation to inquire into what they really mean. It is crucial that professional educators not *dismiss* such phrases without inquiry, and that professionals not *accept* such phrases uncritically. Here is one definition from advocates of multiage grouping: "Developmentally appropriate practice (DAP) means providing curriculum and instruction that address the physical, social, intellectual, emotional, and aesthetic needs of young learners and permits them to progress through an integrated curriculum at their own rate and pace" (Daniel & Terry, 1995, p. 2). If you pull out the pieces, you find that DAP has three basic components: it meets kids' needs, it works through integrated curriculum, and the student sets the pace. As a professional educator, you might raise questions such as the following about the definition:

- Who decides what children need? If needs are not readily observable (such as malnutrition), how do we determine what needs they have? Does the child who is not getting along need lessons in social skills or a nap?
- What categories of needs are the legitimate domain of educators?
- What is an integrated curriculum? How much connecting does it take to make a connected curriculum?
- How do I decide on an appropriate pace for a child? What is the proper place of challenge or pushing a child forward?

These are not easy questions, and they invite discussion with our colleagues. However, these questions represent the kind of critical thinking that a professional is obligated to engage in, as opposed to accepting slogans like DAP without thought. Upon reflection, an educator may decide that DAP is not only defensible, but the only ethical approach to educating children. The key thing is that the professional make that decision through thoughtful inquiry and dialogue, rather than simply accepting the slogan of the day.

Continuous Progress

You may have encountered the phrase "continuous progress" in your inquiry for this problem. What does it mean? What is the teacher's responsibility in this context?

Continuous progress is another means of helping teachers focus less on the groups of children and more on individuals. Thus, a teacher who is committed to "continuous progress" would need to know each child well enough to adapt the curriculum for that child. A student who succeeds at what she is already capable of is not making progress; likewise, a student who is pushed into areas where he cannot succeed is not making progress. The trick lies in knowing each child and guaranteeing that this child, not some hypothetical third-grader, is moving forward. Clearly, having all children do the same work all the time ignores the idea of continuous progress.

The notion of progress goes beyond the realm of isolated teachers, too. If schools are serious about continuous progress, they need to have a good deal of communication among teachers and all who work with the children, especially as children move from grade to grade. The situation in schools, unfortunately, is that such communication is rare. As Stiggins (1995) writes, "The reality is that we rarely talk with one another, redundancy and gaps permeate the curriculum, and continuous progress remains a dream to which we aspire" (p. 244). For this reason, grouping students into multiage communities, advocates say, facilitates continuous progress. Progress is not dependent on some communication that is not likely to take place; progress is assured by the students' staying with one teacher for more than one year.

What do you think? Is "continuous progress" a worthwhile target for educators? Is there a reason to focus on individual children in this fashion, as opposed to establishing, as we do, expectations about what all sixth graders should know and be able to do? And if continuous progress is a worthwhile goal, is multiage grouping the only or the best way to achieve this goal?

Good Teaching?

Perhaps multiage grouping represents a means of reforming teaching practices. In their book on multiage schooling, Daniel and Terry (1995) describe the positive features of the multiage classroom, including curriculum that is integrated around issues instead of focusing on textbook coverage, instruction that is flexible and

individualized, and an environment that supports problem solving and peer tutoring. They raise the following question, rhetorically: Couldn't all this happen in a
single-grade classroom? Of course, they answer, but the pressures are different.
The multiage classroom presses for individualized, flexible instruction, while the
graded classroom encourages all students to continue at the same rate on the same
material.

From this perspective, multiage grouping appears to be a vehicle for introducing good teaching practices. That is, multiage grouping serves to make classrooms into what classrooms ought to be. Perhaps (though Daniel and Terry do not
make this case) the experience of working in a multiage setting would be enough
for teachers to learn better pedagogical practices. Having worked in a multiage setting, teachers learned to alter the organization of their curricula and their patterns
of instruction. These teachers could then apply the principles of good instruction
in a single-grade setting.

What do you think? Would the experience of multiage teaching alter a
teacher's practices? Would an "inoculation" of teaching in a classroom with developmentally appropriate practices guided by the idea of continuous progress protect teachers from the one-size-fits-all teaching infection? Or are the pressures of
tradition and social agreements so strong in schools that only a radical shift, such
as multiage grouping, can make a dent in the way schools work?

Workplace Harmony

The legal language of the teachers' protest to Ms. Watson's plan seems out of place
for the working world of school. It appears from this petition that the teachers
have no interest in a dialogue with their leader. Instead, they appear to be laying
the groundwork for some sort of formal—perhaps legal—action against their
principal.

This situation prompts reflection on the matter of workplace harmony. It is
not only possible, but probable, that you will have disagreements about teaching
practices with your colleagues, the teachers who have official positions of leadership, and your administrative leaders. And there are many things beyond teaching
practices over which you might disagree. What happens in such situations?

A starting point is to contemplate the role of conflict in group situations.
Many people do whatever they can to avoid conflict. Others take all instances of
conflict as personal affronts. Yet there may be good reasons to reconsider this position. Conflict among ideas often sparks the most creative solutions to problems;
conflict also helps to avoid the unthinking conformity that goes with "groupthink"
(Worchel, Coutant-Sassic, & Wong, 1993). Thus, conflict may be a sign of vitality in
an organization rather than disaster (Senge, 1990).

At the same time, no one wants a work environment characterized as conflict-
filled. So the proper balance for a community of professionals may be achieved by
recognizing a few principles. First, there must be a common purpose in the organization. If all the staff members clearly commit to a vision of what the students leaving the school should be like, disagreements on how to get there have every

possibility of resolution. On the other hand, disagreements on techniques and structures are irresolvable when there is no agreed-upon purpose. Second, it is crucial that individuals recognize that the value of conflict lies in the clash of ideas, not assaults on persons. One of the greatest skills you can learn is to disagree with a person in an evidently respectful manner. Of course, you may find yourself working with a principal who does not know how to separate conflict of ideas from personal criticism. In that case, be very cautious about your disagreements until you can help to educate this leader.

Third, learn that there are times when it is best to give in. Obviously, you cannot compromise what you see as your ethical responsibilities. However, there are many occasions when your capacity to compromise will build the foundation for future agreements. Although the best ideas come out of conflict, it is not always wise to enter the fray.

DISCUSSION QUESTIONS

1. The opening scenario recounted the sort of questions teachers had to be able to answer in one place in the early twentieth century. What do they reveal about the expectations of teachers at the time? How do these expectations compare with the sorts of tests you face in your quest to become certified to teach?

2. In examining the issue of multiage grouping, what did you find to be the potential costs and benefits? Do students or teachers gain more? How does this organization create new demands for the teacher? What might schools do differently if children were not grouped according to grades?

3. How do the terms "developmentally appropriate practice" and "continuous progress" help you to understand your job as a teacher? What questions do these phrases raise for you?

4. In part, this PBL experience raises issues of how a school is governed. Where do you think the proper authority for decisions about grouping and instruction lie? Is Ms. Watson an instructional leader?

5. What are the most effective ways to draw good ideas and productive solutions from conflict situations?

6. Considering the PBL process, what did you learn about yourself as a group member through this experience?

FURTHER READING

Chase, P., & Doan, J. (1994). *Full circle: A new look at multiage education.* Portsmouth, NH: Heinemann. Chase and Doan write of their experience as co-teachers in a multiage setting in Maine. They are enthusiastic advocates of multiage classes, building the theme throughout their book that multiage grouping makes a major shift in teaching: Instead of the curriculum driving the learning experience, the children drive it. Chase and Doan see multiage grouping as "developmentally appropriate" and a means to guarantee that teachers attend to individual differences. The authors give examples of their practices, organization, and values. One chapter walks the readers through a typical day in this multiage experience. In another chapter, the authors describe how they use "the little room" as a source of dramatic play for their primary grade students. There are numerous examples of how they do business (e.g., communicating with parents or creating a pumpkin patch project) and what they value (e.g., eliminating grades and providing students with choices). The book also includes a section of voices from other educators, a parent, and a principal about the advantages of multiage grouping. Finally, the book concludes with a research section, summarizing the advantages of multiage education to children in both social and cognitive development.

Connell, D. R. (1987). The first 30 years were the fairest: Notes from the kindergarten and ungraded primary (K–1–2). *Young Children, 42*(5), 30–39.

Her article focuses on only the primary grades, but Connell presents her experience as a teacher facing multiple age groups, ESL students, and children from isolated rural areas. She makes a case that the movement toward higher expectations for children (often with later entry birth dates for kindergarten) does not serve children well. In fact, we damage children's self-esteem and achievement when we see them "fail" the first grade. On the other hand, through multiage grouping, Connell was able to address the varying needs of all her children. She provides examples of the kinds of things she did to be successful with a wide variety of ability levels in her class.

Stone, S. (1995). *Creating the multiage classroom.* New York: Addison Wesley Longman.

Sandra Stone provides a useful guide to how to make multiage classrooms work. Clearly committed to the practice, and drawing on her research on how children learn from play, Stone makes a convincing case. She has a wonderful blend of practical ideas and research information. This is an excellent resource.

WEB SITES

ERIC Clearinghouse on Elementary and Early Childhood Education
   http://ericcass.uncg.edu/virtuallib/achievement/1106.html
   A paper by Susan J. Kinsey on academic achievement and multiage grouping.

North Central Regional Educational Laboratory
   www.ncrel.org/sdrs/areas/issues/methods/instrctn/in5lk50.htm
   The site brings together other resources and some basic information.

REFERENCES

Chase, P., & Doan, J. (1994). *Full circle: A new look at multiage education.* Portsmouth, NH: Heinemann.

Connell, D. R. (1987). The first 30 years were the fairest: Notes from the kindergarten and ungraded primary (K–1–2). *Young Children, 42*(5), 30–39.

Cuban, L. (1989). The "at-risk" label and the problem of urban school reform. *Phi Delta Kappan, 70*(10), 780–784, 799–801.

Daniel, T. C., & Terry, K. W. (1995). *Multiage classrooms by design: Beyond the one-room school.* Thousand Oaks, CA: Corwin.

Kliebard, H. (1975). Bureaucracy and curriculum theorizing. In W. Pinar (Ed.), *Curriculum theorizing: The reconceptualists* (pp. 51–69). Berkeley, CA: McCutchan.

Senge, P. M. (1990). *The fifth discipline: The art and practice of the learning organization.* New York: Doubleday.

Shepard, L. A., & Smith, M. L. (Eds.). (1989). *Flunking grades: Research and policies on retention.* New York: Falmer.

Stiggins, R. J. (1995). Assessment literacy for the 21st century. *Phi Delta Kappan, 77*(3), 238–245.

Stone, S. (1995). *Creating the multiage classroom.* New York: Addison Wesley Longman.

Worchel, S., Coutant-Sassic, D., & Wong, F. (1993). Toward a more balanced view of conflict: There is a positive side. In S. Worchel & J. A. Simpson (Eds.), *Conflict between people & groups: Causes, processes, and resolutions* (pp. 76–89). Chicago: Nelson-Hall.

Yarborough, B. H., & Johnson, R. A. (2000). Nongraded schools: Why their promise has not been realized and should be reconsidered. *Contemporary Education, 71*(3), 42–48.

CHAPTER SEVEN

RAISE THOSE SCORES!

INTRODUCTION AND PROBLEM BACKGROUND

The famous fighting words of the 1983 report, *A Nation at Risk,* set a tone for raising the stakes in educational testing: "If an unfriendly foreign power had attempted to impose on America the mediocre educational performance that exists today, we might well have viewed it as an act of war" (in Berliner & Biddle, 1997, p. 140). Whether that mediocrity was real or imagined, such an accusation prompted all sorts of responses, and the ensuing years have seen increasing emphasis on testing as a means to monitor the progress of American education. Some of this testing is part of a long-term, national attempt to monitor schooling, as is the case with the National Assessment of Educational Progress (NAEP), which predates *A Nation at Risk.* Some of this testing is designed to establish comparisons among various educational systems at an international level. The Third International Mathematics and Science Study (TIMSS) attempts to do this. But perhaps the most immediate, powerful form of testing is that imposed by the states on their own schools to see how well students are meeting mandated standards. When results from such a test have a strong impact on the test-takers or the educators, an impact that is automatically triggered by the test results, this testing is considered "high-stakes" (Madaus, 1999).

There are, of course, a number of possible responses to the pressure implicit in high-stakes testing. The professional educators at a school could continue doing their jobs as they see fit, a business-as-usual approach that says "we know what is best for our students, and the test results are not our chief concern." At the other extreme, professional educators might redesign their curricula and instruction so that what they teach corresponds as closely as possible to the high-stakes test. The unspoken position here would say "we agree that the test is important and worthwhile, so we will guarantee that our students achieve in its terms." Perhaps a more cynical unspoken position takes the "reality" view: "the test may not be worthwhile, but our reality is that we are judged by its results, so we must change."

An increasingly popular approach to dealing with the tests stops short of altering the entire curriculum, but focuses on improving test results through test-preparation activities. Sometimes these activities are as simple as giving students practice with the format of standardized tests. In fact, many supplemental materials from textbook publishers feature tests or quizzes formatted to resemble standardized tests. Some schools create special courses or after-school programs designed to provide coaching and practice on tests. And some schools hire outsiders either to work directly with students, or more frequently, to train teachers on how to improve test performance. Linda McNeil (2000) describes one such program that "makes war" on the tests. Consultants arrive at the school dressed in camouflage clothing, provide participants with camouflaged notebooks of ideas, and carry on this theme of doing battle. McNeil also points out that such activities may raise test scores without improving student learning.

This chapter invites you to look more deeply into the matter of test scores and the impact of such scores on the lives of teachers and students. Though the pressure resulting from standardized tests seems to come in waves, there is little to indicate that the pressure will recede any time soon. The teacher moving into the classroom today must understand enough about the issue of high-stakes testing to enable this teacher to make sound choices as an instructor and to be an informed participant in the crucial decisions being made for our students at the system level.

PROBLEM CONTEXT AND SOLUTION PARAMETERS

Context

Emerson Elementary School was once the only school in the community, so its traditions and allegiance reach back many years. Of course, as the population grew in this Northwest community, new schools developed, and the neighborhood served by Emerson changed from a cross-section of all segments of society to a neighborhood largely populated with working-class people who could not afford the newer, larger houses that appeared as the community spread out. Now, Emerson is just one of fifteen elementary schools in town, and it is sometimes seen as a "troubled" school. That is, while the school doesn't appear in the newspapers for violence and crime, it is sometimes seen as one of the dead weights on the system, especially when it comes to the standardized achievement scores of its students.

The superintendent of schools in the community was hired as a forward thinker, someone who could anticipate what's in store for schools and help to place the city schools "on the map for this state and beyond." Superintendent Hamburg has, as a result, been far more proactive than her predecessors; in fact, some teachers see the superintendent more as a disruptor than a predictor. School principals have worried in private that the superintendent is taking away some of their autonomy in her efforts to make the district a model for the state.

Problem

One area in which Superintendent Hamburg hopes to beat out surrounding school districts is in performance on standardized achievement tests. As a fairly recent immigrant from the state of Texas, Dr. Hamburg knows what a powerful force standardized tests can be, either to build or crush the credibility of the school. And as a forward thinker, Dr. Hamburg can see that the state will be building its own graduation tests similar to the Texas Assessment of Academic Skills (TAAS). For now, student scores on the Stanford Achievement Test (SAT-9) serve a similar purpose. School results on the SAT-9 are published in newspapers and on the state's Department of Education web site. At the very least, real estate agents and potential business relocators are well aware of how schools rank in terms of their test scores.

And the big problem, according to Dr. Hamburg, is that the city's schools don't rank very high. The city averages by grade level were near the state average, certainly not disastrous. However, for a city that wants to sell itself as a model of education for the state and beyond, the scores are simply too low. Worse yet, of all the schools in the city, your school, Emerson Elementary School, the oldest school in town, has consistently scored the lowest of any elementary school. In fact, more than a few administrators have referred to the city's low scores as the "Emerson effect."

Superintendent Hamburg worked with an advisory council to discuss the test issue and she has now come to a decision. As indicated in her memo (which is included here), she is dedicating all professional development funds and a portion of the textbook budget for the next two years to purchasing the services of the STAR test preparation program. From her own experience and from reading the professional literature, Dr. Hamburg concluded that this program was just what was needed to take the city to the next step.

You are a relatively new teacher at Emerson, which makes you a bit reluctant to get too involved in what some of your colleagues are calling a "political issue." On the other hand, you are too idealistic to simply accept a directive without at least looking into its justification and potential effects. When you heard that some of your Emerson colleagues were exploring the issue and had already reserved a speaking time at the school board meeting where the superintendent expected to receive final approval for her plan, you decided to join the investigation.

Solution Parameters

Your team has been allotted ten minutes of the board's agenda time, with up to five minutes for questions and answers following your report. You're not at all sure what should be done at this point. Clearly, the team could endorse Superintendent Hamburg's ideas, offer an alternative plan, or urge a complete rejection. But that is why you have an investigation to conduct first.

··········WORK THE PROBLEM ──────▶

PROBLEM DOCUMENTS

To assist you in understanding various aspects of this situation, the following documents have been provided to you:

7.1 Memo from the Superintendent of Schools

7.2 Letter of support from the Business-Partnership for Effective Schools (B-PES)

7.3 Advertising brochure from the STAR (Standardized Test Achievement Renaissance) test-preparation program

7.4 District test data from the past three years

PROBLEM DOCUMENT 7.1   *Memo from the Superintendent of Schools*

Forest City Schools—
Where Education Still Pioneers!
Bobbi Lee Hamburg, Ed.D., Superintendent

Memorandum

To   Forest City Board Members

Cc   School Administrators and Faculty

From   Superintendent Hamburg

Date   2/10/03

RE   Test Performance

As you recall, I received a very clear charge from the Board on my hiring—to put our city schools on the education map. It is no secret that the vitality of any community is intimately tied to the vitality of its schools. We know that attracting businesses to this community cannot be accomplished without the prior step of building a model school environment. More importantly, we owe it to the fine students of this community to provide them with the best opportunities for education available anywhere in the Northwest.

I believe it is evident from the Annual Report to the Board that I filed in the fall that much progress has been made in this endeavor. Changes in the structure and personnel policies at our high schools have begun to move this community to a position of athletic preeminence in the state. Students from our schools have been recognized across the state for literary and artistic works, and our extra-curricular drama program was honored as the best in state last year.

However, the core of our work as educators remains largely unaffected. I am referring to the academic centerpiece of education—the achievement of our students. As many of you are aware, our state is rapidly joining nearly every other state in mandating a standards-based assessment of student learning as a requirement for graduation. Not only will this affect individual students' life decisions, but it will also affect—most dramatically—the credibility and status of our school system. Best indicators tell us such a test will be in place within two years, perhaps sooner, and our schools simply must prepare for this now.

The standard measure for the state at this time is the Stanford Achievement Test (SAT-9). As you can see by the data I have provided, our schools have been, at best, mediocre in performance on these tests. While we are not a "low-performing district," as the state defines this, we are clearly not a model district yet. However, I have every confidence that the fine educators and tremendous students in this community can move us quickly to a position of prominence on this test—and later on the state exam. All that is needed is for us to devote deliberate, sustained attention to the performance of our students on this exam.

I am, therefore, offering a proposal for the Board's consideration. This proposal is similar to the work I did in Texas, work which the Board acknowledged in its hiring me. The essence of my proposal is that we channel existing resources that have been targeted for professional development of teachers into a focused program of professional development dedicated to enhancing the performance and opportunities of our students. I also recommend that a portion of the money be reserved for incentive bonuses for principals and teachers in outstanding schools.

In past years, professional development monies have been allotted on a formula of FTEs and controlled at the building level. This has resulted in sporadic, fragmented, and inefficient professional development. For example, one member of a high school department might use up the entire department's budget to attend a national convention in the subject area. I do not doubt that this is rejuvenating for that faculty member, but it hardly serves to provide the entire department with professional growth. At one elementary school, the entire professional development budget was turned over to creating a community-intervention program, while another elementary school utilized its budget by allowing teachers to purchase whatever books they wanted with the money. Clearly there is no defined goal or even theme for the expenditure of these monies.

I propose that our district purchase the services of the STAR program. In order to do this, for the next two years, all professional development money must be earmarked to fund this venture. In addition, we should delay the purchase of materials designated for upgrading elementary art programs and eliminate library discretionary funds. This STAR program *guarantees* improvement in student performance on standardized tests. That is, if we find our scores do not improve, the entire expenditure will be refunded to us. If our scores improve, we are moving forward in our goal to become an exemplary district. Either way, we profit.

Having worked with a similar program in Texas, I am completely convinced that this is the best possible use of our resources. When I was a principal, my students' scores jumped by 10 percent in the first year of our contract with the test-preparation firm. Moreover, I believe we provided students with transferable skills to take into other testing situations. Our teachers became better teachers through the principles they learned in their training. Soon after the test-preparation program began, we were recognized as a U.S. Department of Education A+ school!

Perhaps the best element of purchasing the services of STAR is that our teachers can continue their great work, but with the systematic support of experts in the testing field, freeing our teachers to bring the best possible education to our students.

All the logistics of the program are handled by the STAR case managers. In short, we buy opportunities, focus, growth, and success with this investment. I would stake my career on the value of this move.

Letter of Support from the Business-Partnership for Effective Schools (B-PES)

Business-Partnership for Effective Schools (B-PES)

Arthur V. Johnson, Chair

To the Board of Education:

On behalf of the Business-Partnership for Effective Schools (B-PES), I am pleased to write in support of Dr. Hamburg's proposal to purchase STAR services for the city schools. The considerable business acumen represented in the membership of our organization has been put to work in investigating the claims of the various test-preparation companies serving our area, and we are pleased to report that we see STAR as the clear value leader. Not only does STAR provide a comprehensive program, with support materials and the ever-crucial human support element, but STAR also provides a money-back guarantee for its product. As responsible business persons and taxpayers, we see the features of STAR as the sort of investment this school system cannot afford *not* to make!

Indeed, the members of B-PES feel so strongly about this matter that we have organized a matching grant program to assist the schools in this venture. Through contributions of members, we propose to match school district expenses in acquiring STAR at a one-to-ten rate. That is, we will increase your budget for purchasing STAR features by 10 percent as our way of emphatically endorsing this educationally-sound decision.

Why should B-PES concern itself in this matter? Essentially, we have two broad reasons for our involvement. First, we recognize that the children who stand to benefit through this enhancement are our children, the children of our workers, and the children of our clients. We are part of this community, and this is our way of giving back. Second, we also acknowledge that we have a vested interest in the success of our schools. We cannot recruit good workers if the school system has a mediocre reputation; we cannot see a broadening of the business opportunities in this community if the conditions of the schools discourage the potential relocation of complementary business firms. As business people, we are attuned to the "bottom line," which is the most convincing component of any organization's ability to sell itself. For schools, that bottom line is student success. To improve opportunities for our students' success, we are willing to put up a meaningful investment.

It is truly our hope that this moment of community-wide collaboration will engender future partnerships between the business and education communities.

Sincerely,

Arthur V. Johnson

Arthur V. Johnson, Chair

ST★R
Standardized Test
Achievement
Renaissance

Making your students Stars in their own futures!

What's at stake?

By now, education professionals around the country have seen what kind of impact test results are having on the business of learning. State legislatures are clamoring for accountability. Members of the professional and business communities are on the doorsteps of the schoolhouse, not to bring help, but to demand results. Newspapers throughout the nation are plastered with the failures—and rare success stories—of public schools. Principals and administrators are justifiably anxious, and teachers are pressed to add to their already overloaded lives. Nothing short of the survival of schools is at stake here. If test scores do not please the pressure groups, schools will find themselves out of business.

The phrase "high-stakes testing" has more bite to it now than ever before. And help is needed.

What do we offer?

STAR™ is the most comprehensive assistance for high-stakes testing available today. At STAR™, our goal is to provide training and materials to reduce the impact of high-stakes testing. We provide the means for schools to address the test so that learning will not be lost. Here are some of the key features of the STAR™ program:

- On-site in-service workshops for all affected teachers
- Hands-on, activity-based techniques with exemplary facilitators
- Practice drills and activities built from the national standards
- Adaptation of focus to your particular high-stakes environment
- Follow-up sessions on a negotiated schedule at your schools
- Cutting-edge materials to take directly into the classroom for instruction
- Computerized practice tests that are readily scored onsite and reports that offer content and test-taking strategy feedback
- Special guides for family support (family sessions available at extra cost)
- Money-back guarantee!

What have we found?

The results are impressive. Our average gain-score improvement has been .48 standard deviations in the language-use tests, .47 standard deviations in the mathematics tests, and a whopping .62 standard deviations in the reading sections of the tests. These results are reported as standard deviations because of the variety of tests used in different districts. There are also dramatic improvements in tests of other specific content domains, demonstrating the adaptability of the STAR™ program.

Here's what a few of our satisfied customers have reported:

"I'm a convert! I have always disdained prep programs as a waste of time and money. But our teachers report that they can teach even more now that they have confidence in the testing results. We're stars!" Annemarie Westcoat, Superintendent of Schools, Remington, VA

"When they promise, they deliver. Our scores went up from the 43rd [percentile] to the 53rd in just one year. I got a bonus!" Dave Pallinger, Principal, Arnodt Elementary School, Grand Rapids, MI

"My principal practically had to drag me into the first session of the STAR workshop. I thought I knew it all, with twenty years of experience under my belt. But from the first minutes, I saw that I would be getting new ideas not just for getting the kids ready for the Arizona state test, but also for making my own class a better environment for learning. I'd have to say that STAR™ is worth it, even if test scores don't matter that much in your school." Jane Thomas, math teacher, Regent Middle School, Phoenix, AZ

How do we become a STAR™ school?

Our professional staff will work with a school or school district on an individual basis to tailor a program to your needs. Costs are established based on the particular needs of your school and testing situation. Our staff members are experts not only in the test-score enhancement process, but also in creative financing possibilities. Ask a representative about potential grants and cost-sharing opportunities in your region.

Making your students Stars in their own futures!

ST☆R
Box 44723, Orlando, Florida
1-800-KIDSTAR
www.startestprep.com

Grade	Content area	1999–2000			2000–2001			2001–2002		
		%	NPR	ST	%	NPR	ST	%	NPR	ST
03	Reading	80	48	49	84	47	49	92	45	49
	Language	80	46	48	84	45	49	91	43	50
	Math	80	51	53	83	49	53	90	47	53
05	Reading	80	47	50	85	45	50	91	43	51
	Language	81	44	49	85	43	51	93	42	49
	Math	81	50	50	79	53	52	88	51	53
07	Reading	77	48	49	80	44	49	93	41	51
	Language	82	43	50	80	43	50	92	42	52
	Math	79	48	51	82	47	51	95	47	53
08	Reading	75	48	50	81	46	49	91	46	51
	Language	78	49	49	83	49	51	93	47	50
	Math	66	55	51	82	49	52	95	48	52

% = percent of students tested in district
NPR = national percentile rank
ST = state mean

·····PROPOSE A SOLUTION ──▶

SOLUTION SUMMARY

Before proceeding to the reflection section of this chapter, write a brief summary of your team's solution here:

Our team defined the "real" problem here as _____

_____

_____

_____

_____

_____

_____

_____

The key features of our solution were _____

_____

_____

_____

_____

_____

_____

My personal view of the problem and solution is _____

_____

_____

_____

_____

_____

_____

TIME FOR REFLECTION

This PBL experience raises a number of issues for you to consider. Of paramount importance is the role of the professional educator as an informed participant in debates about testing and accountability. The reflection is organized first around issues of standardized testing: its role in schools and school reform, the pressures this testing places on students and teachers, and how we prepare students for the tests. In addition, we will consider the impact of accountability on schools in general. Finally, this section focuses your attention on the professional development of teachers.

The Place of Standardized Testing

With tremendous pressure placed on most schools to perform well on one standardized test or another, it is a commonplace of schooling today to find educators—especially administrators—judging any potential innovation in terms of how it will affect the test scores. Thus, standardized test results become, perhaps unintentionally, the standard by which progress is measured. Consider Tanner's (2000) portrayal of the role of standardized testing: "Nonetheless, the prevailing attitude of the school superintendent and principal is that curriculum is determined at the state level and is manifested by means of statewide achievement tests in the mandated individual core subjects. The clearest path to educational efficiency resides in 'teaching to the test,' and the demonstrated measure of educational excellence resides in the test scores, pure and simple. The job of the teacher is to 'deliver' the curriculum" (p. 193). Tanner's skepticism is entirely missing in similar comments from testing advocates, such as (then Texas governor) Bush's education advisor, Margaret LaMontagne, who said "If you teach to the test, and the test has just what you want the kid to know, it's kind of a 'So what?' deal here in Texas" (Henry, 2000).

At a position quite the opposite of Dr. Hamburg's, some teachers see standardized testing of any form as a dirty word in education. That is, they see such testing as irrelevant in its best forms and insidious in its worst. Such testing is not a measure of progress, they would argue. It is a meaningless measure.

Clearly, information from standardized tests is still information. We can do much with information if we know how to use it well. Some have argued that information from standardized tests can help us target deficiencies among average students to help them move forward (Whitehead & Santee, 1987). Key, however, is finding valuable uses of this information and resisting misuses that don't consider the social and legal implications of test use (Airasian, 1987). Teachers can help their constituents understand what it means to use test data appropriately (Heubert & Hauser, 1999). For instance, teachers can help the public recognize that using one test to compare groups of students who have studied different curricula leads to questionable conclusions. Teachers can help the public remember that not everything that is important to learn can be tested in this manner.

Is Test-Prep "Teaching to the Test"?

Theodore Sizer (1992) writes that "Teaching to the test is eminently sensible if the test is worthy, and a travesty if the test is corrupt or mindless" (p. 113). He uses the word "test" more broadly than the sense of "test" in this problem. However, his words provide us with an important perspective. The idea of "teaching to the test" is widely scorned among educators at the same time that this idea is widely implemented. Does using a test-preparation program necessarily mean we are teaching to the test? And where do we draw the line for ethical behavior here? That is, if we can improve student scores through some sort of test preparation, whether we improve student learning or not, do we owe it to the students to provide them with that assistance? Or do we owe it to the students to protect them from such a perversion of the learning process?

The view expressed by Sizer (1992), of course, assumes that the "test" is something far more significant than an externally-imposed standardized test. Madaus (1999) argues that the very presence of standardized testing that has high stakes associated with it will lead teachers to teach to the test. Airasian (1987) lays out the proposition that "Given the important consequences that ensue from policy-oriented testing, not to teach to a test may be a greater disservice to pupils than to teach to it" (p. 408).

Thus, we have two extremes: we are obligated to teach to the test and we are obligated *not* to teach to the test. The question we must consider is whether we can accept either extreme or work out some middle ground. In his editorial on standardized testing, Gordon Vars (2000) writes that it would be nice if we could turn over the test preparation to someone else and, as teachers, focus on student learning. This is, however, an impossible dream. "The skills and information assessed by even the more poorly conceived test have no value unless they are *applied* in real life. . . . Instruction in the mandated competencies, however trivial they may be, must not be separated from the major goal of educating whole human beings" (p. 1).

The climate of testing doesn't allow much room for educators to simply ignore this question. As a professional, you need to reflect on what position you take. Do you see justification in teaching to the test? How would you address a parent who thought you were neglecting or over-emphasizing test-taking skills?

The Real Pressures on Teachers

To what extent do teachers feel pressure on the question of standardized test scores? Apparently the pressure is real and significant. Survey recent news stories on education, and you will find ample evidence both of the pressure for accountability and of teachers' reactions. In the fall of 2000, voters in Oregon turned down a proposition which had proposed tying teacher pay to the performance of students on standardized tests, and this proposition was not unique to Oregon. Writing against this idea, principal Jan Ophus (2000) of North Bend High School said, "Surely even the angriest voter understands that in education the result of a teacher's skill, effort, dedication, and even love is not always graphable on a chart of student assessment. There are simply too many powerful social and economic factors that get in the way. . . . The hurting, troubled, hungry children who pass into our schools each morning are often better off when they leave at the day's end if only because they've learned they're known and cared for by the adults who work in those schools. Not giving a raise or a cost-of-living increase to a teacher of such children because his students didn't gain a point at the end of the year on a state multiple-choice reading and math assessment is wrong" (p. 7).

Whether the test scores are tied to monetary rewards or simply a part of the work climate in schools, teachers cannot easily ignore such pressures—especially if the pressure is personalized in the form of a bonus-seeking administrator. Innovations in curriculum and instruction are quickly judged by their potential to influence standardized test scores, and even ideas that may promise greater aesthetic development, greater interpersonal success, greater wholeness as a human being, are set aside if they do not lead to improved multiple-choice performances. Teachers have been known to abandon exciting, engaging units for their children in favor of drill for the tests; in some places, recess has been eliminated for primary students in order to provide extra time for practice. As Oakes and her colleagues found in their research on reform in middle schools, standardized testing programs "had a chilling effect on experimentation" (Oakes, Vasudeva, & Jones, 1996, p. 29).

Thus, beyond the merits of being accountable or focusing on student achievement, the testing movement must seriously consider the impact of this pressure on the lives of teachers. And, of course, there is no such being as "the testing movement." Instead, there are politicians and educational leaders and disgruntled community members and committed advocates and even teachers. There are people. These people, loosely drawn together to create a national force called the testing movement, affect the careers and lives of educators and the children they serve. It is crucial that teachers are both aware of the pressure (to deal with it productively) and prepared to be participants in the debates about standardized testing.

Students and Standardized Testing

In virtually every call for accountability through standardized testing, the language of protecting or assisting students comes into play. Perhaps there is a basic distrust of the educational system or of teachers beneath the calls for accountability, but at an overt level, everyone seems to agree that such testing is really put into place for the sake of the children. Is this so? As a participant in the educational venture, you do well to consider this question.

In his article about the role of the state in establishing a vision for education, French (1998) points out that in a society stratified by race and economic status, the lack of standards will doom minority students to an inferior education. Standards, in this context, become a means of guaranteeing that all children have the opportunity to be educated. However, as French points out, when educators discussed implementing standards without a broader vision of the democratic basis for schools, the result was an insensitive, rigid implementation that worsened inequities. His examination of the Massachusetts example found that the original vision for complex, multi-faceted standards was reduced to results on a single multiple-choice test. Instructional practices that had proven to be successful with diverse learners were abandoned in favor of "coverage" to get ready for the tests. McNeil's (2000) investigations in Texas found something similar, with a greater emphasis on how such teaching actually damaged the educational opportunities of minority youth.

You should recognize in the examples given above that there can be contradictions between *standards* and *standardized tests*. It is important, therefore, to be clear about the differences. Standards focus on what students should know and be able to do. These standards can be carefully selected to produce the kinds of graduates we can be proud of. However, in most views of what it means to be well educated, not all standards are reducible to what can measured by standardized tests.

Another issue related to student performance is the actual testing situation and the discomfort it may generate. We know that students find the testing situation generally unpleasant, and increasingly so as they progress through the years (Wheelock, Bebell, & Haney, 2000). We know that some students suffer from serious anxiety about testing, particularly when time limits influence their performance (Woolfolk, 1998). But the same things might be said about making a visit to a physician. Virtually no one enjoys going to the doctor to find out what's wrong; some people have such serious anxiety about the doctor's office that they avoid it altogether, even though they may suffer serious consequences. An argument could be made that the discomfort of the testing situation is a necessary evil in the attempt to diagnose and correct what is "wrong" with any given student.

Of course, we must ask if that is truly how we use the information garnered from standardized testing. Imagine if the information gathered from a visit to a doctor was pooled so that whole neighborhoods received health ratings—even to the extent that we could say that a certain neighborhood was the healthiest in town, while another was the most sick. The information the doctors gathered was not effectively used to help any given patient, but only to label the community. Eventually, business and real estate representatives might start coaching citizens on how to handle the doctor's appointment or even whose information should not be included in the neighborhood report.

As ludicrous as this analogy seems, it is worth some consideration. We have to ask who is benefiting from the information gathered from standardized tests. Are individual students helped or harmed? This sort of question is asking about what some have called "consequential validity" (Gipps, 1994), the idea that we need to consider seriously how the uses of assessment information will affect students' lives. Standardized testing raises some serious questions in this regard. Data from Massachusetts indicate that the implementation of high-stakes testing related to graduation in that state has caused an increase in the dropout rate, especially among African American and Latino students (FairTest, 2000), a finding corroborated in Texas (McNeil, 2000). In fact, nine of the ten states with the highest dropout rates have high-stakes testing; none of the ten states with the lowest dropout rates have such testing (FairTest, 2000). Schools have eliminated arts programs, class meetings, recess periods, electives, and even whole programs in order to focus on the areas covered by standardized tests (Kohn, 2001), and one must raise the question of consequences: Are students better off because of these cuts? Kohn (2001) takes the position that a rise in test scores may actually indicate teachers are doing a worse job of educating children, since they are probably focusing on more superficial matters, or sometimes leaving out important subjects (such as science and social studies) that are not covered by the tests.

The necessary reflection, then, focuses on what such testing does to the children with whom we work. Educators must be guided by this sort of thinking. Given the predictable relationship between test scores and socio-economic status (Kohn, 2001), we must be hesitant to exult in high scores and just as hesitant to condemn low scores.

The Impact on Schools

Perhaps the most important issue we need to reflect on is the kinds of schools we will create for children. Ideally, the schools we create will be places of high engagement, curiosity, and learning. Such schools are likely to produce graduates who will do well on standardized assessments. Drilling students to prepare for tests may improve the scores; the question is whether or not that will make schools places of engaged learning. Seymour B. Sarason (1998) argues that schools ought to be places of productive learning. He phrases well his hope for graduates, a hope that is worth reflecting on. In considering what a person should leave school with, he writes, "*I would want all children to have at least the same level and quality of curiosity and motivation to learn and explore that they had when they began schooling*" (p. 69). Not a bad target!

Professional Development

When I began teaching, I was given some provocative advice: "It's okay to teach twenty years; it's just not okay to teach one year twenty times." I wish I could credit my advisor, but I don't recall who said it. However, the statement highlights a notion that is worth contemplating: How do we develop as professionals?

I was startled to find that there were actually days set aside for teachers to engage in professional development. Like most of my colleagues, I entered the work of those professional development days with mixed emotions: grateful for the break from the routine of the classroom, but ill-prepared to learn in the professional development setting. I had plenty of work to do, and I would have been much more pleased just to be given time to spend grading papers, preparing units, creating bulletin boards, and doing the thousand chores of teaching. I was not receptive to the in-service workshop.

This problem invites you to think about turning over all professional development time and money in a school system to test preparation activities. One question worth contemplating is what would be the opportunity cost of such a bargain? That is, whether or not the workshops were good, what would a teacher give up in professional growth by giving up all other development efforts?

To answer that question, one must reflect on what it means to be a growing professional. Surely a teacher can carry on such growth independently, through readings and taking the odd graduate course. The trade-off would involve the kind of workshop activities most schools engage in, what Quartz (1996) calls marginal expert-driven learning opportunities that don't have much impact on teachers anyway. Quartz argues that most professional development in schools is stabilizing, reinforcing what's going on rather than inviting new ideas. If this is so, and the evidence appears to support it, then perhaps there is no great loss in turning over the paid development time to test preparation activities.

Perhaps. But perhaps not. The idea of a community of professionals joining together to consider their practice and the effects of their practice on their "clients" may be the essence of professionalism. If we take away the conversations about teaching, the structured whole-group conversations that make up professional development in the schools, do we lose important connections? Do we eliminate the chance for ideas to spark?

As a teacher stepping into the classroom and the school community, you must give careful thought to how you will continue to grow as a professional. A moment of honesty with yourself will probably convince you that you, like all beginning teachers, have much to learn about your new profession. Taking charge of your professional development, or at least entering into the opportunities you have with enthusiasm, may make the difference between teaching for twenty years and teaching one year twenty times.

DISCUSSION QUESTIONS

1. If there is a balance to achieve between preparing for standardized tests and just educating your students, how does the professional educator strike such a balance?

2. What ways can individual teachers help to win the public relations battle associated with test scores and schools? How can a school get out its story of student learning in terms other than such scores?

3. One portion of the superintendent's plan for implementing a test-prep program was to create incentives for performance. She suggested the possibilities of bonuses for principals and teachers. What do you see as the potential positive and negative effects of such a reward system?

4. What legitimate role can outside consultants, such as the STAR program, perform in helping schools accomplish their goals? How does a school maintain a shared sense of purpose and commitment with such outside forces?

5. Some students and parents around the country have organized protest boycotts of standardized testing. If such a boycott were promoted in your school, what would you see as the ethical response of a professional educator?

6. In your contacts with model teachers, what have you discovered about their per-
    spectives on professional development? How can this become a priority for the
    busy beginning teacher? How can a teacher who has neglected this make it a part of
    the everyday world of teaching?

7. Considering the PBL process, what did you learn about your tolerance for a differ-
    ent model of learning?

FURTHER READING

Heubert, J. P., & Hauser, R. M. (Eds.). (1999). *High stakes: Testing for tracking, promotion, and graduation.* Washington, DC: National Academy.
Heubert and Hauser represent the Committee on Appropriate Test Use from the National
Research Council in putting together this book. The work addresses a variety of issues in
high-stakes testing, including promotion and retention, tracking, granting diplomas, disabilities, and more. The second chapter, on policies and politics, is especially useful for the
beginning teacher in developing an understanding of what it means to use test data
appropriately.

Madaus, G. F. (1999). The influence of testing on the curriculum. In M. J. Early & K. J. Rehage
(Eds.) *Issues in curriculum: A selection of chapters from past NSSE yearbooks: Ninety-eighth yearbook of the National Society for the Study of Education, Part II,* (pp. 71–111). Chicago, IL: University of Chicago.
This important essay is reprinted from an earlier (1988) NSSE Yearbook, and it's a timely
reprint. Madaus lays out a clear depiction of the issues that follow from what he calls
"measurement-driven instruction" (p. 75). He identifies seven principles that describe
what can happen when tests gain excessive power in the system, and the principles are disturbing from an educator's point of view. In particular, he argues that as the stakes get
higher for tests, the curriculum and instruction narrow, and the control over learning
moves farther away from teachers and students.

Popham, W. J. (1987). The merits of measurement-driven instruction. *Phi Delta Kappan, 68,*
679–682.
In this essay, W. James Popham writes a defense of "measurement-driven instruction,"
arguing that in this practice "we have a potent and cost-effective intervention that can substantially boost the quality of schooling in our nation. It's time to use it" (p. 682). He
acknowledges that, like anything else that is poorly done, MDI can have negative consequences. However, he sees its positive consequences as more convincing. Popham
addresses the concerns of critics who argue (as Madaus does) that such testing will narrow
the curriculum or stifle creativity. Instead, Popham sees such testing as "a powerful curricular magnet" (p. 680) that can pull the schooling experience away from the boring, irrelevant, unmotivating reality most students face. Popham has raised other perspectives in
more recent works (for example, see *Educational Leadership,* Volume 56 Number 6, March
1999, "Why Standardized Tests Don't Measure Educational Quality"), but this essay provides a strong case for accountability.

Wheelock, A. (1998). *Safe to be smart: Building a culture for standards-based reform in the middle grades.*
Columbus, OH: National Middle School Association.
Anne Wheelock takes a positive approach to the standards movement, trying to redeem
what otherwise might be a disastrous trend. She makes a clear case that standards and
standardized tests are not the same thing. She even points out, as Kohn (2001) does, that
practices associated with raising the test scores do not necessarily improve learning, that
such practices may actually harm learning. In the end, Wheelock offers three key ideas

rooted in the notion of a supportive school culture for making standards work to the students' advantage in schools: focus on student work and rich pedagogy, focus on relationships that nurture motivation, focus on teachers' role in a community of professionals.

WEB SITES

Consortium for Equity in Standards and Testing
> www.csteep.bc.edu/ctest
> The mission of this organization is to focus on how standards and tests can be used more fairly.

FairTest
> www.FairTest.org
> This web site is dedicated to challenging the way in which standardized tests may disadvantage certain students. It is an ongoing, up-to-date reference for information on what is going on at the national level in connection with standardized testing. Despite the name, this site maintains a highly critical perspective on testing.

Alfie Kohn
> www.alfiekohn.org
> He has plenty to say about standards and standardized testing.

REFERENCES

Airasian, P. W. (1987). State-mandated testing and educational reform: Context and consequences. *American Journal of Education, 95*(3), 393–412.

Berliner, D. C., & Biddle, B. J. (1997). *The manufactured crisis: Myths, fraud, and the attack on America's public schools.* White Plains, NY: Longman.

FairTest. (2000). MCAS: Making the Massachusetts dropout crisis worse. *MCAS Alert.* Retrieved from www.fairtest.org/care/MCAS%20Alert%20Sept.html

French, D. (1998). The state's role in shaping a progressive vision of public education. *Phi Delta Kappan, 80*(3), 184–194.

Gipps, C. V. (1994). *Beyond testing: Towards a theory of educational assessment.* London: Falmer.

Henry, T. (2000, November 1). 'Teaching to the test' becomes the learning standard. *USA TODAY,* p. 8D.

Heubert, J. P., & Hauser, R. M. (Eds.). (1999). *High stakes: Testing for tracking, promotion, and graduation.* Washington, DC: National Academy.

Kohn, A. (2001). Fighting the tests: A practical guide to rescuing our schools. *Phi Delta Kappan, 82*(5), 348–357.

Madaus, G. F. (1999). The influence of testing on the curriculum. In M. J. Early & K. J. Rehage (Eds.), *Issues in curriculum: A selection of chapters from past NSSE yearbooks: Ninety-eighth yearbook of the National Society for the Study of Education, Part II* (pp. 71–111). Chicago, IL: University of Chicago.

McNeil, L. M. (2000). Creating new inequalities: Contradictions of reform. *Phi Delt Kappan, 81*(10), 728–734.

Oakes, J., Vasudeva, A., & Jones, M. (1996). Becoming educative: Reforming curriculum and teaching in the middle grades. *Research in Middle Level Education Quarterly, 20*(1), 11–40.

Ophus, J. (2000). Measure 95 should be defeated. *Oregon School Administrator, 27,* 6–7.

Popham, W. J. (1987). The merits of measurement-driven instruction. *Phi Delta Kappan, 68,* 679–682.

Quartz, K. H. (1996). Becoming better: The struggle to create a new culture of school reform. *Research in Middle Level Education Quarterly, 20*(1), 103–130.

Sarason, S. B. (1998). *Political leadership and educational failure.* San Francisco: Jossey-Bass.

Sizer, T. R. (1992). *Horace's school: Redesigning the American high school.* Boston: Houghton Mifflin.

Tanner, D. (2000). Manufacturing problems and selling solutions: How to succeed in the education business without really educating. *Phi Delta Kappan, 82*(3), 188–202.

Vars, G. F. (2000). An impossible dream? *The Core Teacher, 50*(4), 1.

Wheelock, A. (1998). *Safe to be smart: Building a culture for standards-based reform in the middle grades.* Columbus, OH: National Middle School Association.

Wheelock, A., Bebell, D. J., & Haney, W. (2000). What can student drawings tell us about high-stakes testing in Massachusetts? *Teachers College Record.* Retrieved November 2, 2000 from www.tcrecoed.org

Whitehead, B., & Santee, P. (1987). Using standardized test results as an instructional guide. *The Clearing House, 61*(2), 57–59.

Woolfolk, A. E. (1998). *Educational psychology* (7th ed.). Boston: Allyn & Bacon.

CHAPTER EIGHT

JUST THE FACTS, PLEASE!

INTRODUCTION AND PROBLEM BACKGROUND

Ask any veteran teacher about some new approach to teaching or learning, and it's likely she or he will tell you that it's been around before. You're likely to hear that every few years some consultant or theorist manages to sell a "new" approach that's already been tried somewhere. Your veteran source may see it as a humorous trapping of the profession or a tragic example of manipulation. You could make a safe bet that the veteran will have an opinion.

And yet some ideas come along that seem to shake the field significantly. One such shaking can be traced to the idea of "constructivist" teaching. That is, the idea might lead to such a shaking of schooling if it were tried. Brooks and Brooks (1999) describe two contrasting classrooms to help illustrate the concept. In a seventh-grade classroom, the teacher works students for the "correct" responses to a poem—what the poet really means, what the poem is supposed to evoke. As students realize they are generally wrong in their interpretations, they shut down, end their participation. In contrast, a ninth-grade teacher turns the students loose to develop their own experiments on how muscle movement is affected by temperature. This teacher challenges the students' thinking and forces them to structure their investigations, to seek relevance in relationships. This teacher is practicing constructivism.

Presented in a number of guises (Perkins, 1999), what most constructivist perspectives seem to hold in common is a de-centering of the teacher and a move toward students making sense of their learning, in the context of relevant issues. Oh, and the seasoned teacher will remind us that the ideas were present in Dewey's, Kilpatrick's, and others' work early in this century.

Just how dramatic this move might be can be imagined when you look at works like John Goodlad's study, *A Place Called School* (1984). Based on thousands of hours of observations, Goodlad concluded that the pattern of education is one where students are passive recipients of information and that this pattern gets stronger as students progress through the grades. Teachers talk; students listen. Goodlad points out that students make few decisions, that they mostly sit passively as members of the whole class, and that their interest wanes as they progress through years of schooling. Moving from a vital interest in kindergarten, students can become jaded cynics before they leave middle school. Students encounter little novelty in their years of schooling. Goodlad goes on to conclude that it is pointless to help teachers get better at what they are already doing way too much of. Yet the pattern of passivity is everywhere and powerful, a pattern that Dewey noted in his 1918 text, *The School and Society* (cited in Phillips, 2000).

So when professional groups such as the National Council of Teachers of Mathematics or the American Association for the Advancement of Science call for a different kind of teaching, they are fighting against a weighty tradition. Is it a futile battle? Can the traditions change? *Should* the traditions change? Is there room for compromise? These are some of the questions you should think about as you address the problem in this chapter.

PROBLEM CONTEXT AND SOLUTION PARAMETERS

Context

Public School #31, Raphaela Martinez Elementary (known locally as "Baskin-Robbins" because of its number—"31"—and its student diversity), is typical of an elementary school in the urban Northeast. The student population is widely diverse, with a higher percentage of second-language learners than most schools in the heartland of the United States. The school has a history of parental involvement, but that involvement diminished significantly in recent years when the district ignored parental opposition to a plan to remove sixth, seventh, and eighth graders from PS31 to open a new middle school. Parents seemed to feel ignored or rejected, and a general cynicism became apparent in the school.

Some teachers argued that the removal of the older children merely pushed misbehavior down in the system. Now, teachers report, students in the fourth and fifth grades act more like the eighth-graders used to act. These children, at the fourth and fifth grade, seem to believe that learning is a waste of their time. School has become more social, and there are certainly more of these students being sent to the principal's office.

After sliding for more than half a decade, with numerous teachers growing more and more hopeless about Raphaela Martinez, the district installed a new principal to shake up the school. Ms. Feverstone came to PS31 from a similar school in the Southeast. Her experience at that school, combined with a powerful experience at a university summer institute, provided her with strong ideas about how to "fix" PS31.

In her first year as principal, Ms. Feverstone created a site council to assist with the decision-making process at her school. She had to recruit heavily to get participants, especially from among the disaffected parents. Her council was made up of five parents, five teacher leaders, two staff members, and a district representative. Ms. Feverstone had no voting membership on the council, but she attended every meeting, set the agenda, and obviously influenced members' decisions. As one long-time second-grade teacher put it, "New principal. New leaders. Same old stuff. She packs the council with yes men and yes women so she can ram her ideas down our throats. What's new about that?"

By the end of that first year, Ms. Feverstone and the site council had agreed to some changes in the school, including the use of student uniforms and an increase in the after-school offerings. But this was not enough. Ms. Feverstone sent all members of the site council to a summer institute at a nearby university. This two-week event focused on brain-based learning and putting "meaning" in the teaching act. Following the institute, the site council made a proclamation that the mode of instruction at PS31 was to change, and change fast. While not all changes could be in place immediately, the council expected that all teachers would be using primarily "constructivist" teaching methods by the second semester.

Problem

Faculty members received a letter from the site council near the end of their summer vacation. This letter, signed by all the members of the council but not the principal, called on the faculty to make significant changes in the way students were instructed at PS31. Some teachers viewed the letter as an attack on their competence, and somehow the letter ended up in the hands of a local editorialist. Much controversy followed, with the principal at first appearing to support the changes called for by the council and later appearing to call for restraint and thoughtful reconsideration of the council's request.

As a teacher at PS31, you see the controversy as a real threat to your school's success. The atmosphere of the school has steadily improved under Ms. Feverstone's leadership, but this may simply be too much. You wonder if the council is actually a means for her to push more changes, or if these "constructivist" ideas are justified. It was one thing to call on the children to wear uniforms; it's another thing altogether to call on the teachers to *be* uniform. At the same time, you suspect that the surface changes at Baskin-Robbins have not really addressed the substance of learning yet.

Your puzzlement about this issue prompted you to volunteer for the task force the principal has asked to form. This group has been given a wide-ranging task: recommend to the site council what to do about teaching at PS31. Your group has also been asked to represent one side of the debate or the other, even if you consider a compromise position to be the best.

Solution Parameters

Ms. Feverstone wants school decisions to be made on the basis of good information, which is why she has asked the site council to reconsider its position. To bring out all relevant information, she has charged a number of task forces with making careful inquiry. Yours is one of these task forces. You will be instructed to make a case *for* or *against* the shift to constructivist practices. Ms. Feverstone has asked that the council will hear the "advocacy" positions from both sides in an attempt to come to a fair and productive decision. She is fully aware that the council may stick with its original ideas, adapt these, or completely abandon them.

The format you will face is as follows: The site council will hear from a variety of groups, each wholly committed to one position. Each group will be given fifteen minutes to present its case to the council. Following this, the council will ask questions, which Ms. Feverstone has characterized as "challenges" to the ideas of the task force. Following the presentation of the various positions, the council will hold an open discussion with all members of the faculty before voting on an action.

Because you may have to suppress your true beliefs in this matter, you will also be asked to write an individual report on the council discussion. In this report, which should be about two pages in length, you will indicate what you see as the best solution for PS31 and your reasons for this opinion.

········**WORK THE PROBLEM** ➡

PROBLEM DOCUMENTS

To assist you in understanding various aspects of this situation, the following documents have been provided to you:

8.1   Letter from the PS31 site council calling for all classes to build on a foundation of responsive teaching; this is the letter that teachers received prior to the beginning of the school year

8.2   The principal's initial ruling on "responsive teaching" at PS31

8.3   Editorial from a community paper concerning the plan to change pedagogy at PS31

8.4   The principal's revised ruling on "responsive teaching" and the need for a task force

8.5   Report by a visiting university professor asked to evaluate the "learning tone" of the school

8.6   Handout from the principal on the "constructive controversy" technique, adapted from ideas outlined by Johnson and Johnson (1994)

PROBLEM DOCUMENT 8.1   *Letter from the PS31 Site Council*

PUBLIC SCHOOL 31, RAPHAELA MARTINEZ ELEMENTARY
A Home for Learning

August 15, 2003

Dear <<teacher first name>>,

As members of the site council for PS31, we are pleased to welcome you back for another year, perhaps the watershed year for our school. What's special about this year? First, you are probably aware that some of the changes we instituted last year have already polished the image and the reality of our school. We think PS31 is a safer, happier place. There is certainly less criticism of the school in local media, and while it is too soon for test scores to show any change, we fully expect these to go up soon—especially as we focus on instruction. Second, there has been a concerted effort this past spring by Ms. Feverstone to hire only the most competent and committed teachers to replace our retiring colleagues. We are pleased to report that for the first time in two decades, we will be starting this academic year with all teaching positions filled with certified teachers! We are grateful to Ms. Feverstone for her energetic recruiting.

Our third reason for optimism is the most powerful of all. As you may know, the council has spent the much of this past summer in careful study of effective teaching methods. We have worked many hours to understand principles of effective teaching as it relates to the children in our school, and we have worked diligently with consultants from State University to be certain we are on the right track. Where teachers have built their instruction around sound principles, the results have been dramatic. We think it's time for dramatic improvements here! Aware that changing established practices is a great challenge for most people, we deliberately choose to disrupt the patterns of instruction at PS31. For too long, we have been a school devoted to holding on to a fragile control of students. Serious learning has taken place in small pockets in our school, but for the most part, teachers have had to fight for control rather than lead into learning. We are calling for ALL classrooms to change this academic year. We are calling for ALL classrooms to implement effective instruction. Specifically, each classroom should provide evidence of the following characteristics of good learning environments:

- Students actively build meanings rather than passively receive information.
- Students actively discuss and cooperate with other students in building internal "meaning".
- Students regularly experience learning in real-life situations and in areas that are relevant to their own lives.
- Students continually see their own growth as lifelong learners.

We have asked Ms. Feverstone to assist in making this transition, and we believe it is only reasonable to allow some transition time. We have also asked Ms. Feverstone to incorporate the above features in all faculty evaluations beginning after the winter break. At that time, the council will expect evidence of these principles in every classroom, every lesson. We are calling for the end to lectures, meaningless worksheets, isolated facts and vocabulary, true-false tests, and mindless video watching. By moving our students to active participation, we expect to transform our school into a model of learning for this community. It is time for responsive teaching at PS31—teaching that responds to the real needs of our children and the realities of how people learn.

We realize that some will believe our decision to be too abrupt. In fact, we are convinced that the only hope to make a real change is to do it now and to do it completely. Half-hearted efforts to reform schools have always failed in our country. To support this change, we have asked Ms. Feverstone, in cooperation with State University, to hold weekly after-school support sessions (alternating Tuesday and Wednesdays, from 3:00 to 4:00).

We are truly grateful for your dedication to our students, and we look forward to working together this year.

(Signed by all the members of the site council.)

The Principal's Initial Ruling on "Responsive Teaching" at PS31

PUBLIC SCHOOL 31, RAPHAELA MARTINEZ ELEMENTARY
A Home for Learning

August 20, 2003

Dear Faculty Members,

I was thrilled to see the proactive, exciting recommendations of our dedicated site council. I believe we should all count ourselves fortunate to be working with a group of people so committed to what is best for children. I hear of site councils that do nothing; ours is a council of action. The action arises from careful study, and that's even more exciting. So a recommendation to use more responsive teaching at PS31 strikes me as the most productive thing a site council could offer a school.

I wish to express my enthusiastic support of the council's call, and I will back this up by providing extra release time for teachers who feel they need further instruction in how to teach with student involvement.

Up to two days' time will be available for any teacher who needs the time to reorganize curriculum or to meet with consultants, visit classrooms, or otherwise carry on the learning necessary to succeed. In addition, our opening-of-school work day will be devoted to "constructivist" techniques for elementary classrooms. We have arranged for a local expert, Dr. Melton, to conduct our workshop.

There are, of course, other issues for us to address this year. Nothing, however, is as important as the transformation of this place into a house of learning, responsive to the needs and interests of our students.

Anne Wallins Feverstone

Anne Wallins Feverstone, Principal

Responsive or Irresponsible?

STAFF EDITORIAL

This paper has gone on record as supportive of site councils in our schools. We believe that giving community members and teachers a venue to join together in creating a school the community can be proud of is a worthy enterprise. When the site council of PS31 (lovingly dubbed "Baskin-Robbins" by the locals) called for uniforms for its students last year, we lauded their decision. This is the stuff of site councils—ways to make a school safe, welcoming, supportive. But it seems the council may have overstepped its credibility and authority in a decision they announced this summer. A letter from the site council came to our attention recently, and it shows just how silly jumping on the bandwagon can be. Deluded by the educational establishment and intoxicated by educational jargon, the Baskin-Robbins site council recently called for an end to teachers' teaching at their school. You read that right—an end to *teaching*! Instead, these wannabe administrators would have us believe that all a school has to do is make a warm place for the kiddies to hang out, and they will "construct" their own understandings. They call it "responsive" teaching, but we see it as merely irresponsible interference.

Who do these amateurs think they are kidding? According to their letter, they would have the teachers abandon any formal instruction. No more spelling lists, for example (a pattern which might explain why our populace has increasingly become unable to spell). In place of instruction, students would be given opportunities to *discover* meaning in relevant experiences. Sounds great if you're the kind of kid who wants a place to hang out and nothing to interrupt your day! One veteran teacher at the school, who asked that her name be left out for obvious reasons, had this to say. "I was hired to teach reading and math and science and social studies because I know these subjects. If my hands are tied so that I cannot explain and teach except in those moments when students find some relevance, I simply can't teach. I came here to be a teacher, not to be responsive, whatever that means." It seems unlikely that the teachers' union will be very supportive of evaluation processes that undercut teaching, but then, teachers' unions have done some pretty surprising things.

As most of us know, the kids at PS31 are already disadvantaged. Now this council wants to throw up yet another obstacle for the kids to have to face. Dump the psychoeducational babble and teach these kids something! Just because most of the students come from poorer neighborhoods doesn't mean they don't deserve an education. Maybe that's what *this* community sees as relevant and responsive to our needs. And, site council, we remind you that it's our school, too.

Perhaps the site council should be reminded of the value in the moniker the school has acquired. PS31 came to be known by the name of a famous supplier of variety, the Baskin and Robbins chain of ice cream stores, offering 31 flavors. Now PS31 would offer only one flavor for everyone, teacher and student alike. What a disaster!

PUBLIC SCHOOL 31, RAPHAELA MARTINEZ ELEMENTARY
A Home for Learning

August 25, 2003

Dear Faculty Members,

I am sorry to greet you with this note on our first day of school, but it has become an urgent matter that I clarify issues surrounding the controversy at PS31 even before our meeting this afternoon. As you are aware, I expressed my endorsement of the ideas of the site council for transforming our school's instructional patterns from passive to active and responsive learning. I believe the mandate from the council was created with the best motives and with solid research backing. In my enthusiasm for supporting such innovation, I'm afraid I was less than sensitive to other forms of expertise and experience on our faculty. For this, I apologize.

It would be rash for us to completely overhaul the evaluation of teachers' work without giving serious consideration to the consequences of such a decision. So, while I maintain my enthusiasm for the ideas of the council, I am suggesting another approach to this problem. I am asking the council to reconsider its position with input from the people affected most by this issue, the teachers. I am also asking for our teachers to investigate this matter more fully. To accomplish this, I would like to adapt the technique known as a "constructive controversy." In this approach to sound decision-making, various people represent the possible positions in a decision. Because these positions are assigned, it is not a matter of representing your own view and winning a debate. Instead, it is a matter of representing a position fully so that all of us can understand it from its best side. Then we will be in a position to decide fairly.

For those of you willing to help with this, you will be assigned to investigate and defend either completely transforming to constructivist teaching or completely ignoring this position. It is my sincere hope that in this spirit of inquiry, we can discover what is best for PS31. When the council has heard both sides represented forcefully, the members (and all interested teachers) will discuss the decision that was announced in the letter of August 15 and proceed to reaffirm, alter, or abandon this recommendation.

If you have any questions, we will be discussing this further at today's faculty meeting.

Sincerely,

Anne Wallins Feverstone

Anne Wallins Feverstone

Excerpts from the PS31 Evaluation Report by Dr. A. T. Melton

Section IV: The "Learning Tone" at PS31

While there are ready measures of achievement for the students at PS31 (standardized tests, state assessments, indices of reading ability, and so on), there are no such ready measures to gauge what some have called the "learning tone" of the school. By "learning tone," I mean what is often characterized as the school culture or climate, but with particular emphasis on how students appear to perceive this place vis-a-vis the atmosphere of learning.

For older students, such information can typically be inferred from student evaluations. While a few of the instructors at PS31 utilize such feedback mechanisms, for the most part, there is a virtual black hole in this realm.

In order to achieve some degree of understanding of this important aspect of the school (consistent with the contractual agreement for evaluation), I engaged in three main activities. First, my assistants and I observed more than forty lessons delivered at all grade levels in the school. I completed an observation protocol that checked for student engagement, student-initiated questions or activities, and student responses. Second, my assistants and I observed the interactions of students outside of formal learning contexts. That is, we watched students interacting in the library, in the lunchroom, on the playground, and so on. Again, we employed a protocol for observations, this one focusing on the valence (positive or negative) of interactions. Third, my assistants and I interviewed students and teachers about the "learning tone" of PS31, with special emphasis on students' perceptions. For example, we asked students questions such as the following (adjusted for the age level of students):

- Tell me about something you learned in school. What helped you to learn this?
- Tell me about a time when you were surprised by what you were learning. What made this surprising?
- Tell me about something exciting that happened in your class. What made this exciting for you?
- What is something important for people your age to know?

These samples demonstrate the open-ended nature of the questions. Our intent was to try to provide students with opportunities to describe directly or indirectly the environment of learning at PS31.

Findings

Our findings were not encouraging. For the most part, observations in the classrooms, with the notable exception of kindergarten classes, revealed that students spent most of their time working alone and most often on "drill" type work. The occasional lapses in the predictability of classroom life were caused by student disruptions rather than deliberate acts on the part of teachers. In general, the older the student, the more likely that he or she could be found working silently or seeking opportunities to disrupt the tedium. Our observations outside of the classroom revealed what one might expect from such a pattern: Students "escaped" their classes and there was virtually no carryover from the class activities to this outside world. No students were observed discussing projects or ideas from their classes. The metaphor our observers developed was that of young factory workers who wanted nothing to do with their "line jobs" once they went on break or were off duty.

Interviews provided yet another confirmation of this negative tone. In general, students were unable to name ideas or concepts they had learned, though they often could identify knowledge such as "spelling," "reading," "how to count," "about volcanoes," "science and stuff," and so on.

When asked about excitement in the classroom, virtually all answers identified disruptions and irregularities, such as an evacuation drill or a student's defiance, as the moment of excitement. In short, students appear not only to fall into a humdrum predictability early in their school experience, but also to accept this as normal. If there is a developing awareness of what it means to be a learner, it seems to be a matter of following instructions and "being good in class" rather than understanding issues. We were surprised at how awkward it was for students to discuss what it means to know something.

Teacher interviews focused on what it means for students to learn at PS31. The teachers appear to believe that what serves these students best is to enhance basic skills such as reading, spelling, writing, and arithmetic. They also believe that students must learn to cooperate, follow instructions, and become "good citizens," though it is not always clear what is involved in such citizenship. A dominant theme among the teachers was that the children were capable of acquiring "survival" knowledge, and that was what the school should aim for.

To summarize this section, the "learning tone" at PS31 strikes the outside observer as gloomy at best. While the school maintains a relatively positive climate of human interactions, particularly for an urban site, it appears to offer little challenge or stimulation to its students. It is a safe place, a calm place, but a place that lacks any spark for the learners.

PROBLEM DOCUMENT 8.6   *Handout from the Principal on the "Constructive Controversy" Technique*

Constructive Controversy Procedure
Anne Wallins Feverstone
Adapted from *Joining Together* (Johnson and Johnson)

The point of a constructive controversy is to build a process that can allow the *best* solutions to emerge without tying those ideas to individual people. Because people advocate for positions whether or not they agree with these positions, the best reasoning from all perspectives comes out.

In a true constructive controversy, teams work together and eventually argue for both sides of a controversial issue. Our process at PS31 will be as follows:

1. Volunteer teams are assigned to take strong positions (either for the recommended changes or against them).
2. Teams research their positions.
3. A team presents its case at a site council meeting.
4. Council members (me included) challenge these ideas in a spirit of inquiry.
5. Another team presents the opposite case.
6. Again, council members challenge these ideas.
7. Drawing team members from both extreme positions together with the council, an open discussion of the best points of each is held.
8. Each team member presents his or her personal view in writing (formed as a result of the debates and discussion).
9. The council considers the written responses and decides on a course of action.

SOLUTION SUMMARY

Before proceeding to the reflection section of this chapter, write a brief summary of your team's solution here:

Our team defined the "real" problem here as _____

_____

_____

_____

_____

_____

_____

_____

The key features of our solution were _____

_____

_____

_____

_____

_____

_____

My personal view of the problem and solution is _____

_____

_____

_____

_____

_____

_____

TIME FOR REFLECTION

This PBL experience gave you the opportunity to explore how a theory of learning might have an impact on a school. In reflecting on the issues raised, this section examines the following topics: constructivism in the schools, how schools make decisions about innovative practices, evaluating a school, whether unity in teaching leads to a negative uniformity, and how schools change. The last section focuses on the constructive controversy as a learning/teaching technique.

What Is Constructivism?

In her essay to answer that question, Constance Kamii (1991) reminds us that constructivism is really a theory about *learning*, not teaching. She elaborates on three kinds of knowledge that we all acquire: physical (which amounts to the empirical or sense observations we make), social (which are agreed-upon issues, such as the designation of a certain season of the year as "Spring") and logico-mathematical (which consists of the web of relationships a learner constructs inside her or his head). This last form of knowledge is how we make sense of the world, how we make meaning. And this last sort of knowledge cannot be delivered to students, Kamii says, though the actions of teachers can either encourage or block the construction of such knowledge. As Eric Jensen puts it, "Ultimately, everyone has to make his or her own meaning out of things" (1998, p. 98).

In the writing about constructivism, one generally finds some common features. These features include the following: students control some of the learning focus and activities, teacher-centered strategies such as lectures are minimized, multiple ways of knowing (through arts, for example) are honored, learning activities and assessments are often rooted in authentic situations, and much learning occurs in groups. These elements are extrapolated from our understanding of cognitive psychology. In other words, these features of practice are logical outgrowths of a view of learning found in cognitive psychology.

Some writers remind us that there really is no such thing as a "constructivist technique," though various techniques can be used in a constructivist manner (Howe & Berv, 2000). A fair question for teachers to raise is this: Are the logical applications of cognitive psychology supported in the actual research conducted in schools? Do we see evidence that students learn more from teachers using constructivist ideas? Some work in this area has revealed that students using "constructivist" methods do better than "traditional" classes in terms of achievement (Lord, 1997, 1999). The videotape studies connected with the Third International Mathematics Science Study (TIMSS) revealed that high-achieving classes in Japan, for example, were using the constructivist techniques recommended by the National Council of Teachers of Mathematics (U.S. Department of Education, 1999), whereas U.S. classrooms were not.

Of course, the controversy about what counts as constructivism suggests teachers have a great deal of flexibility in using so-called constructivist techniques. An appropriate line of inquiry might be to compare your own personal beliefs about learning with what the "constructivists" claim. See where your beliefs match or depart from the constructivist approach. Then consider how your teaching practices can be consistent with what you believe to be the central principles of how people learn. But notice something powerful here: As soon as you begin to focus on the learning as opposed to your actions as a teacher, you will find tremendous growth possibilities for your students.

A final thought about this focus on learning. Seymour Sarason presented a powerful goal for our educational systems when he wrote what he would want for graduates of our schools: "I would want all children to have at least the same level and quality of curiosity and motivation to learn and explore that they had when they began schooling" (1998, p. 69). We do well to consider how our teaching keeps such curiosity alive.

Decision Making in Schools

This problem began with the proclamation of a site council, which was part of a whole school-reform package instituted by the principal to help this struggling school. There was a suggestion on the part of at least one teacher that the council was nothing more than a tool for the principal to accomplish her own goals, but to disguise this in a committee room. Whether the council was exercising its own powers or masking the principal's power, it does raise a question about the role of such decision-making groups in schools.

In recent years, there has been a greater and greater emphasis placed on what is sometimes called site-based decision making (SBDM) or site-based management. Some states and/or districts require this to take place. The form of SBDM varies. Generally, community members and other staff members (such as a secretary or cafeteria worker) are involved as well as teachers. Some theorists have claimed that there is no evidence that such decision-making has any effect on students (Johnston, 1995; Midgley & Wood, 1993; Weiss, 1993), especially if the focus is on *who* decides rather than *what* is decided. Other theorists argue that site-based decision making, done well, is the best avenue for reform (Lange, 1993). If such councils have authority and are careful to communicate with their constituencies, they can succeed (Guskey & Peterson, 1995–1996; Wohlstetter, 1995). However, there are always risks involved with the new roles and responsibilities in teachers' making decisions that they may not be accustomed to making (David, 1995–1996).

In the context of this problem, how effective was the site-based decision making? The site council seemed to be an important element in the reform of PS31, as evidenced by its push for school uniforms in the previous school year. This is clearly consistent with the best hopes for SBDM. At the same time, it is apparent that the council alienated some teachers and community members by its decision to change the way instruction was handled at PS31. Did it overstep reasonable boundaries in calling for a change in the dominant model of teaching at the school? Or, as some would argue, was it necessary for the council to call for a radical change to be made immediately rather than hope that gradual, incremental change might work? In essence, educators need to decide if they want such councils to make decisions with the potential to alter practices, policies, and environments radically, even if this is contentious, or if such councils are to be symbolic means of legitimizing others' decisions.

As a teacher, you may find yourself in a position to participate in such decision-making bodies. In this capacity, perhaps more than in any other role, you are called on to see the school from the perspective of the students and to think in terms of the "big picture." Teachers grow accustomed to concerning themselves with their own classrooms or grade level, but participating on some sort of site council calls on teachers to think differently. In this capacity, information such as that provided by Dr. Melton's evaluation becomes important. It does no good for an individual teacher to dismiss such information as applying to someone else; the site council must focus on the whole school experience.

Related to the issue of decision making and school change, this PBL experience gave you a glimpse of a school leader's role. Ms. Feverstone appears to be a respected, change-oriented leader. She certainly could not be accused of being an old-school, stuck leader. At the same time, she also appears to have shifted positions or backed off of her initial support. What might explain this? What sorts of pressures do school leaders face that cause them to have to reverse themselves? We can only speculate, but some of the forces that might have influenced this school leader include the pressure of the newspaper editorial, concerns from the school district offices, protests made by the teachers' association, and even the reactions of respected faculty members. Ms. Feverstone may have found herself in the position of advocating for changes, but not considering the implications of her advocacy carefully enough. Does her backing down on the decision indicate weakness as a leader or humility?

Evaluating Your School

The information provided in the school evaluation reminds us that schools can and should seek feedback about the job they are doing with children. In the case of PS31, this information was sought from the perspective of a "critical friend," an outsider who viewed the school both sympathetically and critically. If you were a teacher at PS31, how would you receive Dr. Melton's report? Do you think such information would cause you to become defensive about your school and your practices, or would this information inspire you to change? You might re-examine the kinds of questions Dr. Melton's team asked. Do you think these questions are effective measures of what is important in a school? What do you think the newspaper editorialist featured in the problem documents would think of these particular questions?

Schools don't always have the opportunity to seek outside feedback from formal evaluations. Still, information can be gathered. Two key sources of such information are the parents and the children in your school. However, beware of the patterns of information-giving. In general, urban schools are far less likely to receive input from the parents than other schools, and any school should take steps to make sure that all parents are heard from, not just those who are comfortable interacting with school personnel. There is, for example, evidence that some cultural groups are more likely to see a sharp division between school and home and therefore view it as interfering to tell teachers what to do (Deyhle & LeCompte, 1994). Yet their children are affected, and schools should not assume that silence is consent.

Teachers can also seek feedback from their students. While this is more common in secondary schools, creative elementary teachers find ways to determine how students view their learning experiences. Students can respond to simple prompts ("Write down one thing you learned today") or color in pictures that reflect their feelings. If Glasser (1993) is correct about his view of quality schoolwork, then such work always feels good to the students. We need to know if they feel good about their work.

Some cautions may be in order, though. Students provide some information, but they have limitations in their perspectives that cause us to temper this information. For example, out of habit, students may prefer rote work to critical thinking (Haberman, 1991). Even so, is there a role for feedback about learning from our learners?

Unity or Uniformity?

Another issue raised by this problem goes beyond the circumstances of how the decision about instruction was made. Instead, our focus shifts to the decision itself, and the implications of a whole school moving in one direction for instruction. How sound is it for a school to adopt a central theme or approach to instruction? For example, should a school be known as a "cooperative learning" school, where all teachers use a form of cooperative learning daily? And what about those teachers who have seen successes without using cooperative learning or arts-based education or whatever technique is advocated?

We do know that a characteristic of successful schools is that there is a unified vision for learning (Lockwood, 1996) and an understanding of the "big picture" for the school as a whole (Felner, Kasak, Mulhall, & Flowers, 1997), though some, such as Michael Fullan, see vision as overrated (1996).

So, should a school adopt a single vision? As you visit schools and converse with your colleagues in the field, you might ask whether the school itself has a central vision. If so, what is the role of this vision in the school's success?

It is well worth remembering that the patterns of pedagogy that teachers hold on to may be nothing more than the traditions they are accustomed to. Seymour Sarason observes that "Teachers teach the way they have been taught to teach, but what they have been taught produces the polar opposite of a context for productive learning" (1998, p. 76). Thus, to get teachers to consider alternatives to the traditional patterns of teaching is potentially revolutionary.

It may be that the issue of instructional methods is only a tiny portion of the problem or solution. Perhaps the unity that promises healthy reforms for schools is a unity of school culture, with a diversity of techniques. In her comments about how to move forward in school reform, Deborah Meier writes, "The next phase will do well not to ignore the lessons learned: it's easier to design a new school culture than to change an existing one. And it's the whole school culture—not this or that program—that stands in the way of learning" (1995, p. 372).

School Change

The problem presented here arises from an energetic principal's attempt to change a school. Teachers at all levels, particularly beginning teachers, wonder about their roles in changing schools. If the continuum for change attitudes ranges from "If it ain't broke, don't fix it!" to the Japanese notion of *kaizen* (continuous improvement), some would say it seems sensible for new teachers to stay near the former end. After all, you've just arrived on campus. Do you want to greet your new colleagues with this message: "Hi. I'm glad to be here. Now let's fix this mess!"?

On the other hand, even if you had a great experience in school, isn't there a nagging sense that things could be better? Couldn't we do more to make students learn and to make this place of learning more inviting and effective? That's why, paradoxically, even though schools are very similar to what they were like generations ago, there is always pressure to make changes in the way schools are.

Developing a perspective on change may be an important feature of your professionalism. One doesn't have to be negative or critical to be a change agent. In fact, it is often the negative staff members who block change with cynicism and inaction. It does help, however, to be purposeful about change. That is, your job is not to try out every new idea that passes through the popular and educational literature. In contrast, your job is to have a learning disposition (Darling-Hammond, 1998; Senge, 1990) and a commitment to making the whole school—not just your little piece of it—a great place to work and learn. Fullan and Hargreaves (1991) argue that there is "an overwhelming need for greater involvement of teachers in educational reform outside as well as inside their own classrooms, in curriculum development and in the improvement of their schools" (p. 15). The provocative title of their book, *What's Worth Fighting For? Working Together for Your School,* suggests that teachers can be active participants in school change, not victims of the way things have always been. In another book, Fullan (1991) points out the importance of making personal meaning of potential changes, again emphasizing that teachers can do something. While you would be wise not to enter a new school as a crusader, recognizing your own obligation to improve the schools is a powerful aspect of becoming a professional.

The Constructive Controversy Process

The principal in this PBL experience made something of a unique proposal. She recommended that teachers use a teaching method (the constructive controversy) to address a real problem. In a sense, this is a reversal of the way most people, including teachers, view school: real life can actually gain something from school techniques. The method in question has been used in the business world as a way to assist in making good decisions (Johnson & Johnson, 1994), but it still would probably surprise most teachers to have a teaching technique proposed to them as a means to solve a problem.

There is a sort of radical endorsement of an instructional method when the learners apply it beyond the confines of the classroom. When teachers apply the principles of effective problem solving to their interactions over real problems, it says that the principles really work. So, Ms. Feverstone's recommendation of the constructive controversy served to demonstrate that she believed it was more than an exercise. What did you learn from the process? Were you able to separate your personal beliefs and opinions from the task of advocating for a particular position? How does such a separation allow you to develop a new perspective on the issue? Could you use the technique in your classroom and beyond?

DISCUSSION QUESTIONS

1. What elements of "constructivist" teaching and learning did you see as appealing to you as an instructor? How would you implement these? Are there elements of constructivism that you see as negative from the perspective of a classroom teacher? What limitations do you perceive?

2. What may be some potential advantages to students of a school with a consistent and united approach to instruction? What might be the potential losses to students in that situation? Is a vision important to a school as opposed to a teacher?

3. What is the teacher's role in the issue of school change? How do you balance the competing pressures to conform and to be a change agent?

4. Having been at the sending end of student evaluations for some time, how do you view the practice as a means of improving instruction? Are there ways that teachers can guide students to write more effective and relevant evaluations? What would you want to learn from your students?

5. How do schools make the best use of research and evaluation to improve the experience of learners? Are outside evaluators essential to this process?

6. Considering the PBL process, what did you learn about collaborating with colleagues?

FURTHER READING

Brooks, J. G., & Brooks, M. G. (1999). *In search of understanding: The case for constructivist classrooms.* (2nd ed.). Alexandria, VA: Association for Supervision and Curriculum Development.
Brooks and Brooks provide a three-part structure to their "case." First, they describe why schools should change, based primarily on how children learn. Second, they lay out key principles of constructivism with chapters on each principle. Finally, they address what needs to be done to make the changes. Of particular interest is Chapter 9, which provides a dozen suggestions about what constructivist teachers do.

Educational Leadership, 57(3), November 1999. "The Constructivist Classroom."
This issue of the journal is devoted to constructivism—what it means and what it looks like. In addition to an article by David Perkins that clarifies various versions of constructivism, there are articles about constructivism in general, constructivism in literature, PBL, mathematics, art, science, brain-based learning, interdisciplinary connections, and research in constructivism.

Jensen, E. (1998). *Teaching with the brain in mind.* Alexandria, VA: Association for Supervision and Curriculum Development.
Eric Jensen draws on research about the brain's functioning to help us improve the classroom. He has a number of inspiring ideas, especially about how to enrich the classroom environment through such means as the arts, movement, and music. I appreciate his caution: 'let's not jump to embrace any idea just because someone, somewhere has labeled it as 'brain compatible'" (p. 6). See especially Chapter 4, where Jensen describes how to enrich the environment.

Nagel, N. G. (1996). *Learning through real-world problem-solving: The power of integrative teaching.* Thousand Oaks, CA: Corwin.
Nagel situates her model of integrative teaching and learning within the constructivist framework, and she draws on elements of problem-based learning. Following a discussion of what integrated real-world learning consists of, Nagel provides a rationale for its inclusion in schools. She includes a series of cases from actual classrooms. These cases take on

special significance because they are the work of intern teachers, cooperating with regular classroom teachers. The cases focus on a second-grade landscaping unit (involving wetlands), a fifth-grade unit on shoe production, another fifth-grade unit on the coexistence of humans and salmon, and a middle school pre-algebra unit on truth in advertising. These units demonstrate the value of local relevance for helping students to construct meaning. Nagel follows the cases with a discussion of assessment for such units and guidance on how to create integrative problem solving units.

Tomlinson, C. A. (1999). *The differentiated classroom: Responding to the needs of all learners.* Alexandria, VA: Association for Supervision and Curriculum Development.

For anyone considering widespread changes in the way instruction looks in a school, Tomlinson's book offers some helpful guidance. Her overall theme is that teachers should create learning environments and experiences that help students grow and succeed. With a focus on differentiating, she provides many examples of different ways of teaching, ranging from stations and centers to PBL to investigations. She gives ideas about how to make change happen in a school, and offers ways of accommodating the real pressures on teachers while making such change. One important point she makes is the value of situating change in the collaboration of teachers rather than in independent work.

Woolfolk, A. E. (1998). *Educational psychology* (7th ed.). Boston: Allyn & Bacon. See especially pp. 277–281 and 346–367.

Woolfolk provides a good overview of the range of ideas about teaching that fit in the "constructivist" perspective. She notes differences, such as the distinction between exogenous, endogenous, and dialectical constructivists, and she gives examples of the kinds of teaching strategies she considers to be constructivist. In addition, she has sections on constructivism in reading, writing, mathematics, and science.

WEB SITES

The Association for Supervision and Curriculum Development (ASCD)
> http://webserver2.ascd.org/tutorials/tutorial2.cfm?ID=27&TITLE=Constructivism
> A tutorial on constructivism.

School Improvement in Maryland
> www.mdk12.org/practices/good_instruction/constructivism.html
> Gives a different, more graphic exploration.

REFERENCES

Brooks, J. G., & Brooks, M. G. (1999). *In search of understanding: The case for constructivist classrooms* (2nd ed.). Alexandria, VA: Association for Supervision and Curriculum Development.

Brooks, M. G., & Brooks, J. G. (1999). The courage to be constructivist. *Educational Leadership, 57*(3), 18–24.

Darling-Hammond, L. (1998). Teacher learning that supports student learning. *Educational Leadership, 55*(5), 6–11.

David, J. L. (1995–1996). The who, what and why of site-based management. *Educational Leadership, 53*(4), 4–9.

Deyhle, D., & LeCompte, M. (1994). Cultural differences in child development: Navajo adolescents in middle schools. *Theory into Practice, 33*(3), 156–166.

Felner, R. D., Kasak, D., Mulhall, P., & Flowers, N. (1997). The project on high performance learning communities: Applying the land-grant model to school reform. *Phi Delta Kappan, 78*(7), 520–527.

Fullan, M. (1996). Professional culture and educational change. *School Psychology Review, 25*(4), 496–500.

Fullan, M. G. (1991). *The new meaning of educational change* (2nd ed.). New York: Teachers College Press.

Fullan, M. G., & Hargreaves, A. (1991). *What's worth fighting for? Working together for your school.* Andover, MA: Regional Laboratory for Educational Improvement of the Northeast and Islands.

Glasser, W. (1993). *The quality school teacher: A companion volume to The Quality School.* New York: Harper Collins.

Goodlad, J. I. (1984). *A place called school: Prospects for the future.* New York: McGraw-Hill.

Guskey, T. R., & Peterson, K. D. (1995–96). The road to classroom change. *Educational Leadership, 53*(4), 10–14.

Haberman, M. (1991). The pedagogy of poverty vs. good teaching. *Phi Delta Kappan, 73*(4), 290–294.

Howe, K. R., & Berv, J. (2000). Constructing constructivism, epistemological and pedagogical. In D. C. Phillips (Ed.), *Constructivism in education: Opinions and second opinions on controversial issues* (Vol. 1, pp. 19–40). Ninety-ninth yearbook of the National Society for the Study of Education. Chicago, IL: University of Chicago.

Jensen, E. (1998). *Teaching with the brain in mind.* Alexandria, VA: Association for Supervision and Curriculum Development.

Johnson, D. W., & Johnson, F. P. (1994). *Joining together: Group theory and group skills* (5th ed.). Boston: Allyn & Bacon.

Johnston, S. (1995). Curriculum decision making at the school level: Is it just a case of teachers learning to act like administrators? *Journal of Curriculum and Supervision, 10*(2), 136–154.

Kamii, C. (1991). What is constructivism? In C. Kamii, M. Manning, & G. Manning (Eds.), *Early literacy: A constructivist foundation for whole language* (pp. 17–29). Washington, DC: National Education Association.

Lange, J. T. (1993). Site-based, shared decision making: A resource for restructuring. *NASSP Bulletin, 76*(549), 98–107.

Lockwood, A. T. (1996). Preliminary characteristics of productive schools. *New leaders for tomorrow's schools, Fall.* Retrieved from www.ncrel.org/cscd/pubs/lead31/31prdlst.htm

Lord, T. R. (1997). A comparison between traditional and constructivist teaching in college biology. *Innovative Higher Education, 21*(3), 197–216.

Lord, T. R. (1999). A comparison between traditional and constructivist teaching in environmental science. *Journal of Environmental Education, 30*(3), 22–27.

Meier, D. (1995). How our schools could be. *Phi Delta Kappan, 76*(5), 369–373.

Midgley, C., & Wood, S. (1993). Beyond site-based management: Empowering teachers to reform schools. *Phi Delta Kappan, 75*(3), 245–252.

Nagel, N. G. (1996). *Learning through real-world problem solving: The power of integrative teaching.* Thousand Oaks, CA: Corwin Press.

Perkins, D. (1999). The many faces of constructivism. *Educational Leadership, 57*(3), 6–11.

Phillips, D. C. (2000). An opinionated account of the constructivist landscape. In D. C. Phillips (Ed.), *Constructivism in education: Opinions and second opinions on controversial issues* (Vol. 1, pp. 1–16). Ninety-ninth yearbook of the National Society for the Study of Education. Chicago, IL: University of Chicago.

Sarason, S. B. (1998). *Political leadership and educational failure.* San Francisco: Jossey-Bass.

Senge, P. M. (1990). *The fifth discipline: The art and practice of the learning organization.* New York: Doubleday.

Tomlinson, C. A. (1999). *The differentiated classroom: Responding to the needs of all learners.* Alexandria, VA: Association for Supervision and Curriculum Development.

U.S. Department of Education. (1999). *National Center for Education Statistics, Third International Mathematics and Science Study, Videotape Classroom Study, 1994–95.* Retrieved from http://nces.ed.gov/pubs99/timssvid/index.html

Weiss, C. H. (1993). Shared decision making about what? A comparison of schools with and without teacher participation. *Teachers College Record, 95*(1), 69–92.

Wohlstetter, P. (1995). Getting school-based management right: What works and what doesn't? *Phi Delta Kappan, 77*(1), 22–26.

Woolfolk, A. E. (1998). *Educational psychology* (7th ed.). Boston: Allyn & Bacon.

CHAPTER NINE

RETENTION OR PRETENSION?

INTRODUCTION AND PROBLEM BACKGROUND

Each year in the United States, around two million people visit state parks in Wyoming, fish in the Great Lakes, participate in organized ice hockey, work as engineers, fly between Los Angeles and San Francisco (U.S. Department of Commerce, 2000)—and just over two million children are retained in the same grade (Canter, Carey, & Dawson, 1998). At the extremes of a controversy on this issue are those who argue that retention does no student any good and those who argue that social promotion is a sign of the declining state of American education. Then-president Clinton, in his 1999 State of the Union Address, identified the key problem in education to be social promotion.

Certainly, retention continues to be a popular notion for "fixing" children who haven't succeeded in schools. There's a nearly impeccable logic behind the practice: If achievement in a grade level counts for anything, we can't discount such work by passing along children who don't achieve. While most educators view retention as a means to help a child who may need some maturation or extra help, children have always seen retention as *flunking*, and they view this as a punishment (Byrnes, 1989), perhaps even a well-deserved punishment.

As you are forming your perspectives on the host of issues that face you as a teacher, consider how you will view the retention issue. Does holding a child back a grade fit your philosophy of education or does this action contradict what you see as the greater purpose of schooling? Does retention serve children? teachers? parents? None of the above?

This PBL experience invites you to dig into the retention question from the vantage point of educators facing one of the tricky issues related to holding back children. As usual, there may be a variety of other issues that emerge from the problem, just as there would be in the complex "real" world of practice.

PROBLEM CONTEXT AND SOLUTION PARAMETERS

Context

Your school is an amiable place to work. Housed within a massive urban building, the Learning Center is one of eight schools-within-the-school. The idea behind this structure is that no school ought to be so large that the principal can't know each child—yet the huge buildings of an earlier era must be put to good use. Thus, nearly 3,000 students in the full range of grades troop daily into the Ellington Building, though no more than 500 children are in any of the schools housed there.

In general, you have been thrilled to be a part of the Learning Center, however presumptuous its name might seem to the other schools sharing this space. (What, after all, do teachers in *Arts and Language Magnet Elementary* center their school around?) Your first dissatisfaction has come about from your willingness to volunteer for a spring committee. Thinking that it would be a good professional growth opportunity, you raised your hand when the principal asked for teachers who would assist with the "retention review committee." As Mr. Ollestad presented this committee, it was "a chance to put the Learning Center philosophy into action." What you didn't realize was that it was also a chance to face one of the more uncomfortable dilemmas available to teachers.

Problem

Your committee has been handed its first case, one that seems relatively straightforward to most of your colleagues. Jamal Williams is in many respects an average second-grade boy. His interests range from sports to art to stories about huge battles in just about any war. He knows details about the big battles that most beginning teachers wouldn't know. But school doesn't appear to be one of Jamal's interests. He does not have the basic skills in reading, writing, and arithmetic that a child heading into the third grade should have. He frequently finds himself in conflict with other children and with his teacher, and these conflicts escalate whenever Jamal feels pressured to perform.

Jamal's mother has expressed numerous concerns about her son. Many of these concerns are related to life outside of school, but she frequently comments on Jamal's lack of interest and lack of progress. She has hinted that there may be a lawsuit in the making if Jamal does not move forward in skill development.

Jamal's teacher, Ms. Scofield, has recommended that Jamal not be promoted to third grade. She argues that it would be a disservice to pass him along without attending to the serious deficiencies in his skills. To pass him to the next level, Ms. Scofield asserts, would be to doom him to falling ever farther behind.

Mr. Ollestad has determined that in the Learning Center, no decision as significant as retaining a child will be made in isolation. This is where your committee comes in. Mr. Ollestad has charged the retention review committee with overseeing all decisions regarding "nonpromotion." Jamal is your first case.

Solution Parameters

The committee has been provided with a number of documents to assist its decision-making process. In addition, committee members have been urged to go beyond the particular cases in order to "help formulate a defensible position for the school." You will be asked, as a committee, to rule on Ms. Scofield's request that

Jamal be retained for another year in the second grade. You will present your decision and justification in an oral format to a panel consisting of Mr. Ollestad, Ms. Scofield, and Ms. Freeman. They would also like your recommendations for a policy in the form of a one-page handout.

▪▪▪▪▪▪▪WORK THE PROBLEM ⟶

PROBLEM DOCUMENTS

To assist you in understanding various aspects of this situation, the following documents have been provided to you:

9.1 Mr. Ollestad's instructions to the "retention review committee"

9.2 Ms. Scofield's request for retaining Jamal Williams

9.3 Jamal's second-grade progress report, covering the first three reporting periods (The final period has not been completed, pending the outcome of the committee's deliberation.)

9.4 Notes from the school counselor's interview with Ms. Freeman at the time of a disciplinary intervention for Jamal

9.5 The school psychologist's summary of a special education conference about Jamal conducted at the end of his first-grade year

---

PROBLEM DOCUMENT 9.1   *Mr. Ollestad's Instructions to the "Retention Review Committee"*

the learning center
focusing on the core of what schools are about

<u>Memorandum</u>

From: A. T. Ollestad, principal

To: Retention Review Committee

Date: 5/11/03

Re: Committee Purpose

I wish to express my sincere appreciation to all the members of this crucial committee for volunteering their time to help move the school forward in this arena. As most of you know, we have been gradually developing procedures and policies that allow us to act as a Center, a place with a single sense of purpose. It takes time to build the sorts of policies and procedures that allow us to do this.

This year, one great leap forward for us will be to come to grips with the question of retention. As a *learning* center, we cannot in good conscience pass along children who have not *learned* what they need. At the same time, to retain a child in grade is a most serious matter, and while we have not encountered any serious difficulties in allowing teachers to act on their good judgment, it is better for us that we move such decision making into the center.

I acknowledge that this committee may very well face some of the toughest questions any of us face in this learning center. Still, answering such questions is a chance to put the Learning Center philosophy into action. And that's why we all joined the center—to put a powerful learning philosophy into action!

So the charge of this committee is twofold. First, in the leisure of reflection, to consider what a justifiable position on non-promotion would be for our school. I would expect that the committee would develop some ideas and bring those to the faculty as a whole so that our unity on this matter is solid. Second, as individual cases arise, the committee will consider the matters and make a recommendation on action to me, the teacher, and the family involved. I think the objective, removed perspective of the committee will give credibility to our decision making. Obviously these two charges overlap, since the committee's understanding of the retention issue will certainly impact decisions about any individual cases.

In conjunction with this charge, I am asking the committee to examine the case of Jamal Williams. I have included relevant documents for your perusal.

Mr. Ollestad,

I am strongly recommending that Jamal Williams be retained for another year of instruction in the second grade. I have several reasons for this, which I am listing below. But it is important to state at the beginning that I have made this decision only after heart-wrenching anguish. I do not ever like to retain children, but it is so much in the best interest of Jamal that I have to recommend this. Here are my reasons:

1. Jamal has fallen far behind his peers in emotional maturity. It may seem like Jamal is more grown up than he is because he has a degree of street smarts. He does make his way around the school and neighborhood with confidence. But Jamal shows his immaturity when he is in a classroom situation. He cannot sit still for instruction; he continually distracts his classmates. When other children settle down to work, Jamal is out of control. I am well aware of the active nature of second-grade boys, so it is not that my expectations are too high. Jamal stands out, and *the other children notice* his behavior as not fitting with the class. Unless we give him this opportunity to catch up, I'm afraid he will never be able to relate on an equal level with his peers.

2. Jamal's reading and writing skills are well below what a beginning third-grader needs to succeed. I worry that Jamal would find himself falling further and further behind his classmates as the work outstripped his skill level. As we all know, when a child is frustrated with schoolwork and in danger of losing self-esteem, that child tends to act out more. So Jamal's problem of immaturity would be made worse because of his skill level. He would become more of a discipline problem and experience greater isolation from his peers. The academic weakness would create a vicious cycle of failure and behavior problems. Is this in his best interest?

3. Jamal appears to have many distractions outside of school. He seems to me to be an ideal candidate for gang involvement. There is still time to prevent this, but only if we keep Jamal away from some of the older influences in the school. Traditionally, gangs have left the children in first and second grade alone in our school. We can preserve Jamal from possible gang influences while strengthening his connection to positive forces in the school.

As I said, I rarely support retention. I do think that the issue is entirely an individual one, and that in circumstances such as Jamal's, it makes sense to intervene to rescue this child.

You may not be fully aware of Jamal's difficult home life. School provides him with a safe haven and a sense of stability. I suspect that unless we take this step to ensure his success, Jamal will have no safe place at all.

Thank you for your consideration.

Yvette Scofield

Yvette Scofield

the learning center

Our Learner's Progress Report

Child's name: Jamal Williams

Grade: Two

Teacher: Yvette Scofield

Note to parent: The progress report you receive from *the learning center* is probably unlike any you've seen before. We believe that progress is always the goal, and that children should be rewarded for that progress. You won't find letter grades on our reports; instead, you'll find a mark (X) indicating where your child's work fits on a continuum of progress. You will also find brief comments from your child's teacher, and these comments are supported by the extensive portfolios of student work our teachers collect as students move through *the learning center.*

Subject	Skill Progress by Term

Reading

Comments:
1. I'm very excited that Jamal will be reading with me this year.
2. Jamal must learn to sit still for story time.
3. Jamal displays little interest in reading.
4.

Writing

Comments:
1. Jamal has a few beginning skills.
2. Jamal shows limited improvement in clarity of penmanship.
3. Jamal resists writing.
4.

Subject	Skill Progress by Term

Arithmetic

Comments:
1. Jamal has shown arithmetic skills in money games.
2. This term, Jamal began to understand subtraction.
3. Jamal still does not understand subtraction.
4.

Art

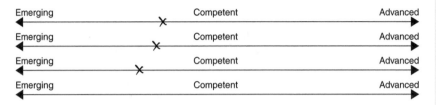

Comments:
1. Jamal has a well-developed sense of different colors.
2. Like many boys his age, Jamal has difficulty with fine motor skills.
3. Jamal is selecting art activities less often than he used to.
4.

Physical activities

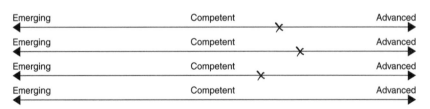

Comments:
1. Good work
2. Talented boy.
3. Good work, but follow rules more.
4.

Social studies

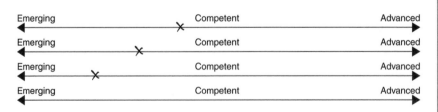

Comments:
1. He shows a good starting interest in social issues.
2. Most of the group learning activities become an occasion for Jamal to disrupt.
3. Jamal is not engaged in our social studies work, and he has not met the standards.
4.

Spelling

Emerging		Competent	Advanced
←—————X————————————————————————————→			
Emerging		Competent	Advanced
←————X——————————————————————————————→			
Emerging		Competent	Advanced
←————X——————————————————————————————→			
Emerging		Competent	Advanced
←————————————————————————————————————→			

Comments:
1. Jamal clearly needs to practice in this area.
2. Continue practice.
3. Jamal should be working more at home on skills.
4.

Penmanship

Emerging		Competent	Advanced
←————————X——————————————————————————→			
Emerging		Competent	Advanced
←————————————X——————————————————————→			
Emerging		Competent	Advanced
←——————X————————————————————————————→			
Emerging		Competent	Advanced
←————————————————————————————————————→			

Comments:
1. Generally about at the right level.
2. Little progress has been made.
3. Jamal should be practicing more. He tends to make his letters too quickly, with little care.
4.

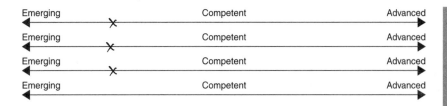

PROBLEM DOCUMENT 9.4

Notes from the School Counselor's Interview with Ms. Freeman

Present: Ms. Scofield, classroom teacher
  Ms. Freeman, parent
  Mr. Ericson, counselor (providing notes)

Ms. Scofield opened the conference with a summary of strengths Jamal has displayed. She noted that Jamal has improved in his relating to adults in the school. In particular, Jamal seemed especially resistant to female teachers at the start of the year, but he now appears to demonstrate more respect for these teachers, though perhaps still preferring male teachers (only his physical activities are facilitated by a male). Ms. Scofield also noted Jamal's enthusiasm for sports and physical activities.

Ms. Scofield then identified areas of concern about Jamal. These are the main areas she identified:
  1. Skill development. Jamal is not reading at the level he should be, and he is not writing to level yet. Jamal will be facing the District Benchmark System (DBS) at the end of the third grade, and Ms. Scofield worries that his skill level will create problems.
  2. Immaturity. Ms. Scofield expressed support of Jamal's enthusiasm, but said that he often acts younger than his age-mates. He has been known to crawl off into a corner of the

room and "make strange noises" that get children's attention. He appears to be losing his ability to relate equally with peers, and as others grow toward the third-grade attitude, Jamal acts out like a kindergartner.

3. Attitude. Ms. Scofield worried that Jamal is feeling defeated by school, and that this attitude would only be reinforced by his low skill level and the demands that third grade (especially the DBS) require.

Ms. Scofield asked Ms. Freeman if she had any questions.

Ms. Freeman: Why is the school telling me this now instead of a long time ago?

Ms. Scofield: We give the students the benefit of the doubt, hoping that their development will improve over time. You can see a decline in the pattern of Jamal's work if you look at his progress reports.

Ms. Freeman: I don't think I got a progress report lately.

Ms. Scofield: You had one about four weeks ago.

Ms. Freeman: I don't remember it.

Ms. Scofield: You signed it.

Mr. Ericson: Maybe the date isn't too important, but I'm worried that you say you didn't know about this.

Ms. Freeman: Well, I guess I knew there was some trouble. I wondered about this reading. Jamal doesn't ever hardly want to read anything.

Ms. Scofield: It's frustrating. He can't read yet, and I'm not sure he's getting the idea of reading.

Ms. Freeman: I'd like him to be a reader and to finish school.

Ms. Scofield: That's what we all want, and that's why we've talking about this now.

Mr. Ericson: Do you see Jamal showing interest in books at home?

Ms. Freeman: We don't have a lot of books or anything. We've had to move a lot, and it's hard to keep books.

Mr. Ericson: I knew you moved in September. Was there more?

Ms. Freeman: Oh yes. We were in that place for September and October. We spent a little time in a shelter. Then we tried another apartment, but that didn't work. We had a different shelter round about Christmas. Now we're with my sister, but her place isn't too big or anything. So there isn't a lot of books or anything.

Ms. Scofield: Do you think those moves might have made school hard for Jamal?

Ms. Freeman: I don't think so. We've been moving a lot his whole life, and he adjusts. We stay in this area, just different places to hang a coat up. Jamal's fine about moving. He's a big help.

Mr. Ericson: Does he talk about the moves? Does he worry?

Ms. Freeman: He don't say much about moving. I think he likes living with my sister, because there's cousins to play with all the time. And he says he sleeps better when there are more people in the house.

Mr. Ericson: What sorts of things does Jamal do outside of school?

Ms. Freeman: Oh, you know, the things boys do. He's mostly playing outside with his friends and cousins. Jamal has lots of friends.

Ms. Scofield: Are they his age?

Ms. Freeman: Mostly I'd say. They're out and about playing all over the neighborhood. But Jamal comes home when I want him. He's a good boy.

Mr. Ericson: What does Jamal tell you about school?

Ms. Freeman: Mostly he's glad about it. He sometimes says it makes him feel dumb, but he doesn't say much to me about school. I tell him as long as I don't hear from the school, that means he's doing his job.

Mr. Ericson: Does he seem frustrated with school?

Ms. Freeman: Frustrated?

Ms. Scofield: Does he say the work is too hard?

Ms. Freeman: No, he doesn't worry much about the work. He sometimes shows me a picture, and he was real excited about some dinosaur story you read him.

Ms. Scofield: Thanks.

Mr. Ericson: Does Jamal write at home?

Ms. Freeman: Doesn't have much occasion to write.

Mr. Ericson: Does he watch a lot of TV?

Ms. Freeman: Doesn't watch more than anybody else. He likes cartoons. And he likes a shoot-em movie, but I don't like those so we don't have them on too much.

Mr. Ericson: Do you understand why we are considering holding Jamal back?

Ms. Freeman: I guess, but it worries me.

Mr. Ericson: Why?

Ms. Freeman: I want him to finish school, and holding back doesn't seem like moving forward.

Ms. Scofield: But it might be the best way for Jamal to move forward. If he goes on to the third grade without the skills he will need, he is more likely to fail.

Ms. Freeman: I thought you were saying he's failing now.

Ms. Scofield: Holding him back doesn't mean he's failing.

Ms. Freeman: That's sure what it meant when I was in school. We called it flunking. There wasn't anything worse a kid could do than flunk, and flunking the second grade would have made me feel about as dumb as anything.

Mr. Ericson: What Ms. Scofield means is that we need to think about Jamal's success in learning—what's important for his life. If he goes on to third grade now, it might seem like he's succeeding. But if he doesn't know what he needs to know, then he's set up for failure.

Ms. Freeman: What makes you think doing second grade again will help him?

Mr. Ericson: We hope that he can mature a little and have some extra time to get the skills.

Ms. Scofield: Some kids just need more time, or they aren't quite ready to learn certain things. It's not a failure to need a little more time. In fact, quite a few kids need more time, and repeating a grade is a time-tested way to help children do their real best.

Ms. Freeman: What happens if all his friends go on to third grade?

Ms. Scofield: He can still see his friends.

Ms. Freeman: Of course he'll see them. That's my worry. They're going to make it awful hard on Jamal.

Mr. Ericson: We work hard with our children to prevent teasing and that sort of thing.

Ms. Freeman: Well it's not working yet. Ask any child in this school and they'll tell you there's teasing all the time. Now if Jamal has to be the kid who flunked second grade, what's that going to be like for him?

Ms. Scofield: Children can be mean, but we can help stop that by talking to them. Usually, after the first week or so, everyone forgets who was supposed to be in what grade.

Ms. Freeman: That's not how it was when I was in school. My brother got held back in fourth grade, and he got so tired of hearing about flunking fourth grade that he just quit going to school after seventh grade.

Mr. Ericson: Does Jamal have a good relationship with his uncle?

Ms. Freeman: He's dead. Jamal wouldn't remember him at all. He was shot.

Ms. Scofield: I'm sorry.

Ms. Freeman: It's a while ago.

Mr. Ericson: So are you willing to give this a try for Jamal's sake?

Ms. Freeman: I'd do just about anything for that boy. If this is the best thing for Jamal, I'm ready. But I'd like to give it the weekend to think about. Can I do that?

Mr. Ericson: Of course. We really want the best decision, and if we can get that with a little more time, it's worth it.

NOTE: Ms. Freeman telephoned the counseling office the following Monday and said she did not want Jamal retained.

| PROBLEM DOCUMENT 9.5 | *The School Psychologist's Summary of a Special Education Conference about Jamal* |

the learning center

SPECIAL EDUCATION CONFERENCE REPORT

Student Name: Jamal Williams   Date of Conference: 5/7/02

Age: 7   Grade: 1   Recorder: Janet Rivera-Thomas, Ed. D.

REASON FOR CONFERENCE: Jamal had displayed delayed development through the year, causing his teacher to initiate a request for a testing battery on Jamal.

SUMMARY OF CONFERENCE/DISCUSSION: Dr. Rivera-Thomas reviewed the results of a psycho-educational assessment of Jamal. His scores on the WISC-III indicated he was below average in his IQ, while the results of the Woodcock-Johnson, 3rd Ed., revealed a student achieving at the beginning first-grade level. However, the two assessments taken together portray a student meeting expectations, with performance consistent in all areas. That is, reading, computation, and nonverbal scores matched predictions based on Jamal's IQ score.

   Ms. Acosta, Jamal's teacher, reported that Jamal's behavior had steadily declined throughout the spring, and that she suspected a learning disability was prompting frustration. Ms. Freeman, Jamal's mother, reported that Jamal did express frustration with schoolwork, but added that certain "personal and challenging" issues at home were also a problem for his concentration. Mr. Ollestad suggested that Jamal might require further testing for emotional disabilities, but Ms. Freeman indicated she would not permit such assessment.

RECOMMENDATIONS: Initially, Ms. Acosta suggested that Jamal might profit from another year in the first grade, but with a different teacher. Ms. Freeman expressed a concern that this might not serve her son, and Mr. Ollestad echoed her concern. Ms. Acosta suggested that Jamal might receive support from special education aides, but both Dr. Rivera-Thomas and Mr. Walters, the special education representative, indicated that this was not within the realm of accepted responses, based on the testing that has been done. In the end, the team agreed to support Jamal's placement in the second grade, but with more systematic monitoring of his performance and behavior in the subsequent school year.

THE FOLLOWING PERSONS WERE CONSULTED OR PARTICIPATED AS A TEAM TO DISCUSS THE RECOMMENDATIONS.

Signature	Agree/Disagree
Arlene Freeman	*Agree*
Parent	
A. T. Ollestad	*Agree*
Principal	
Angela Acosta	*Agree*
Teacher	
Pat Walters	*Agree*
Spec. ed	
Therapist	
D. Ericson	*Agree*
Counselor	
Janet Rivera-Thomas	*Agree*
School Psychologist	
District Rep.	
Translator	
Other	

••••PROPOSE A SOLUTION ➡

SOLUTION SUMMARY

Before proceeding to the reflection section of this chapter, write a brief summary of your team's solution here:

Our team defined the "real" problem here as _____

_____

_____

_____

_____

_____

_____

_____

The key features of our solution were _____

_____

_____

_____

_____

_____

_____

_____

My personal view of the problem and solution is _____

_____

_____

_____

_____

_____

_____

_____

TIME FOR REFLECTION

As often happens in PBL, there are main issues and side issues raised in this problem. The reflection takes on both. The main issue of the problem provides the initial reflection as we consider retention in grade. However, we will also examine what constitutes effective meetings with parents and the school-within-a-school model. The final reflection offers you a chance to think about homelessness among school-aged children.

Grade Retention

At the heart of this issue is a difficulty educators often have to face: While some actions seem reasonable and like the common-sense thing to do, we have to ask whether the evidence supports such conclusions. Do we know that retention in grade helps students become better learners, more productive citizens, and more eager participants in the school community? Or is retention the curricular counterpart to the stereotypical ugly American tourist addressing a vendor in a foreign market: they didn't get it the first time, so we say the same thing louder and slower?

Much of the research about retention is speculative, since schools don't regularly keep data on this issue. Instead, we can infer something about retention rates by looking at figures for how many students are overage for their grade (Roderick, 1995; Shepard & Smith, 1989b). For example, a typical fifth-grader is ten years old. A ten-year-old child in the spring of her third-grade year is overage and probably was retained at least once. Given that limitation, we can infer that there is a lot of retention taking place. Estimates vary, but a fairly common view is that between 20 and 25 percent of students in school have been retained at least once (Martinez & Vandegrift, 1991; Roderick, 1995). And that figure is somewhat misleading, since many retained students have dropped out of the system. New York City schools, for example, reported a 19 percent dropout rate in the high schools in 2000, and many of the children who did drop out reported that a key reason was being overage in their classes (Hartocollis, 2001).

Retaining students has been a popular strategy for addressing student weaknesses throughout the modern era of schooling, though recent decades have seen the highest retention rates since the advent of compulsory graded schooling. In the 19th century, when the philosophy of schooling was merit-based, there was a 70 percent retention rate (Shepard & Smith, 1989b). Teachers appear to believe that immature children get an opportunity to mature and catch up by virtue of retention (Smith, 1989). Again, this seems to be common sense, particularly if it matches one's view of learning. If learning is a linear, sequential process in which a person must learn A before B before learning C and so on, then retention appears to be not only justified, but obligatory. What self-respecting school system can pass students along to the next step in a learning sequence without first helping that child succeed in the current step? A well-known court case, *Peter W. v. San Francisco Unified School District*, in which a school system was sued for graduating a student without the basic skills, brought educators to the realization that there can be serious consequences if a student is moved through a school system without acquiring basic skills (Shepard & Smith, 1989b).

On the other hand, a different view of learning may be worth a few moments' thought. Susan Ohanian wrote that as a third grade teacher, she refused to prepare her students for the rigors of fourth grade (1996). Indeed, viewing the learning process as a more individual progression for students, as opposed to a completion of graded hurdles, suggests that retention is absurd. A "constructivist" view of learning, one in which the learner builds meaning rather than simply acquiring it sequentially, suggests a different response to a child's inadequacies. Peterson (1989) contrasts two metaphors for learning. In a linear, sequential model, learning is like building a tower out of blocks. You have to build the bottom row carefully before progressing, and if you are missing something in the foundation, the whole tower crumbles. A constructivist metaphor for learning is a tinker toy edifice. The structure is a matter of connections, and the more connections one makes, the stronger it is. However, there are multiple connections, and one can build connections at any time. Consider which model better explains your own understanding of this important notion.

The research evidence is always worth investigating. Rather than recount it all here, perhaps the best approach is to raise some questions in this regard:

- What happens to retained children in the short term, for the first year or so after being retained?
- Further into the school career, what are the effects of children's being older than peers? For example, is there a relationship between retention and dropping out of school?
- What do we know about the achievement or learning of retained students?

An issue like retention is one where the professional educator must be certain to know enough to address the common cultural views of the issue.

Parent Meetings

There is a certain irony to the preparation most teachers experience. While the time spent learning how to teach a lesson or how to manage unruly children is indispensable, often the toughest dealings a teacher will face occur with a different kind of "client." Teachers also must deal with administrators and custodians and district personnel and counselors, but above all, with parents. The range of parents will be astounding: some will know all the laws associated with whatever issue brings them to see you; some will know more about whatever subject you are teaching than you do; some won't realize how important they are to helping their child succeed in learning; and some won't even have a clue that their child is a bully or terrified or desperately lonely. But you will have to deal with all sorts.

So how does a teacher develop competence in dealing with parents? First, whenever possible, observe your mentors in their interactions with parents. You can learn much from the experience of those around you. Second, learn to approach parents with a humility that honors their place in life. A mistake beginning teachers make far too often is to try to impress parents with some mysterious knowledge. Some beginners use language that is unfamiliar to parents, perhaps in an effort to boost the teacher's confidence or credibility. However, it is usually more effective to communicate in a straightforward, honest manner. And it is important to remember that a meeting with parents ought to be a source of information for you. They generally know more about the children you face than anyone, so it serves you well to learn from them.

Schools-within-Schools

The structure of the Learning Center in this problem connects with what some have called the "small school movement." Advocates of small schools have helped us to think about ideas of smallness and community even when we are saddled with buildings that attempt to draw thousands of children into one place. Among other things, small school advocates cite improvements in student achievement, the success of "at-risk" students, better long-term bonds among individuals, and more innovative approaches to education (Raywid, 1997/1998).

Perhaps the most famous of the small schools is Central Park East Secondary School. Founded by Deborah Meier, a former kindergarten teacher, this school lives out the philosophy of smallness. Meier makes a case that as children get older, educators pay less and less attention to those children's interests. However, in small schools, educators have the opportunity to adjust to the children. She writes, "Simple changes that are impossible to make in a mega-school can be decided in one afternoon and implemented the next morning in a small school" (Meier, 1995, p. 372).

In his account of creating the ideal school, Sizer (1992) emphasizes the possibilities of using "houses" or schools within larger schools. Such small organizations can provide focus for students and teachers; most importantly, small schools promote conditions in which students are no longer anonymous (Wasley & Lear, 2001). In small schools, the environment is humanized by virtue of the opportunity to know and care for others. The Coalition of Essential Schools, founded by Theodore Sizer, has as a core principle this notion of smallness.

In the Learning Center, the ideas of focus, smallness, and caring are given the opportunity to flourish. While the problem offers us only a glimpse of the kind of unique school that might have been created within a massive inner-city building, it allows us to contemplate the possibilities. What the Learning Center teaches us indirectly is that the rules for what makes a school are not set, that educators have the chance to break away from traditions and the dictates of efficiency in order to design the sort of learning environment that can serve children well. This sort of dreaming is a good start for beginning teachers.

Homelessness among School-Age Children

Consider the comment of a 12-year-old occupant of a Los Angeles homeless shelter, quoted in Seltser and Miller, 1993, p. 52: "Look at all the Skid Row bums. . . . It's dull and dumb and, if it was my world, I would set it on fire. . . . I feel like a dead cat."

In a perfect world, we wouldn't have to reflect on this issue at all. Civilized nations, it seems, would make the idea of a homeless child an unthinkable oxymoron. In fact, many children, a great many children, qualify as homeless. And, as Yvonne Rafferty reports, "Children in the United States do not have a legal right to housing, to emergency shelter if they lose their home, to adequate nourishment and freedom from hunger, to preventive or curative health and mental health care, or to a quality public education" (1995, p. 55).

Our stereotype of the homeless person is a ragged old man who smells of alcohol and street filth. He wanders the public thoroughfares in search of handouts during the day; he huddles in a doorway each night. But the picture is broader than that. According to some estimates, almost a quarter of the homeless in America are families with school-age children, with some 500,000 homeless youth (Daniels, 1992). Whereas many homeless youth have fled dysfunctional homes due to physical or sexual abuse (Smollar, 1999), there are many others who stay connected to families in their homelessness. Indeed, even defining *homelessness* presents some challenge. States vary in who they identify as homeless, ranging from only occupants of shelters to those who are doubled up with relatives. New York state did not count runaway youth living in shelters as homeless until 1991 (Rafferty, 1995).

In general, to be considered homeless, a child spends time either in a shelter or in an impermanent setting such as a hotel room. The child may move frequently from one dwelling to another. Success in school, under these conditions, may be difficult to attain, with challenges in attendance, performance, acceptance by peers and staff, and having the basic necessities such as supplies and clothes (Rafferty, 1995). True, the school may be the one source of stability and a sort of haven for children who otherwise face many uncertainties (Daniels, 1992), but even if school serves such a purpose, chances for academic success are low.

The Stewart B. McKinney Homeless Assistance Act of 1987 requires that states provide professional development for educators to raise awareness of the issues of homelessness and to respond appropriately to their needs (Rafferty, 1995). However, it is unclear whether this legislation has had a significant impact on educational opportunities for children. As a member of the professional community at a school, you will want to consider what impact you can have in terms of raising awareness of the problem of homelessness. Far too often educators find fault with such children rather than solutions for the children's lives. As educators increase their awareness of the issues of homelessness, they are more likely to become a force for emotional and academic stability for children who suffer the consequences of this bizarre situation (Rafferty, 1997/1998).

DISCUSSION QUESTIONS

1. Having inquired into the issue of retention, what do you see as the most defensible stand for an educator? How would you communicate this to the parents you work with? For those who oppose retention, does this create a problem in motivating children?

2. How can professional educators create the necessary dialogue at their schools to re-examine issues such as retention? What provides the trigger point for opening discussions about matters with long traditions in the schools?

3. What do you see as the virtues of "small schools" and what do you see as the potential losses in such an organization? How would you help a community to investigate this idea?

4. Given the schools' obligation to address issues of homelessness, what do you see as the individual teacher's role in meeting this obligation?

5. What particular challenges does the teacher face in dealing with the parents of a child who may need to be retained? Are there principles suggested by this problem that help you define how you might successfully communicate with parents?

6. Considering the PBL process, what did you learn about determining the relevance of different and sometimes competing information? How effective were you at filtering information?

FURTHER READING

Alexander, K. L., Entwisle, D. R., & Dauber, S. L. (1994). *On the success of failure: A reassessment of the effects of retention in the primary grades.* New York: Cambridge University.
   This book reports on a study of some 800 children in the Baltimore City schools over an eight-year period. The authors take a position they regard as at odds with what most researchers conclude about retention. They find that retention helps children achieve at a higher level academically, and without serious consequences to their self-esteem. The book provides a distinctly positive perspective on retention, concluding that "although the weight of sentiment in the research literature would have us believe otherwise, having children repeat a year can and does help academically; moreover, at least for children like those in Baltimore, it does not compromise self-regard" (p. 233).

Harber, C. (1996). *Small schools and democratic practice.* Bramcote Hills, Nottingham, UK: Educational Heretics Press.
   The claim of the publishing house is worth noting in consideration of this book: "Educational Heretics Press exists to question the dogmas of education in general, and schooling in particular." Clearly, this book comes from a tradition that does not hesitate to challenge the way things are in schools. Harber writes a brief book with three main sections: First, he looks at the many benefits of small schools (which he says are superior by any measure); then he examines ways of making large schools smaller (and getting large-school benefits to small ones); finally, he addresses how small schools can promote democracy. The book is an easy read, made especially valuable to North American readers because of the numerous international examples Harber provides.

National Association of School Psychologists. (1998). Position statement: Student grade retention and social promotion. Bethesda, MD: Author.
   This position paper (available from NASP, 4340 East West Highway, Suite 402, Bethesda, MD 20814) provides a quick review of research on the issue of retention. The paper lists about nine disturbing research findings in relation to retention. The paper also lists some potential benefits of retention and alternatives to the practice. NASP also has handouts available for teachers and parents to help all parties understand the implications of retention and possible alternatives. The handout authored by Canter, Carey, and Dawson (1998) is especially useful.

Rafferty, Y. (1995). The legal rights and educational problems of homeless children and youth. *Educational Evaluation and Policy Analysis, 17*(1), 39–61.

This paper provides a concise examination of the situation of homeless children and youth. Rafferty explains the role of the McKinney Act as well as the problems with its implementation at the state level. Moreover, she reviews the numerous obstacles homeless children face in their school lives. (Rafferty published a similar paper in the December 1997/January 1998 issue of *Educational Leadership,* pp. 48–52.)

Seltser, B. J., & Miller, D. E. (1993). *Homeless families: The struggle for dignity.* Chicago, IL: University of Illinois.

This book helps break down the stereotype of a homeless person. Seltser and Miller interview 100 homeless persons, many of whom are parts of homeless families, to understand the experience of homelessness. The fourth chapter, on life in shelters, is especially helpful in understanding this condition. Seltser and Miller point out that the homeless population seeks dignity, as do all humans. The authors highlight four key requirements for dignity: autonomy, predictability, self-expression, and social stability.

Shepard, L. A., & Smith, M. L. (1989). *Flunking grades: Research and policies on retention.* New York: Falmer.

This collection of reports examines issues of retention, including the relationship between retention and dropping out; the attitudes of teachers, students, and parents; teachers' beliefs about retention; and the effects of retention on learning. The general picture in the book is that whereas there is strong support for retention, this support survives in the face of overwhelming evidence against the practice. In fact, one of the authors (Ernest R. House) writes that "Few practices in education have such overwhelmingly negative research findings arrayed against them" (p. 204). This book argues that there are no real benefits for retention, except in cases where retention includes individual attention and remediation for students. The collection also offers some evidence that teachers can change their beliefs and practices in regard to retention. The final chapter, a recapitulation by the editors, may be the best section for beginning teachers.

WEB SITES

Consortium for Equity in Standards and Testing, Spotlight Issue on Retention
www.csteep.bc.edu/CTESTWEB/retention/retention.html
Anne Wheelock provides more information on the topic.

National Association of School Psychologists, Position Paper
www.nasponline.org/information/pospaper_graderetent.html

Northwest Regional Laboratory
www.nwrel.org/nwreport/may96/small.html
A report of research on small schools.

National Association for Small Schools in the United Kingdom
www.smallschools.org.uk
Dedicated to preserving small schools.

REFERENCES

Alexander, K. L., Entwisle, D. R., & Dauber, S. L. (1994). *On the success of failure: A reassessment of the effects of retention in the primary grades.* New York: Cambridge University.

Byrnes, D. A. (1989). Attitudes of students, parents, and educators toward repeating a grade. In L. A. Shepard & M. L. Smith (Eds.), *Flunking grades: Research and policies on retention* (pp. 108–131). New York: Falmer.

Canter, A., Carey, K., & Dawson, P. (1998). Retention and promotion: A handout for teachers. Bethesda, MD: National Association of School Psychologists.

Daniels, J. (1992). Empowering homeless children through school counseling. *Elementary School Guidance and Counseling, 27,* 104–112.

Harber, C. (1996). *Small schools and democratic practice.* Bramcote Hills, Nottingham, UK: Educational Heretics Press.

Hartocollis, A. (2001, March 22). Not-so-simple reasons for dropout rate. *New York Times on the Web.* Retrieved from www.nytimes.com/2001/03/22/nyregion/22/DROP.html?pagewanted=all

Martinez, B., & Vandegrift, J. A. (1991). *Issue: Failing students—Is it worth the cost?* (At-Risk Research: Issues & Answers, Issue Paper #3 ERIC Reproduction Services Document # ED359666). Tempe, AZ: Morrison Institute for Public Policy.

Meier, D. (1995). How our schools could be. *Phi Delta Kappan, 76*(5), 369–373.

National Association of School Psychologists. (1998). Position statement: Student grade retention and social promotion. Bethesda, MD: Author.

Ohanian, S. (1996). Is that penguin stuffed or real? *Phi Delta Kappan, 78*(4), 277–284.

Peterson, P. L. (1989). Alternatives to student retention. In L. A. Shepard & M. L. Smith (Eds.), *Flunking grades: Research and policies on retention* (pp. 174–201). New York: Falmer.

Rafferty, Y. (1995). The legal rights and educational problems of homeless children and youth. *Educational Evaluation and Policy Analysis, 17*(1), 39–61.

Rafferty, Y. (1997/1998). Meeting the educational needs of homeless children. *Educational Leadership, 55*(4), 48–52.

Raywid, M. A. (1997/1998). Small schools: A reform that works. *Educational Leadership, 55*(4), 34–39.

Roderick, M. (1995). Grade retention and school dropout: Policy debate and research questions. *Phi Delta Kappan Research Bulletin* (15). ERIC Reproduction Document Services No. ED 397213.

Seltser, B. J., & Miller, D. E. (1993). *Homeless families: The struggle for dignity.* Chicago, IL: University of Illinois.

Shepard, L. A., & Smith, M. L. (Eds.). (1989a). *Flunking grades: Research and policies on retention.* New York: Falmer.

Shepard, L. A., & Smith, M. L. (1989b). Introduction and overview. In L. A. Shepard & M. L. Smith (Eds.), *Flunking grades: Research and policies on retention* (pp. 1–15). New York: Falmer.

Sizer, T. R. (1992). *Horace's school: Redesigning the American high school.* Boston: Houghton Mifflin.

Smith, M. L. (1989). Teachers' beliefs about retention. In L. A. Shepard & M. L. Smith (Eds.), *Flunking grades: Research and policies on retention* (pp. 132–150). New York: Falmer.

Smollar, J. (1999). Homeless youth in the United States: Description and developmental issues. *New Directions for Child and Adolescent Development, 85,* 47–58.

U.S. Department of Commerce (2000), *Statistical Abstract of the United States: The National Data Book 2000,* (120th ed), Washington, DC: Author.

Wasley, P. A., & Lear, R. J. (2001). Small schools, real gains. *Educational Leadership, 58*(6), 22–27.

CHAPTER TEN

HYPER KID, HYPER MOM, HYPER TEACHER—WHO'S HYPER?

INTRODUCTION AND PROBLEM BACKGROUND

Imagine living in a world where the slightest stimulation drew your attention away from whatever you tried to focus on. A simple task, such as driving a car down the street, becomes complicated almost beyond endurance. You are thinking about the pressure on the gas pedal that will get you to the speed you want, but an annoying smell drifts up to you from the floor of the back seat, reminding you that you need to clean the car. The fluttering of leaves on trees near the street seems to create a visual noise in your brain. You shake your head and shake each arm as though flicking off drips of moisture. A dog sniffing along the sidewalk demands that you look at it, but you coach yourself back to the task of maintaining your speed and watching the road. The dog barks, and you can't help but look over, as the car slows down. You watch to see if the dog is after something, or if it is going into one of the yards where the rhododendrons are blooming bright pink. Where was that passing car's license plate from? Somewhere in the distance there is a flashing light that reminds you of danger, though you are not sure why, and you pull your foot off the gas pedal and lightly press the brake. The car behind you honks and you jerk forward, noticing that the road seems somehow rougher as you speed up.

Of course, the complexities of driving are enormous. When we drive we receive thousands of pieces of information, but most people learn quickly that they must filter out irrelevant information in order to focus on the important matters. The color of flowers can be of interest to us, but the motion of the dog towards the street sends a much more powerful, urgent message. The task of driving would be much more difficult and dangerous if every possible piece of information came to us with equal value—so that we were virtually incapable of sorting through the mess.

For some children, it seems that the experience of school is much like driving without the ability to filter information. Each stimulus, whether a sound or a smell or the decorations on a wall or the motion of a nearby student, quickly draws the interest and attention of these students. Rather than focusing exclusively on the school tasks before them, such students fidget, whirl, and forget what they were doing as they latch on to what comes into view. Such students may suffer from what is known as attention-deficit hyperactivity disorder (ADHD), a disability affecting 3 to 5 percent of the population (Brock, 1998).

Or they may not. There is some controversy surrounding the issue. Many teachers have wondered if a child's misbehavior warrants a federally-sanctioned label—ADHD, or a socially-sanctioned label—BRAT. And once the label has been accepted, the controversy doesn't end. Some say we over-diagnose and over-medicate ADHD sufferers. Others say we don't do either enough.

The theoretical and research debates move into the background for both the families struggling to deal with ADHD and the teachers who have to cope with the challenges on a daily basis. Teachers worry about the sense of safety and order they create in a classroom, and the student who threatens that order demands a great deal of the teacher's attention. For such teachers, it is not a matter of academic debates about the issue; it's a matter of doing something that works and doing it now. In one of those rare moments in life, there may be a magic pill that can fix the problem: a psychostimulant, such as Ritalin. The child takes the pill, and behold, order!

The controversy remains, because this magic pill has also been accused of causing dramatic changes in personalities, prompting suicide, and laying the groundwork for a lifetime of drug dependency. Is ADHD real? Is it something that should be addressed with a prescription? What do teachers need to know about this disability? These are some of the questions you are invited to pursue as you consider this PBL experience.

PROBLEM CONTEXT AND SOLUTION PARAMETERS

Context

Rothsfield Elementary School has well-established policies and procedures in place for addressing issues that arise in relation to special education. Consistent with the laws in this midwestern state, the school diverts every request for assessment to an established student study team (SST). At Rothsfield, this team consists of the school counselor, nurse, special education teacher for the grade level, school psychologist, and one regular education teacher who receives release time and a stipend to serve on the team for a year. Each special education referral results in a preliminary meeting of the SST, which may call in other participants, such as the child's classroom teacher or parent. The outcome of this meeting varies. Sometimes the team recommends a formal evaluation; sometimes the team recommends no action; sometimes the team recommends a plan to accommodate the needs of a child. If the issue is not resolved by the preliminary meeting, the counselor (who chairs the team) calls for a follow-up meeting. Most often, this sets in motion the formal evaluation of the child by the school psychologist. After completing the evaluation, the psychologist reports to the team, this time with parental participation, and an individualized education plan (IEP) is drawn up for the child.

In most cases, the process works efficiently. Keeping together a single team for at least a year has allowed Rothsfield to be very consistent in how it addresses special needs issues. The principal, Madeleine Foster, feels that the school is able to comply with state and federal regulations and to meet the needs of children because of this team's expertise. But it doesn't always go smoothly.

Problem

Ellen Mannington came to Rothsfield mid-year in the fourth grade. While she struggled some at that time and seemed distracted, her teacher saw nothing unusual for a child who has gone through a radical change (moving away from her home and father in Texas). In the fifth grade, her teacher, Rondee Carter, began to see behaviors that indicated a possibility of attention-deficit hyperactivity disorder (ADHD). After some initial attempts to address the problem in class and through phone calls with Ellen's mother, Miss Carter followed school procedure and referred the case to the SST. This team met and approved a student accommodation/ intervention plan for Ellen. The plan did not address the issue of medication, which Miss Carter felt was a necessary element of any plan to assist Ellen. The follow-up report from Miss Carter indicated that the plan was not working, and she strongly urged a formal evaluation with consideration of appropriate medication in Ellen's case. Ellen's mother, Andrea Easton-Mannington, then expressed her strong opposition both to the evaluation and to the medication.

Anticipating difficulties in the next meeting, the SST chair has asked a group of educators at Rothsfield to examine the case and make a recommendation. Mr. Anderson, the chair, has made this unusual request because the letter of concern from Ms. Easton-Mannington indicates that she believes the committee to be biased in some way. Mr. Anderson hopes that the participation of outsiders, whatever their recommendation, will give credibility to the outcome of this situation.

Solution Parameters

Your team of educators will make a brief recommendation to the SST regarding Ellen Mannington. Your job is to examine the available documentation in light of what we know about the purported diagnosis (ADHD) and indicate what would be the best solution. You will have ten minutes to address the team, followed by up to five minutes of questions and answers. You are free to recommend any appropriate course of action—ranging from no action to special education programs to medication. Be sure to justify your recommendations with connections to established research.

········WORK THE PROBLEM ⟶

PROBLEM DOCUMENTS

To assist you in understanding various aspects of this situation, the following documents have been provided to you:

10.1 Letter from Ms. Easton-Mannington explaining why she will not permit a formal evaluation of her daughter and her opposition to the use of medication in this case

10.2 Written summary of the original student study team (SST) conference regarding Ellen Mannington

10.3 The SST-approved Section 504 plan for Ellen that has come into question

10.4 Miss Carter's follow-up report on Ellen's performance after implementing the SST plan

10.5 A page from Ellen's reading journal that her teacher found relevant. The book discussed is *The Westing Game,* a book with a reading level slightly beyond most students in this grade level. Miss Carter points out that sample entry exhibits typical lack of organization on the part of Ellen.

10.6 Notes from the school's psychologist's interview with Ms. Easton-Mannington

10.7 A classroom observation of Ellen's behavior, filed by the school counselor; contact was initiated by Dr. Tyrrell after receipt of the letter prohibiting a formal evaluation

---

PROBLEM DOCUMENT 10.1 *Letter from Ms. Easton-Mannington*

1/23/04

To the members of the Rothsfield Elementary Student Study Team:

As you are well aware, I expressed my opposition to medication at the earliest opportunity in addressing the school's difficulties in dealing with my daughter, Ellen. I continue that steadfast opposition, and I will detail why in this letter. First, I would like to chronicle the events surrounding my daughter's case.

At the beginning of this school year, Ellen, who has a superlative record both at this school and at her former Texas elementary school, experienced conflict with Ms. Carter. Some attempts to address this were made by Ms. Carter, although her ideas struck me as patronizing and unprofessional. In late October, a "student study team" convened at Rothsfield to discuss this case. I have made known my objection to this team's meeting without my presence, so I don't need to belabor that point here. The team made some suggestions about how to address Ellen's needs, but did so without fair consideration of the school's role in creating Ellen's difficulties. It seems to me that the team accepted Ms. Carter's view of a pseudo-diagnosis: attention deficit disorder. Most of the recommendations of the team were palatable, so I did not object strenuously to the outcome.

After following the team's recommendations for barely a month, Ms. Carter returned to her theme of medicalizing Ellen's situation, claiming that the 504 plan had been ineffective. As before, Ms. Carter continued to seek a label for Ellen and to call for radical intervention. It is here where I draw the line.

167

As anyone who has looked into the matter knows, not even the professionals can agree on what this attention deficit disorder is. The central guidebook of the American Psychiatric Association, the *Diagnostic and Statistical Manual of Mental Disorders,* has changed its presentation of the condition with every revision of the manual. Sometimes the manual will emphasize motor issues; sometimes, attention issues. While this condition has little clarity about it, what *is* starkly clear is that the ailment Ms. Carter describes is a male condition. However you define it, it appears that males are about ten times more likely to experience this than females. The question of medication for this ill-defined ailment is even murkier! There is, perhaps, some evidence that males can profit from medication. I know of no evidence that suggests females profit from the use of drugs for ADD. On the other hand, there appears to be mounting evidence that the use of drugs leads to a host of problems for the victims: future drug use, personality disorders, altered behavior, and diminution of creativity.

It is this last point that especially concerns me. Ellen does not suffer from some "disorder" in need of treatment. Ellen suffers because she is a creative, energetic, exciting young woman who is being suffocated by a school interested in nothing more than churning out drones who can fill in blanks and conform to stifling uniformities. I realize how inflammatory that sentence is, but I must speak the truth here. What the schools are calling a disorder has been shown time and again to be nothing more than non-conforming creative behavior. Unable to allow for such differences, the schools call this a disorder. And when the behavior modification programs don't work, they drug our children to silence them.

I know my rights as a parent. No one at Rothsfield can perform a formal evaluation of my child unless I approve it. No one can tell me she needs drugs to become "normal," when I see a spark of light in her that shames your normality, a spark that I won't let you extinguish with drugs.

Your job is to provide a learning environment for my child, not to mold her into a clone of the perfect worksheet-completer. If the school spent one-tenth the time looking at how to make learning an exciting venture as it spends trying to find the problems in the children, this would be a dynamic institution.

I'm not sorry to say it: I won't let you off the hook. I refuse to have Ellen drugged and I refuse to let you try to condemn her to special education. Do your job.

Sincerely,

Andrea Easton-Mannington

Andrea Easton-Mannington
36 Weller Court

Written Summary of the Original Student Study Team (SST) Conference

Irwin Rothsfield Elementary School

Student Study Team Summary Report

Michael X. Anderson, Chair

Student Name: Ellen Mannington   **Meeting Date:** 10/13/03

Grade: 5   **Teacher:** Rondee Carter

Date Report Sent to Parent/Guardian: 10/18/03

Reason for initiating the SST meeting: Miss Carter initiated the request based on observations of Ellen's classroom behavior. Miss Carter indicated Ellen had the following problems: difficulty sitting still for class work, poor organizational skills, missing assignments, frequent disruptive behavior, and low self-esteem.

Executive Summary of SST Meeting: After careful consideration of Ellen's situation, the team recommended a number of accommodations, consistent with Section 504. A copy of the recommended accommodations was sent to the teacher and parent.

Special Education Accommodations (check):

_____ YES ___X__ NO _____ UNABLE TO DETERMINE AT THIS POINT

Document interventions attempted prior to this meeting: According to Miss Carter, she attempted four basic interventions with the student and one with the parent. To assist Ellen in focusing her attention, Miss Carter required Ellen to complete a daily notebook. To assist Ellen with planning, Miss Carter required a summary assignment sheet. To assist Ellen in complying with behavioral expectations, Miss Carter required Ellen to evaluate her own actions in light of classroom rules through a weekly conference and a daily reflection sheet. Finally, Miss Carter required Ellen to stay after school to reinforce the consequences of violating rules. To enlist parental support, Miss Carter requested that Ellen's mother provide consequences at home when Ellen did not complete her assignment sheet (but Ellen's mother did not participate).

Document options considered at this meeting:

1. In-class modifications (selected as best option).
2. Conducting formal evaluation for special education placement.
3. Use of a full-time aide/assistant.
4. Behavior management plan.
5. Assignment to a different classroom.
6. Counseling alternatives, including one-on-one counseling or group counseling.
7. Referral for medical assessment (recommended).
8. Out-of-school placement.
9.
10.

List all Recommendations from the SST:

1. File recommendations as a 504 plan.
2. Daily assignment report form (signed).
3. Weekly grade/behavior check (signed).
4. Time out activities for "fidgety" moments (errands, library trips, classroom tasks).
5. Seating change option (teacher maintains an unoccupied desk near the back of the room for student's use).

6. Shorten lengthy assignments.

7. Computer use for writing assignments.

8.

9.

For further information, contact Michael X. Anderson, School Counselor, Irwin Rothsfield Elementary School.

The SST-Approved Section 504 Plan for Ellen

Irwin Rothsfield Elementary School

504 Student Accommodation-Intervention Plan

Student Name: Ellen Mannington   **Date:** 10/13/03

Grade: 5   **Teacher:** Rondee Carter

Description of disability:

Ellen's inattentive behavior, impulsivity, inconsistency with academic work, and difficulty in staying in her seat indicate she may experience an attention-deficit hyperactivity disorder.

Specific accommodations:

Ellen will be provided with and complete daily assignment report forms. These are to indicate what work must be done by the next day, signed by her teacher and counter-signed by her parent.

On Friday of each week, Ellen will collect a grade/behavior check form from the counseling office (form rack). She will take this to Miss Carter and any special teachers from the week (music, PE, art, etc.). Her teachers will indicate a current grade, any missing work, and any behavior problems. This will be taken home with Ellen, and her parent will assign consequences appropriate for the report (positive rewards for good results; negative consequences for poor results).

Ellen's teacher will provide "time out" activities to provide alternative sources of stimulation in those times when Ellen is in need of motion and variety to her routine. Acceptable activities include making trips to other areas of the school for the teacher, performing educative classroom tasks (such as animal/plant care, organizing materials), or other appropriate activities.

For times when Ellen requires the stimulation of motion but the classroom activities require continued focus, her teacher will provide an alternative seating arrangement. An empty desk in an unused portion of the room will be available for Ellen to move to as she feels the need to move around. Ellen will continue the class work from this alternative seating assignment.

To maintain Ellen's focus during unusually long written assignments, the teacher will adapt the work by shortening the length expectations for Ellen. For example, if the class does fifty vocabulary words, Ellen might be expected to do thirty-five appropriate to her achievement level. If the class is assigned a ten-page report, Ellen's expectation might be eight pages.

Given that Ellen has expressed an interest in the use of computers for writing activities, the teacher shall make the classroom computer available for Ellen whenever a written assignment is made.

Review date:
Review of this plan will take place four months from its initiation or earlier if one or more parties indicates a need to do so.

Participants:

Michael X. Anderson, Counselor   Jermaine Jefferson, Special Education Teacher

Priscilla Tyrrell, Ed. D., School Psychologist   Arthur West, School Nurse

Theresa Nelson, Regular Education Teacher Representative

Distribution:
White copy: District Special Education office   Yellow copy: School counselor   Pink copy: Parent

---

PROBLEM DOCUMENT 10.4   *Miss Carter's Follow-up Report on Ellen's Performance*

Irwin Rothsfield Elementary School

Follow-up Log for Section 504 Accommodations

Student Study Team, Michael X. Anderson, Chair

Student: Ellen Mannington   **Date of Report:** 11/17/03

Teacher/evaluator: Rondee Carter

Part I

Recommendation	Action
File recommendations as a 504 plan	Accomplished by SST
Daily assignment report form (signed).	Initiated form, and provided daily copies. Ellen was inconsistent in her completing of form, and mother did not sign.
Weekly grade/behavior check (signed).	I signed two weekly checks (using the form from the guidance office). Beyond that, none were presented to me, and no parental follow through.
Time out activities for "fidgety" moments	Ellen was given errands, such as taking notes to the office, when she seemed to need to move. She also assisted with in-class chores, such as watering plants, straightening shelves, and so on.
Seating change option	I set up an extra desk near the back. Given the large student count, this was a crowded area.

Shorten lengthy assignments	The assignments are generally not long. I did reduce a four-page report to three pages for Ellen.
Computer use for writing assignments	There is one computer available in the classroom. Ellen had first option to use this for writing.

Part II: Assessment of Plan's Effectiveness

I have more than 20 years experience teaching the elementary grades, with 12 in the fifth grade. I have worked through many accommodation plans, and rarely have I seen one that was less effective. It is clear to me that the real problem with Ellen's behavior is not being addressed by the attempts we have made so far. The failure appears at every step of the plan.

First, the attempts to establish school-to-home communication and consistency were a disaster. Apparently the mother did not support this idea at all. While some assignment sheets came to me for checking, I never saw a single parent signature during the time of this plan. Ellen's consistency in not turning in the sheets was matched by her inconsistency in doing assignments. Her work showed no improvement, with roughly 50 percent of the assignments never reaching completion. I indicated this on the two weekly grade checks that Ellen presented to me, but this also appeared to be irrelevant at home. Ellen's mother did not sign (or Ellen did not return) either sheet; after the second week, I saw no checks. When I telephoned Mrs. Mannington, she told me that the weekly check sheets were a waste of her daughter's time. This accommodation was worse than nothing.

Second, I implemented actions to help Ellen manage her hyperactivity. Ellen appeared to respond positively to errands (such as taking notes to the office or other teachers). Of course, I have no idea what she actually did while out of the room. She came back happier, and it solved my problem with the disruptions. On the other hand, she was very disruptive when asked to do classroom tasks such as watering the plants. She would perform her tasks in a noisy manner, gathering the attention of the students around her. She sometimes bumped or jostled students in the area of the task, and it inevitably caused a classroom disruption. The use of the extra desk at the back of the room was no more productive. Whenever I suggested to Ellen that she might like to work at that desk, she sighed loudly and stomped back to the desk, muttering "Here I go to Siberia again!" She "performed" at the desk by being just as noisy and disruptive as anywhere else.

Finally, the adjustments to academic work appeared to be futile. It is hard to know whether shortening assignments is helpful or not, as the assignments so rarely come in. Ellen did like working at the computer, but once again, it became an opportunity to draw attention to herself. Other students wondered why Ellen always got the computer first, and she made the most of it. She seemed to work deliberately slowly, commenting on her work while she did so. "I wonder what word might go here," she might say while other students worked quietly.

In summary, the plan has been utterly ineffective. Ellen clearly needs a more appropriate response. In my experience with similar children, medication is extremely effective, leading to academic and social success instead of repeated failures.

Sample Page from Ellen Mannington's Reading Journal

Here we are again writing from Siberia. I am at the OUTPOST in the tecchy corner by the idiot queen NAME BLOCKED OUT *. If my dad would answer a letter I might break out of this place and get away from jailer MISS Carter. MISS Carter would be pleased as punch with that I bet.*

Oh I'm supposed to be writing about that stupid Turtle Wexler, right? Let's see. She wants to kick box or bomb knees I guess. She has the right idea. If I had to live in that dumb apartment bulding I would to. I like my house even if it was lived in by a cereal killer. I don't see any reason to move again unless it's back to Texas.

So Turtle gets along with Sandy better than the other charicters do. She is old for her age if that makes any sense. I can see that she has stuff figured out. She can make people act how she wants them to act, which is as they say the way to get ahead in this world. If I was Turtlle I would be sneaking around to get everyone else's cluse so that I could win the prize and use the money for myself. I'd get out of that apartment and maybe travel around, but first I'd have a great big house built with my own pool like Amanda's back home. And I would have a TV in my room that mom could never say shut it off.

But I guess that's all for know since I haven't finished the book and I don't feel like reading right now. I would rather be kicking knees myself or anything else for the fun of it in stead of sitting in the boring land of SIBARFIA.

Notes from the School Psychologist's Interview with Ms. Easton-Mannington

I began the conversation by apologizing for not including Ms. Easton-Mannington in the initial SST. I explained that our school customarily conducts such meetings without parental participation, but that this is a pattern based on community expectations rather than any attempt to exclude a parent. Ms. M. was not satisfied with this.

I asked about Ellen's behavior at home. Ms. M. indicated that she found Ellen's behavior to be perfectly normal and appropriate for a girl her age. She indicated that Ellen was much like she had been as a child, and that while there were some struggles at times, Ms. M. had managed to make it through the system, earning an M.F.A. in design. She said that Ellen is not particularly organized, that her room is often a mess, but that this seemed fitting for her age. Ms. M. is, she says, far more concerned about nurturing the creative spark in her child than in creating a factory worker.

I inquired about the family situation, but Ms. M. was reticent on this matter. She indicated that she and her husband had finalized an "amicable" divorce a little over two years ago, though she would provide no further details about this. When I inquired about Ellen's response to the divorce, Ms. M. said that Ellen was much better off without her father around. She would not elaborate. She said that the divorce had not altered Ellen's behavior in the least and that, if anything, Ellen was a better person now.

The subject of Ellen's 504 seemed to evoke much hostility from Ms. M. She said she could not support the accommodations because they were done without consultation and they ignored the true problem in this case, which she believes is the teacher, not the student. She commented that Ellen's teacher had been "duped" into thinking that drugs were the answer for every problem. She said that Carter had no idea what problems she was creating for children by opening the door to drug use—and she hinted that she had had some very negative drug experiences herself. When I tried to pursue this, she said this was not relevant to Ellen's situation.

Finally, we closed our conversation on the topic of Ms. M's refusal to allow a formal evaluation of her daughter. She appears to be well acquainted with regulations for special education, and she spoke of a friend who had successfully sued a district in Texas. She remains steadfast in her opposition to any labeling of her daughter with special education terms. I noted that she was especially hostile to any implication that Ellen might be "hyperactive."

PROBLEM DOCUMENT 10.7 | *A Classroom Observation of Ellen's Behavior*

Classroom Observation

Conducted by Michael X. Anderson, 11/3/02

Context
The observation was performed for 35 minutes during a mathematics lesson on multiplication. The primary means of instruction was direct instruction, with teacher explanation and guided practice for the students.

Narrative account
Miss Carter began the lesson with a homework check from the previous day's lesson. Students were asked to correct a neighbor's paper. Since Ellen had no assignment, she was not permitted to mark a classmate's paper. She fidgeted during the corrections, making occasional comments. Miss Carter gave her nonverbal cues to desist (extended eye contact and a finger to the lips).

After correcting the papers, Miss Carter asked for questions. Several students asked questions. Ellen raised her hand, but Miss Carter did not call on her. She reminded Ellen of the question-assignment rule ("you can't ask a question if you don't have a ticket").

Immediately after the questions, Miss Carter began explaining the lesson for the day. Ellen did not appear to take any notes, and she seemed angry (perhaps due to the comment about tickets). When Miss Carter asked for volunteers to try problems at the board, most children raised hands to participate. Ellen did not. While students went to the board to write problems, Ellen sharpened her pencil twice and moved to the empty desk at the back.

After examining the student problems on the board, Miss Carter made an assignment for the next day and the students began to work. Apparently they are not to talk during this time, since students immediately became quiet after finishing the board work. Ellen went to the board and began erasing the problems, and Miss Carter said, "Thank you, Ellen." After finishing the boards, she went to Miss Carter, who was assisting students at their desks. Ellen asked if she could get a drink. Miss Carter asked if Ellen had tried any problems yet, and Ellen responded that she couldn't do her work if she was thirsty. Miss Carter gave her permission to get a drink.

Ellen was gone approximately five minutes. Upon returning, she sharpened a third pencil and asked a student near her desk what they were doing. The student shushed her, and Ellen made a comment about an "idiot queen." Ellen then asked a boy near her desk what they were doing. He showed her the pages in the textbook, and Miss Carter said, "James, we are working on our own today."

Ellen turned away from the teacher and mouthed the words she had just spoken to the students near her. I could not see their reactions.

Ellen began to work on the assignment, but not more than three minutes passed before Miss Carter announced it was time to do a social studies lesson. Ellen slammed her math book shut noisily and dropped it on the floor. Miss Carter said that was enough for a day and asked Ellen to go see Mr. Prentice (the principal). The observation ended.

····PROPOSE A SOLUTION ➡

SOLUTION SUMMARY

Before proceeding to the reflection section of this chapter, write a brief summary of your team's solution here:

Our team defined the "real" problem here as _____

_____

_____

_____

_____

_____

_____

_____

_____

The key features of our solution were _____

_____

_____

_____

_____

_____

_____

_____

My personal view of the problem and solution is _____

_____

_____

_____

_____

_____

_____

_____

TIME FOR REFLECTION

A number of issues should have surfaced in your explorations for this PBL experience. The reflections begin with ideas about hyperactivity in the classroom. We will also consider what the evaluation process is for students who may have ADHD, and this leads to a discussion of medication for ADHD—an important issue teachers will encounter in their classrooms. Finally, the reflection invites you to think about what happens when parents and teachers disagree about what is best for children.

Hyperactivity in the Classroom

The documents associated with this PBL experience don't provide a lot of description of Miss Carter's classroom, but one can infer some features of the learning environment both from her comments and the narrative description provided in Mr. Anderson's observation notes. While she may be very effective with children, it appears that Miss Carter has a low tolerance for activities in the classroom. She appears to prefer quiet, orderly learning activities, and with the exception of the board work, she appears to prefer having students work alone. A parent might make the case that normal childhood activity would seem like hyperactivity in this context. So what constitutes hyperactivity?

Children are wonderfully adaptive, capable of recognizing where different kinds of behavior are appropriate. Watch any class spill out onto the recess grounds, and you will see children demonstrate their understanding of how and when to let loose. Children also manage to fit with a variety of teachers' styles, so that the demands for passivity from Mr. Stern are no more difficult to meet than the permission to play from Mr. Soft. Certainly children have preferences, and they may be more *comfortable* or more *successful* with one style of teacher than another, but they usually can survive.

Hyperactivity becomes an issue in the child who cannot read the context and adjust accordingly. The personal fidgeting and distracting of others stand out for this child, and such actions threaten that child's performance. Kamphaus and Frick (1996) provide a definition of hyperactivity as "the tendency to be overly active, rush through work or activities, and act without thinking" (p. 123). This fits most of us at times, so it is important to remember the norm-referenced feature of the definition. That is, a child is "overly active" in comparison to peers (age and gender).

A responsible teacher ought to ask if there is anything about her or his classroom that is causing children to act out due to boredom or lack of stimulation. Armstrong (1999), for example, argues that making classrooms more accepting of the multiple intelligences perspective would allow us to channel energy that is otherwise seen as hyperactive into productive activities. There is a place for us to consider how we might contribute to general hyperactivity. However, when an individual stands out for his or her hyperactive behavior, it is probably time to initiate an evaluation process.

Evaluation Processes

One of the myths that Barkley (2000) addresses in his book is the notion that if ADHD were real, there would be a simple lab test for its presence. We could, for example, take a blood sample that would show a person has this disability. Barkley reminds us that there are no such tests for anxiety disorders or alcoholism, though these conditions are not questioned. So how do we know about the presence of something like ADHD?

Students suspected of having disabilities are generally referred to specialists in the school for formal evaluation. Current law requires that parents give permission for such evaluations. In the case of ADHD, there is a good deal of wiggle room in the process. The most important features for diagnosing ADHD come from observations and rating scales of the student's behavior. Included in this process is some indication of early onset of ADHD.

While the specific features of evaluating a student for ADHD are not important to pursue in this reflection (though perhaps a worthwhile avenue of inquiry for your solutions), it is important to have a general sense of what the teacher's role is in this process. Generally, a school psychologist will conduct the assessment of a child, relying a good deal on the teacher's description of the child's behavior. (The parents' description will also be important in this process). It is crucial that the teacher learn to observe students dispassionately and carefully, so that the information provided for the evaluation is useful. What about Miss Carter in this case? Does she seem able to provide objective observations of the student? Has her long experience in the classroom sensitized her to the issues surrounding ADHD or has it reinforced counterproductive views of children like Ellen?

Early in my classroom career, I had a physician phone me to ask if I thought a certain child had ADHD and should be medicated. At the time, I thought this doctor was ludicrously incompetent to be asking a mere teacher such a question. Of course, my time with the child gave me so many more opportunities to observe and so many different contexts to see the child's behavior that I was in a much better position than the doctor to provide reliable data. It is crucial that teachers recognize their importance in this evaluation process.

Medication?

A large portion of this problem arose because of disagreements about whether or not to medicate a child. Teachers do form opinions on such matters, though they must be very cautious given the lack of expertise they have in this area. While some researchers, like Barkley (2000), believe that fewer children are medicated than should be, others disagree. In fact, Ritalin has become a popular drug for students to abuse in school (Wen, 2000), with one study revealing that 13 percent of Massachusetts high school students had used the drug without a prescription. The controversial nature even of properly prescribed Ritalin is demonstrated in Wen's article: "Congress has held hearings on the issue, and class-action suits against the drug have been filed in several states, led by some parents and psychologists who say the diagnostic criteria for attention-deficit disorders are so broad that nearly every feisty child qualifies."

Given the high incidence of ADHD, you will almost certainly encounter children who are being medicated for this disability. You may be asked your professional opinion about whether a child needs medication, however inappropriate that question may strike you. It is important that teachers are observant of children's behavior, careful to note variations so that discussions of the effects of medication can be helpful to all involved. Be cautious. You are on fairly safe ground when you describe a child's behavior; you very quickly move into dangerous territory when you label that behavior and offer medical solutions.

When Parents and Teachers Disagree

As a teacher, you think one response to a child's action is correct. Her parent opposes your plan. What happens now?

That teachers and parents don't always agree is hardly surprising. Both have interests in the behavior of a given child, but from radically different perspectives. The parent is almost always an unequivocal advocate for the child—even if that advocacy may sometimes *not* serve the best interests of the child. The teacher, on the other hand, must always temper advocacy for a given child with responsibility for the welfare of the larger learning community.

Koenig (2000) argues there are three categories of parents: those who are actively involved in their children's education, those who are not actively involved but can be drawn into a more active role, and those who have no involvement at any level. Such categories are always risky, since they may disguise other issues. For example, Deyhle and LeCompte (1994) point out that Navajo parents typically practice noninterference with their children by the middle school years. White educators frequently interpret this as an attitude of not caring, while the cultural meaning behind Navajo parents' noninterference is a granting of adult status to the children. Thus, we must be careful in assumptions about what motivates parents. Nevertheless, Koenig's categories help provide some guidance for dealing with parents. Ironically, while the first category provides the most support for teachers, it is also the group of parents with whom a teacher is most likely to clash. Koenig emphasizes an important theme that promises to reduce parent–teacher conflict: communication.

This PBL experience provides some evidence that Miss Carter communicated with Ellen's mother. Was the communication enough? Was it *early* enough? How did Ms. Easton-Mannington develop the view that her daughter's teacher had a personal issue with Ellen as opposed to a professional issue? And, more importantly, what can you learn about communicating with parents in a timely manner so that teachers and parents can work together in a problem-solving alliance rather than a tug-of-war over a child's learning?

DISCUSSION QUESTIONS

1. Teachers play a vital role in the student study teams that decide how to help children succeed. How can teachers prepare for such meetings? What sort of participation by teachers is most effective in the mix of other professionals? How do teachers maintain a student-focused perspective even when the child is incredibly frustrating?

2. Experienced teachers have a good sense of what is "typical" behavior for a given age group. How do teachers develop this notion of "typical" behavior in order to identify children in need of intervention? Is it important that colleagues develop such understandings together as a check on what they observe?

3. Teachers develop strong opinions about such things as the role of medication in a child's plan. However, teachers do not have the last word in this matter. How does a teacher respond when she or he disagrees with the proposal for a child? How does a teacher avoid undermining the plan that goes against that teacher's best judgment?

4. Much of Ellen's mother's case appears to be a criticism of Miss Carter's classroom. Do you see this as a diversion from Ellen's real problems or a legitimate complaint? How does one judge the responsibility of teachers for students' acting out?

5. Considering the PBL process, what did you learn about your ability to work with messy details in an unstructured situation?

FURTHER READING

Armstrong, T. (1999). *ADD/ADHD alternatives in the classroom.* Alexandria, VA: Association for Supervision and Curriculum Development.

Armstrong takes a "holistic" view of the ADD/ADHD question. He sees biology as one part of this issue, but not the core. Thus, while he doesn't actually oppose the use of medication for the disability, he certainly discourages it as the first response. Instead, he addresses ways of helping people with the disability to cope with the problem, not just the symptoms. He indicates that the use of Ritalin may prevent people from seeking other ways of managing ADHD. He also cites several potential negative consequences of using the medication: diminishing children's sense of responsibility, teaching children to turn to drugs to solve problems, the side effects (feeling weird, nauseous, different), and the possible disqualification from the military or intercollegiate athletics. Armstrong's "alternatives" draw on the multiple intelligences theory of Howard Gardner. For example, he calls for incorporating more movement in the education of children rather than stifling the impulse of the ADHD child. He also calls for alternative means of expressing oneself.

Barkley, R. A. (2000). *Taking charge of ADHD: The complete, authoritative guide for parents.* (Revised Edition). New York: Guilford.

Although written for a nonacademic audience, this book provides a good deal of useful information. Indeed, its audience may be a virtue for the text, since the language is clear and without jargon. Barkley has divided the book into four parts: understanding ADHD, being a successful parent, coping at home and at school, and medications.

Three sections may be of particular interest in light of this PBL experience. The first part, understanding ADHD, provides a theoretical perspective for understanding possible causes and effects of ADHD. The book provides five problems that people with ADHD have in controlling their own behavior. Barkley takes the position that ADHD is "a disorder of self-control, willpower, and the organizing and directing of behavior toward the future" (p. 62). He also suggests that persons with ADHD may be more creative due to their emotional expression (p. 57).

The second section of the book that may prove useful is devoted to school issues, Chapters 15 and 16. There are some practical suggestions for managing the disability, such as building home-based reward programs. This section also includes a description of the world of ADHD through the eyes of a fifteen-year-old who has been diagnosed with ADHD (pp. 228–231). It can be powerful to see the world through such eyes.

Finally, Barkley describes—in layman's terms—the medications associated with ADHD. It is evident from his book and the studies he cites that he sees medication as a viable option, indeed, an option that is underused.

Barkley's more academic work on ADHD, *Attention-Deficit Hyperactivity Disorder: A Handbook for Diagnosis and Treatment* (1998, Guilford), presents a clear picture of the research associated with this disability, though it goes into depth beyond what most teachers seek.

Brock, S. E. (1998). *Helping the student with ADHD in the classroom: Strategies for teachers* [Handout]. Bethesda, MD: National Association of School Psychologists.
On behalf of the leading association for school psychologists, Brock has created a quick read on generic strategies that might help with ADHD. The guide emphasizes that each child's case is different, requiring that teachers select appropriate strategies. Among the ideas listed are auditory cues, use of a token economy, breaking down complex instructions into simple step-by-step procedures, and incorporating novelty. The paper also emphasizes the importance of positive reinforcement as opposed to punishment.

Kamphaus, R. W., & Frick, P. J. (1996). *Clinical assessment of child and adolescent personality and behavior.* Boston: Allyn & Bacon
Chapter 18 of this technical text provides a brief but thorough description of ADHD from the perspective of diagnosing the disability. The authors discuss the changing definition of ADHD and the importance of multi-source assessment for the disability. In addition, the authors explain potential problems that co-occur with ADHD and other possible explanations for ADHD-like behaviors. While this is intended for specialists, the chapter helps a classroom teacher understand the nature of ADHD.

WEB SITES

The ADHD Owner's Guide
www.edutechsbs.com/adhd
A site assembled by a physician. Includes such things as the feeling of having ADHD and teacher tips.

Mental Health Net
http://mentalhelp.net/poc/center_index.php?id=3
Information on ADHD and its treatment.

Parent Soup Education Central
www.parentsoup.com/edcentral/LD/add.html
Gathers together definitions, resources, and ideas in terms that are readily accessible to parents.

REFERENCES

Armstrong, T. (1999). *ADD/ADHD alternatives in the classroom.* Alexandria, VA: Association for Supervision and Curriculum Development.

Barkley, R. A. (2000). *Taking charge of ADHD: The complete, authoritative guide for parents* (Revised edition). New York: Guilford.

Brock, S. E. (1998). *Helping the student with ADHD in the classroom: Strategies for teachers.* [Handout]. Bethesda, MD: National Association of School Psychologists.

Deyhle, D., & LeCompte, M. (1994). Cultural differences in child development: Navajo adolescents in middle schools. *Theory into Practice, 33*(3), 156–166.

Kamphaus, R. W., & Frick, P. J. (1996). *Clinical assessment of child and adolescent personality and behavior.* Boston: Allyn & Bacon.

Koenig, L. (2000). *Smart discipline for the classroom: Respect and cooperation restored* (3rd ed.). Thousand Oaks, CA: Corwin.

Wen, P. (2000, October 29). "As easy to get as candy": A new Massachusetts study finds wide teen abuse of Ritalin. *The Boston Globe,* p. A01.

■ ■ ■ ■ ■ ■

CHAPTER ELEVEN

BULLY TROUBLES, OR "BOYS WILL BE BOYS"?

INTRODUCTION AND PROBLEM BACKGROUND

An almost certain way to make the headlines in the United States is to commit a major act of violence in a public school. It may be true that many more such acts occur each week outside of school, but the pathway to the headlines is through the schools. Part of the reason for this is that we expect our schools to be havens of safety, and, indeed, by almost any measure, they are. Still, for many children, attending school means daily facing fears that few adults could stomach. And often that fear is associated with the face of a bully. Consequences of bullying reach out in many directions, but one purported consequence is that the victims of bullies react with violence, with as many as 66 percent of thirty-seven recent school shootings committed by young people who had felt bullied (Carroll, 2001).

A quick search on the Internet will tell you that bullying appears to be a universal experience, a common ground in the diverse, international world of schooling. Web sites from the United Kingdom, Australia, the United States, and Canada, among others, testify to the miseries children experience in their daily lives at school. An interesting common complaint is that the teachers do not see a problem with bullying, that, perhaps, the "victims" have a warped view of how they are treated. Consider Alexandra's comment about how bullying was handled at her Canadian school when her mother tried to get action:

> The principal talks to the teachers, the teachers talk to the kids. The kids laugh. It feels like they're laughing at me. My mom got a bullying message around the school. The kids snicker in class, while the teacher is talking about bullying. They don't care, they will keep harassing kids; cause they don't seem to care. (www.bullying.org/alexandra.html)

Alexandra's comments echo many of the victims' voices registered from all over the world on the web site *Bullying.Org: Where You Are Not Alone!* (www.bullying.org). And she helps to remind us that dealing with this issue is not a matter of issuing a simple directive from the principal's office that will alter the behaviors of bullies. It's not that easy.

Almost any flaw appears to be enough to generate the bully's interest: too fat, too thin, too smart, too dumb, too weak (though never too strong!), glasses, acne, puberty, no puberty, race, religion, no religion, parents, and neighborhood. At the same time, there is a kind of banter that goes on back and forth among school children, where all these same taunts come into play among even the best of friends. So how do we draw the line for what constitutes bullying and what constitutes banter?

In light of the much-publicized acts of violence in U.S. schools, anything that might contribute to further violence is a serious matter. This PBL experience invites you to reflect on and inquire into the nature of bullying in a middle school, though the behavior is not limited to the middle level. Indeed, the British Broadcasting Company cites a report that indicated 10 percent of primary and 4 percent of secondary students are bullied once a week (www.bbc.co.uk/learning)! That would mean more than 350,000 eight to ten-year-olds bullied each week in the United Kingdom alone. Younger and older children are also experiencing this grief. By some accounts, fully one-fifth of the students in schools in the U.S. report having been bullied (Skiba & Fontanini, 2001).

PROBLEM CONTEXT AND SOLUTION PARAMETERS

Context

East Valley Middle School (EVMS—called "Evil" by some students) serves a community on the outskirts of an urban center. As a result of its location and tradition, EVMS draws almost equally from students bused out of an urban environment and in from a suburban area. Few students actually live in the neighborhood of the school, which developed after the school's construction and consists largely of recently-developed, small industrial operations. The joke at the district office is that EVMS got a bargain on its site because the superintendent at the time relied on crystal balls to predict the future rather than zoning laws.

For all its geographical isolation, the school does not suffer from a lack of involved parents. Indeed, the site council at EVMS is one of the most active in the city. This has been especially true in the last several years, because the parent who chairs the council has grown increasingly impatient with the school's principal, retired Army captain Owen Gallagher. Mr. Gallagher was heavily recruited by a number of schools in the city after he graduated from an "administrative cohort" program created as a partnership between the school district, the military, and the local university. As a star of the program and a man with a spotless record in the military, Mr. Gallagher offered the district an opportunity to get public support for its program, as well as to address the critical shortage of administrators in the area.

Ms. Lomax, the chair of the site council, supported Mr. Gallagher to begin with. However, as time has gone on, she has formed an opinion, shared with a large support group, that Mr. Gallagher is simply insensitive to the needs of children at this age level. She has been quietly, but actively, lobbying with teachers and the central administration for the replacement of Mr. Gallagher with one of his assistant principals, Dr. Ella Baker, who Ms. Lomax sees as a person who can express developmentally appropriate care for the students. Mr. Gallagher, according to Ms. Lomax, is a product of his past, and what works with soldiers is disastrous with impressionable young people.

In the midst of this subtle conflict for power, an accusation of serious bullying has been made against some of the children in the school. While this is certainly not the first instance of bullying at EVMS, the issue has the potential to inflame the struggle for leadership at the school.

Problem and Solution Parameters

Ms. Emilie Thompson has been teaching reading at EVMS since the program began, a few years ago, when the poor performance of students on the required state exam led to the creation of a formal reading program for all three grades at the school (6 to 8). Ms. Thompson had previously worked in a suburban elementary school, and she was one of Mr. Gallagher's first hires. He was attracted to her view of the importance of phonics instruction for all children, even in the later elementary years.

One student in Ms. Thompson's class, Edward Johnson, appeared to be experiencing some difficulties in getting along with the other children in the class. Ms. Thompson counseled with Edward about his behavior, urging him to be a little more adaptive in the classroom as a means of making friends. However, Edward somehow made his way past the counseling office into an interview with Dr. Baker, the assistant principal. After that interview, Edward's father contacted the classroom teacher with certain demands and expectations. For a few days, Edward appeared to be smug about this, according to Ms. Thompson, but that changed abruptly and with no explanation. Ms. Thompson welcomed the change, assuming that Edward's situation had improved and that the accusations were at an end.

She was surprised to hear that Edward's father had lodged a formal letter of complaint against the school for the "bullying" that Edward was enduring. Even though she was not asked to do so, she provided her principal with an explanation of how she viewed the situation as soon as she heard that the site council would be considering an "anti-bullying" policy.

You are a member of the faculty at EVMS. As a new teacher, you hope to make some contribution outside of your own classroom, so you have agreed to volunteer for the committee to consider the policy at EVMS (see Mr. Gallagher's memorandum). As a member of this ad hoc task force, you will work with your team to investigate the issues raised by the various participants in order to make a recommendation to the site council about the question of a school policy. Your report to the council should be no longer than ten minutes, and you should be prepared to answer questions from the council for another five minutes. In addition, you are expected to provide the key points of your recommendations on a one-page handout for all members of the site council. These members include Ms. Lomax, Mr. Gallagher (nonvoting), Dr. Baker (nonvoting), Mr. Wells (parent), Mrs. Silcox (staff member), Mr. Redding (teacher), Ms. Forrester (teacher), Mrs. Short (parent), Amanda Larsen (student), and Ms. Dorman (district representative).

·······**WORK THE PROBLEM** ➞

PROBLEM DOCUMENTS

To assist you in understanding the problem and in formulating a solution, the following documents have been provided for you:

11.1 Ms. Thompson's management plan

11.2 Mr. Johnson's letter of complaint to the principal of EVMS, Mr. Gallagher

11.3 Note from Alicia Lomax (Site Council Chair) to the principal of EVMS, Mr. Gallagher

11.4 Mr. Gallagher's memo to faculty on the bullying issue

11.5 Ms. Thompson's unsolicited written response to the complaint

11.6 Results of a student survey conducted by the counseling office

---

PROBLEM DOCUMENT 11.1   *Ms. Thompson's Management Plan*

7th Grade Reading, Classroom Rules
Ms. Thompson

This class is built around mutual respect, respect between students and the teacher. Your job is to demonstrate that respect; my job is to remind everyone of the importance of respect.
   To make respect real in this class, we must follow these rules:

1. Respect others.
2. Do your best work.
3. Do not eat candy or gum in class.
4. No hitting.
5. Complete your homework on time.
6. Do your best (it's worth repeating).
7. Raise your hand when you want to talk.

In case you have trouble following these rules, I have some consequences to remind you of what we are here for.

1. If you are late to class, you have 15 minutes of detention after school.
2. Any acts of violence will earn you an instant pass to the principal's office.
3. If you are not doing your best, something needs to be fixed and we will have a conference to discuss this.
4. Gum or candy gets a warning, but then you will have a 15-minute detention after one warning.
5. I reserve the right to call your parents/guardian if there is a need.

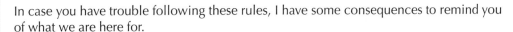

Dear Principal Gallagher:

My son, Edward Johnson, is a seventh-grader in your school. I am sorry to have to report to you that I believe the bullying at East Valley Middle School is out of hand, and that my son's experience at EVMS demonstrates this clearly.

Let me give you some background. Edward has consistently been a "good" student, and this has never before been a source of trouble for him. In previous years, Edward's teachers have generally indicated that he is well behaved and that his performance is exemplary. Ironically, since Edward has come to EVMS, his performance has been a source of shame for him. That's right, SHAME. Edward tells me that throughout the fall term, he was ridiculed for bringing books home to study (a practice he gave up some weeks ago, now). Edward attempted to hide good scores on tests or assignments from his friends, even though this sounds absurd. He was fairly effective at the practice, except in cases where the teachers made his ruse impossible. For example, in his reading class, the teacher has the benighted practice of giving students quizzes on reading materials and then doing peer corrections. She also has students complete numerous worksheets, which their peers grade. Students are actually required to read their scores aloud so that the teacher can enter grades in a book (and save her the effort of actually looking at the papers). Edward must either lie about his scores (he's a superior reader) or suffer the consequences.

This particular class, the reading class, is where Edward encounters his most difficult moments. I understand that kids are hard on each other and that there is always a possibility of being made fun of. That's the nature of junior high, and I remember it well from my own experience. However, there appear to be several bullies in Edward's reading class, and his teacher is unwilling to do something about it. I am loathe to name names here, but the severity of this is such that Edward is afraid of going to school—largely due to the bullying in this classroom. A child by the name of Tom Ramos appears to be the ringleader, accompanied by Jermaine Saunders and Ronald Petrovich. Edward reports that these boys have threatened him physically, that they take every opportunity to knock his books down, to punch him, and worst of all, to deride him incessantly.

I have spoken twice with Mrs. Thompson about this situation. I'm not sure whether she is a good-hearted Pollyanna or naive beyond belief. She tells me she has witnessed NO incidents of bullying. In addition, she recites tales of the woes that these boys have "overcome" so that she might excuse their misbehavior. Ramos, she tells me, has a troubled past and a difficult situation. She says he is improving every day. But what she does not see is the disastrous effect of this bullying on Edward and other sensitive children like him. If Ramos is improving, what's happening to Edward?

I also contacted your counseling office to acquire a copy of the school policy on bullying. Imagine my surprise to discover that NO SUCH POLICY EXISTS! In light of school shootings across this country, most often attributed to bullying, I find this inexcusable. Can you let this continue in good conscience?

I am torn between contacting the police and pulling Edward for another form of education. I understand a charter school will be opening in the fall, and you can be sure I will be looking carefully at this option. In the meantime, I expect some action. It is clearly time that the school does something about the rampant bullying going on, and it needs to happen in such a way that children like Edward are protected. If ever there was a time where compassionate leadership was called for, now is that time.

By the way, Edward does not know I am writing this letter. He worries that the bullying will get worse if I try to intervene. I would like to have you address this without any identification of Edward.

However, I want to be very clear. I don't intend to be a Klebold Harris parent, and I won't let your school turn my child from scholar to victim to vigilante the way other bully targets have gone.

Sincerely,

Clay Johnson

Clay Johnson

Cc: Alicia Lomax, EVMS Site Council Chair; Dr. Baker, Assistant Principal

---

Note from Alicia Lomax (Site Council Chair)

Mr. Gallagher,

I was embarrassed to read the letter from Edward Johnson's father. I agree that we must do something about this. I am putting the issue of bullying at the top of our next Site Council agenda, and I will be pushing hard for a school policy.

Do we really want the next school shooting here?

A. L.

Mr. Gallagher's Memo to Faculty on the Bullying Issue

East Valley Middle School
Home of the Gladiators

Memorandum

To: All Faculty members

From: Owen Gallagher, Principal

Date: 11/11/03

RE: "Bullying" at EVMS

As many of you have heard, the Site Council for EVMS will be taking on the issue of "bullying" in our school at its next regular meeting. This is an important topic, so I am hoping to get your input for that meeting.

As we used to say in the service, facts first. I'd like to get the facts straight about any bullying problems before we go into that meeting. I'd like to know what you've seen, and whether you think there is a real problem in our school. It seems to me that we have to draw clear lines between whining about the good-natured rowdiness of the young men and women in our charge and anything that goes beyond what you'd expect from people this age. I won't have any bullying on my watch. But I also won't support the kinds of crazy witch hunts we've witnessed across this country. I've already asked the guidance department to pull out any questions from last year's student survey that might help us resolve this issue.

Based on the facts, we can make a reasonable decision about what needs to be done. After three years here, I think I've made my views crystal clear. I don't want a unit bogged down in a lot of red tape. I'd like to just deal with problems, and you can bet there won't be bullying in this outfit. But I've also learned that things operate differently in the public sector. The Site Council is part of our operation, and we need to support that. So I'm asking for a task force to report out to the Site Council. I think we're in a much stronger position if we walk into that meeting with facts and a recommendation than if we let someone else call the shots.

I will be grateful for the volunteers who step forward to help out in this important endeavor. Leave your names with my secretary.

| PROBLEM DOCUMENT 11.5 | *Ms. Thompson's Unsolicited Written Response to the Complaint* |

Mr. Gallagher,

I feel compelled to write something in my defense, even though you have not asked me to do so or publicly identified me. I am well aware that the bullying issue has arisen because of a student in my class, Edward Johnson, and the letter his father wrote in complaint. I appreciate the fact that you have taken some action on this, but I would like you to know some of the facts that have prompted the whole affair.

Edward Johnson is a quiet, somewhat standoffish child in my seventh-grade reading program. While it is true that Edward has conflict with some other boys (more on that below), I believe the real problem in this situation relates more to teaching than student behavior. I have used a strictly-sequenced reading program for my students, including review of important phonics principles. Many of our students have gone through elementary schools that appear to have forgotten about the importance of phonics, and our children suffer for this. Edward has revealed some weaknesses in phonics in his oral recitation, and when I placed him in remedial work for this purpose, his father came "unglued." He appears to support some form of whole language, group work (he spoke about Jane Atwell or someone like that and "reader's workshops"). I think the bullying issue is a smokescreen to get his son out of my class because of my approach to reading.

What about the bullying? It is true that Edward appears not to get along with other children. I don't see any particular singling out of Edward, and I believe that a little more willingness to go along with what we are trying to accomplish would serve Edward well. No other children seem to challenge the work of the class. And as for the so-called bullies, consider the lives of these young men. Ronnie Petrovich comes from a family where three older brothers have dropped out of school. Ronnie's dad has run a bulldozer for 25 years, and he told me he wants one child to make it. At the beginning of the year, Ronnie had detention almost daily. He is now seeing that he can be successful. Jermaine Saunders comes from a home with no father present, and he has had to be the man of the house for five siblings. He seems gruff, but who wouldn't? And Tom Ramos has the hardest time of them all. He is being raised by a grandmother because his mother is in prison. This is a kid who witnessed the shooting of his father in his own house and who watched drug transactions in the front yard. When Tom came to my class, he could hardly speak without a string of obscenities, but now he is learning social skills. His reading is still delayed, but what would you expect?

So I have three young men who are progressing towards being productive members of society. They have rough edges, but they are getting better all the time. Edward, who comes from a privileged family, wants to change the way class is working. It is no surprise that he is unpopular, but is he a victim? I don't see it. I worry that perhaps this notion has been encouraged by some members of our staff who are discontent with other things at the school, including my approach to reading.

Emilie Thompson

Results of a Student Survey Conducted by the Counseling Office

East Valley Middle School
Home of the Gladiators

Selected Survey Results: The Climate at EVMS

Conducted by the Guidance Department

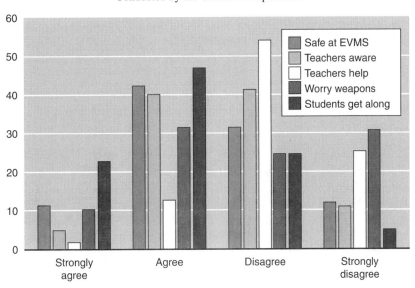

Questions included:

3. I feel safer at EVMS than on the streets.
7. My teachers are aware of the conflicts between students.
8. My teachers help me in dealing with conflicts.
17. I am worried about students who bring weapons to school.
21. Student get along well at EVMS.

SOLUTION SUMMARY

Before proceeding to the reflection section of this chapter, write a brief summary of your team's solution here:

Our team defined the "real" problem here as _____

_____

_____

_____

_____

_____

_____

_____

_____

The key features of our solution were _____

_____

_____

_____

_____

_____

_____

_____

My personal view of the problem and solution is _____

_____

_____

_____

_____

_____

_____

_____

TIME FOR REFLECTION

The potential "messiness" of problems in PBL may have been apparent in this experience. On the most basic level, the problem focuses on bullying, and the first sections of the reflection follow this focus with these topics: bullying versus messing around, the teacher's responsibility in bullying incidents, and the potential value of a schoolwide response. Among the secondary issues that may have arisen in this problem are the following focal points for reflection: school choice, ownership of instructional methods, ex-military personnel in the schools, and grandparents acting as custodial parents.

Bullying or Just Messing Around?

In coming to a resolution of this situation, your group certainly had to wrestle with the question of just what constitutes bullying. While even mentioning "bullying" arouses certain emotions in people, it is far less clear what one actually means by the term. In fact, it is no easy task to define "bullying" in a way that will help solve the problems associated with the issues.

For example, Skiba and Fontanini (2001) write that "A student is being bullied or victimized when exposed, repeatedly over time, to intentional injury or discomfort inflicted by one or more other students" (p. 1). They clarify that the injury might be physical, verbal, or emotional—even a gesture or a facial expression. What does such a definition accomplish? Is it clear enough in the contexts of schools to allow us to protect young people without creating a climate of surveillance that is oppressive? Farrell (1999) cautions us that when we broaden the definition of bullying too much, we run the risk of diverting attention from the real suffering of victims. As with other definitions, the definition of bullying is only useful if it both includes some behaviors and excludes other behaviors.

Perhaps a key portion of the definition above is the idea of "repeatedly over time." Is it the repeated *pattern* that becomes the defining feature of bullying? If so, what about the one-time act of violence against someone? Is that bullying? Ken Rigby, in a paper on his web site (www.education.unisa.edu.au/bullying/define.html), works through a number of the conditions of bullying to develop this definition: "Bullying involves a desire to hurt + hurtful action + a power imbalance + (typically) repetition + an unjust use of power + evident enjoyment by the aggressor and a sense of being oppressed on the part of the victim." Does that provide an adequate definition of bullying?

These are not easily answered questions. As you talk to other teachers, you will find that they develop differing views on the issue of bullying. All teachers witness conflict among students, and they interpret these conflicts in different ways. It appears that they see little actual bullying, considering that teachers intervene in only 4 percent of what others report to be incidents of bullying (Skiba & Fontanini, 2001). So what are the teachers seeing? Surely they are not supportive of bullying behavior.

As you consider your own position on this issue, you might consider why there is such a disparity between the incidents of bullying and the teacher interventions. Part of the answer may lie in what teachers actually see (were they even there?), what victims perceive and experience, and how others react. Parents of victims are typically angry and under great stress (Rigby, 2001), while teachers view the issue with more personal detachment. Parents see the unique circumstances of their children, while teachers develop a notion of what is typical behavior for the students they deal with. Do teachers become hardened on the issue? Or do they merely develop realistic expectations?

You will learn that children at every age have ways of relating to one another that often seem destructive and negative. Part of our job, as teachers, is to help the children learn to see the effects of their actions on others. As the responsible adults helping young people get along, teachers must play a role in showing how quickly one crosses over from messing around to bullying.

Teachers' Responsibility in Bullying

Despite the surprisingly low rate of teacher interventions in bullying, teachers do have an obligation to act when they know that bullying is taking place. In fact, students may interpret a lack of response from the teacher to be a tacit approval of bullying (Froschl, Sprung, & Mullin-Rindler, 1998). The teacher's responsibilities include protecting victims, providing a source of support for victims, and raising awareness of the issue.

Rigby (2001) identifies five ways that teachers can help the victims of bullies. His suggestions focus on the teacher as a listener and one who can prompt thoughtful dialogue about the issue. Interestingly, he argues that "It is, in fact, always better for victims to solve the problem of being bullied themselves, if this is possible" (p. 328). Perhaps this is a recognition that when others intervene for victims rather than working to eliminate the conditions that support victimization, the authority figures really don't help the victim in the long run.

Moreover, acts of bullying often arise from wounds and pain. A teacher must maintain some balance in responding to incidents of bullying. As Newman, Horne, and Bartolomucci (2000) write, "an overly sympathetic response toward the victim (by teacher or classmates) could humiliate the victim or result in the bully's attempting to gain further negative attention by continuing to focus on the victim" (p. 104). Thus, finding a balance of support for the victim, support for positive conditions in the school, and support for the bullies in order to reinforce productive behavior is the real task for teachers.

Above all, however, teachers must be very careful that they do not model bullying behaviors themselves or provide bullies with tacit permission to continue in their ways. Consider ways you have seen teachers "bully" their students. How can a teacher avoid this? Also, what can a teacher do to ensure that his or her words and behaviors do not provide subtle permission for bullies to carry on? In those moments when your own annoyance with a particular child is at its height, it is crucial that you *not* be seen by the other children as willing to allow that child to be harmed.

A Schoolwide Response

While individual teachers can do much to stem the problems associated with bullying, it may be the schoolwide response that is most important (Froschl et al., 1998; Newman et al., 2000; Smith, Shu, & Madsen, 2001). One British web site on bullying policies (www.bullying.co.uk/school/bullying_policie.htm) lists a variety of policy responses schools have implemented, including the following: the no-blame approach (where bullies are not identified or punished), the Pikas method (a counselor speaks to the bullies and then the victims without threat of punishment), circle time (children play for a time and then discuss the issue in a circle), and peer counseling.

One clear advantage of a schoolwide response is that individual teachers have limited opportunities to witness what goes on between children. While a particular teacher might assume that an act of aggression is a harmless, one-time event, a schoolwide perspective places all such acts in a category of unacceptable behavior. Moreover, the system-wide response provides support for all teachers to be consistent.

Still, a teacher might find that the schoolwide policy places that particular teacher in an awkward position. Teachers do tolerate different levels of conflict among their students; teachers differ in their views of bullying behavior. There appear to be advantages and disadvantages to the schoolwide approach. Which do you see as more effective and in keeping with your view of teachers' obligations to their students?

Advocates of the middle school model (NMSA, 1995; Stevenson, 1992) argue that advisory periods for all students provide an important opportunity to help young people learn to relate effectively to one another. Typically, advisory periods involve mixing students in ways unlike other classes: Students from various groups, ability levels, even grade levels join together daily under the guidance of an adult. In advisory periods, students are able to discuss such things as goal-setting, study habits, service to the community, and effective ways of dealing with peers (including conflict resolution). The advisory period allows students to explore important elements of their social world in a relatively safe environment. The advisory period offers a place to tackle bullying beyond the realm of official policy setting.

School Choice

In his letter of complaint, Mr. Johnson implies that one of the pressures he can bring to bear against his son's school is the threat of moving his son to a charter school. Clearly, one of the forces for change in public education is the charter school movement.

Where the charter school movement has taken hold, the public has been supportive of differing models of school organization. For example, a charter school—which is *not* a private school—might be created to serve children who are interested in careers in the arts. This sounds like a magnet school, and it is, in fact, a form of a magnet. However, the magnet school is likely to be a part of a school district and subject to the regulations of that district. Charter schools, in most cases, are freed from many of the rules that guide school districts. In Arizona, for example, charter schools receive public funds yet they are not required to hire teachers certified by the state.

Mr. Johnson's threat does not suggest that charter schools will be bully-free. Rather, the threat of moving his son to a charter school demonstrates a new pressure that schools must face in serving the public. In a sense, the presence of charter schools becomes a bargaining chip for any discontented parent, since the funding formula for public schools means that loss of enrollment causes a loss of operating funds.

Of course, there may be solid educational purposes for parents and children to seek charter school experiences. In this example, however, does it seem that the charter school is presented as an educational option? Have parents found a new pressure point for influencing schools with the charter threat?

Instruction—Who's in Charge?

You may have read the comments about reading as a red herring in this problem. That is, as often happens in real problems, you may have seen the information as irrelevant to the actual issue. Ms. Thompson suggests that all the fuss about Edward as a victim is in reality a vehicle to get action because Edward's father disagrees with her approach to teaching reading. She appears to believe that Mr. Johnson has a strong view of what constitutes good reading instruction, and it is more along the lines of "whole language" than the phonics-based approach she advocates.

The debate over reading instruction is perhaps the most predictable controversy related to public schooling. Why can't Johnny read? Everyone has an answer to that, whether it is that Johnny didn't get enough phonics in elementary school or that Johnny got too much phonics or that Johnny's parents are poor or that Johnny is undisciplined or didn't learn English soon enough or whatever. Doubtless your preparation to teach has acquainted you with the debate; you have probably encountered passionate and persuasive advocates on both sides.

Is it possible that the true issue for Mr. Johnson is a question of reading pedagogy? If Ms. Thompson used the "reader's workshop" approach (Atwell, 1987), would this eliminate the concerns about bullying? Is it likely that Edward was an agent of change in the reading wars and this provoked his victim status?

However one views the core question of bullying, it is true that teachers need to be well prepared to justify their approaches to instruction. In this case, the focus on phonics at the middle school level is unusual. Ms. Thompson does well to support such a decision with a sound basis.

In addition to her unorthodox approach to middle school reading, Ms. Thompson uses a somewhat unusual set of rules. Examine the class rules again and see if they appear to be supportive of the needs of young adolescents. Are these rules clear enough for the children to understand? Are they clear enough for the teacher to be able to provide consistent enforcement?

School Leaders or Teachers from the Military

A minor point in this PBL experience relates to the military background of the principal, Mr. Gallagher. In fact, as teacher shortages have become more widespread, schools have turned to former members of the military for teacher recruits. The same is true for addressing the shortage of administrators. *Troops to Teachers* is perhaps the best-known program designed to track retired military personnel into schools, though other programs invite them as well.

In addition, some major school systems (for example, Seattle, Washington and Jacksonville, Florida) have drawn on military figures to serve as heads of the entire system. Given the differences between military careers and the nature of schooling, does such a recruitment pool raise concerns? If you found yourself a colleague of a former career military person or the subordinate of one, how might this affect your relations with that person? Are there ways to draw the strengths of such recruits and avoid some habits that might be counterproductive in schools?

Perhaps more important to the way this problem plays out is the apparent struggle over leadership at the school. Mr. Gallagher was recruited to fill a leadership void. Once on site, he did not match the expectations of some other school leaders. You can read some of Ms. Lomax's actions as attempts to shift the power in the school. Indeed, Mr. Johnson's letter seems to be a weapon in this struggle for leadership, and he seems to have been "coached" on who to send copies of the letter. Indeed, it is possible that the "real problem" at this school is that some forces want new leadership, and the bullying is merely a vehicle for change. This certainly casts the problem in a different light.

Grandparents as Parents

We see one child in this situation whose aggressive behavior is attributed to a difficult home life. Tom Ramos lives with a grandparent because of his mother's incarceration. More than 5 percent of school-aged children live with a grandparent as a primary caregiver (Bryson & Casper, 1999). These children are more likely to be poor and more likely to lack health insurance than other children. The grandparents raising such children can be active participants in the school lives of their grandchildren, but often they are not. Teachers can benefit from awareness of the special stresses on grandparent-maintained households.

A secondary issue—or perhaps it is the primary issue here—arises due to the reason for Ramos's living with his grandmother. Like some 2.1 percent of the minor population in the United States (Mumola, 2000), Tom's mother was in prison. Typically, mothers in prison are there due to drug-related crimes, and some 20 percent of parents in prison report that their children live with a grandparent (most imprisoned parents report the child lives with the other parent). All the issues for a child living with a grandparent are compounded by the fact that mom or dad is in jail. Indeed, there is evidence that the children of incarcerated parents suffer from a variety of related effects, with those at about Tom's age increasingly likely to end up in the criminal justice system themselves (Johnston, 1995). A study of such children in Philadelphia found that "Violence had become an acceptable, though frightening, part of their daily lives" (Rogers & Henkin, 2000, p. 227).

Often the children of incarcerated parents are taught to conceal this fact, to hold it in rather than to speak about it (Johnston, 1995), and this can lead to a sense of shame and stigma. Such children often have more difficulties working with others and with achievement in general. Some, like Tom perhaps, become aggressive. And teachers are not likely to know about the parents' situation, given that children overwhelming do not reveal this information.

Grandparents can be helped by support groups, such as Grandparents as Parents (GAP) (Poe, 1995) or economic and psychosocial support (Porterfield, Dressel, & Barnhill, 2000). An example of a comprehensive support program is "Grandma's Kids" in Philadelphia (Rogers & Henkin, 2000). This program not only provides children with support through such means as after-school tutoring and summer camps, but it also provides support for the grandparents acting as parents. And, perhaps most important for our purposes, the program offers training for teachers through three primary means: sensitivity workshops, feedback about the progress of the children, and invitations to events for kinship caretakers. Such supports form a productive way for the school to help grandparents succeed in their role as parents (Silverstein & Vehvilainen, 2000).

A word of caution is in order. However good her intentions were, Ms. Thompson must be very careful about what information she passes along to others. Do you see ethical implications in her decision to tell others that Tom's mother is in prison? Even if this creates sympathy and understanding, is it right for a teacher to reveal such private information?

DISCUSSION QUESTIONS

1. How does a teacher balance compassion for the child with the "rough" background who is making progress with concern for the child who might be the victim of such a child? Is there a way to be supportive of both?

2. What ways might you incorporate lessons and experiences that teach respect for all your children?

3. Does the system-wide response to bullying seem like a positive solution to you? What dangers do you see in this? What promising features?

4. What different approaches might you use to relate effectively to a child's grandparent as opposed to the typical parent of one of your students? What would you look for as a sign that such children may be in distress?

5. How might you address parents who find issues to criticize in your work, when their real concern relates to a different aspect of your teaching?

6. Considering the PBL process, what did you learn about your patterns of problem solving? For example, do you find a desire to move to a solution quickly, or are you comfortable playing with the details for a time? How would you describe your problem-solving approach?

FURTHER READING

Froschl, M., Sprung, B., & Mullin-Rindler, N. (1998). *Quit it! A teacher's guide on teasing and bullying for use with students in grades K–3.* New York: Educational Equity Concepts, Inc. and Wellesley College Center for Research on Women.

This is one of three books in a series. This volume and the one directed at fourth and fifth graders (Sjostrom & Stein, 1996) offer teachers many ideas, activities, and reproducible handouts to work with students at the elementary level. The basic perspective of the books is that teachers need greater awareness of teasing and bullying, and that classroom activities can help students address the problem. The authors focus on gender issues and building self-esteem of all persons. The activities are promising, and the books are easy to use.

Newman, D. A., Horne, A. M., & Bartolomucci, C. L. (2000). *Bully busters: A teacher's manual for helping bullies, victims, and bystanders.* Champaign, IL: Research Press.

An excellent, readable source for considering how to deal with bullying. The authors set the big picture clearly in their introduction, followed by "modules" that work to raise awareness and prompt actions on the parts of teachers and students. Each module includes classroom applications and activities that work to build the self-esteem, empathy, and self-control of the children.

Module 4 is especially valuable. It details how to take charge through interventions for bullying behavior. The book takes an empathetic view, that bullies are themselves "walking wounded" (p. 101). The authors describe four R's of bully control: recognize that a problem exists, remove yourself if you can't intervene effectively, review the situation, and respond (p. 102). Among the general principles for intervention are building a positive environment, enforcing rules, acting quickly, using positive interpersonal skills, examining your own response, providing a way out of conflicts, letting students know they are important, and empowering students to take positive actions to eliminate bullying.

Rigby, K. (2001). Health consequences of bullying and its prevention in schools. In J. Juvonen & S. Graham (Eds.), *Peer harassment in school: The plight of the vulnerable and victimized* (pp. 310–331). New York: Guilford.

Rigby reports on his and others' research about the health effects of bullying on the victims. It is particularly interesting that he found "suicidal ideation" (thinking about killing oneself) to be much higher among the victims of bullying. Rigby describes other health complications from bullying, such as anxiety, depression, and social dysfunction. He then provides some ideas about how schools and teachers can help address the problem. Rigby's web site (www.education.unisa.edu.au/bullying/define.html) also offers helpful perspectives.

WEB SITES

Bullying.Org: Where You Are Not Alone!
http://www.bullying.org

British Policies on Bullying
www.bullying.co.uk/school/bullying_policie.htm

REFERENCES

Atwell, N. (1987). *In the middle: New understandings about writing, reading, and learning.* Portsmouth, NH: Heinemann/Boynton-Cook.

Bryson, K., & Casper, L. M. (1999). *Coresident grandparents and grandchildren* (Current Population Reports P23–198). Washington, DC: U.S. Department of Commerce.

Carroll, D. (2001, August 14). From bully to buddy. *The Arizona Republic.*

Farrell, M. (1999). *Key issues for primary schools.* London: Routledge.

Froschl, M., Sprung, B., & Mullin-Rindler, N. (1998). *Quit it! A teacher's guide on teasing and bully-ing for use with students in grades K–3.* New York: Educational Equity Concepts, Inc. and Wellesley College Center for Research on Women.

Johnston, D. (1995). Effects of parental incarceration. In K. Gabel & D. Johnston (Eds.), *Children of incarcerated parents* (pp. 59–88). New York: Lexington Books.

Mumola, C. J. (2000). *Incarcerated parents and their children* (Bureau of Justice Statistics Special Report NCJ 182335). Washington, DC: Bureau of Justice Statistics.

National Middle School Association. (1995). *This we believe: Developmentally responsive middle level schools.* Columbus, OH: National Middle School Association.

Newman, D. A., Horne, A. M., & Bartolomucci, C. L. (2000). *Bully busters: A teacher's manual for helping bullies, victims, and bystanders.* Champaign, IL: Research Press.

Poe, L. (1995). A program for grandparent caregivers. In K. Gabel & D. Johnston (Eds.), *Children of incarcerated parents* (pp. 265–267). New York: Lexington Books.

Porterfield, J., Dressel, P., & Barnhill, S. (2000). Special situation of incarcerated parents. In C. B. Cox (Ed.), *To grandmother's house we go and stay: Perspectives on custodial grandparents* (pp. 184–202). New York: Springer Publishing.

Rigby, K. (2001). Health consequences of bullying and its prevention in schools. In J. Juvonen & S. Graham (Eds.), *Peer harassment in school: The plight of the vulnerable and victimized* (pp. 310–331). New York: Guilford.

Rogers, A., & Henkin, N. (2000). School-based interventions for children in kinship care. In B. Hayslip, Jr. & R. Goldberg-Glen (Eds.), *Grandparents raising grandchildren: Theoretical, empir-ical, and clinical perspectives* (pp. 221–238). New York: Springer Publishing.

Silverstein, N. M., & Vehvilainen, L. (2000). Grandparents and schools: Issues and potential chal-lenges. In C. B. Cox (Ed.), *To grandmother's house we go and stay: Perspectives on custodial grandparents* (pp. 268–282). New York: Springer Publishing.

Sjostrom, L., & Stein, N. (1996). *Bullyproof: A teacher's guide on teasing and bullying for use with fourth and fifth grade students.* Wellesley, MA: Wellesley College Center for Research on Women and National Education Association Professional Library.

Skiba, R., & Fontanini, A. (2001). *Bullying prevention: Early identification and intervention* (Safe & Responsive Schools, Indiana University). Bethesda, MD: National Association of School Psychologists.

Smith, P. K., Shu, S., & Madsen, K. (2001). Characteristics of victims of school bullying: Develop-mental changes in coping strategies and skills. In J. Juvonen & S. Graham (Eds.), *Peer harassment in school: The plight of the vulnerable and victimized* (pp. 332–351). New York: Guil-ford.

Stevenson, C. (1992). *Teaching ten to fourteen year olds.* New York: Longman.

■ ■ ■ ■ ■

CHAPTER TWELVE

WHO SAYS NO TO A BOOK?

INTRODUCTION AND PROBLEM BACKGROUND

Teachers rightly get squeamish when the word "censorship" is uttered. For some, there are visions of Puritanical inquests along the lines of Arthur Miller's *The Crucible*. For others, there are images of nine-year-old boys chortling in a group around a computer screen while viewing pornography on line. The whole issue may be one of the most emotional of all the issues teachers face. Probably no other issue, short of high school athletics or school shootings, generates as much community controversy.

It's not always an easy issue, either. Some calls for censorship might strike us as silly. One parent group in the United Kingdom objected to the teaching of *Black Beauty* because the title implied racism. Hmm. Dr. Seuss's *The Lorax* was challenged in a community that was sustained by logging practices. But the parent who objects to *Roll of Thunder, Hear my Cry* (by Mildred Taylor) because she doesn't want her sixth-grade daughter exposed to people calling someone a "nigger" seems to demand more careful consideration. The parent who objects that his ten-year-old son has learned how to practice oral sex through the readings on AIDS deserves a careful hearing from school officials. In short, there is a *possibility* that censorship is not the black-and-white issue it often seems. Censorship may be an issue that deserves thought instead of automatic reactions.

Indeed, the issue of censorship is characterized as an attack by the "right" in most cases. Even this may not be true. For example, J. D. Salinger's *Catcher in the Rye*, a staple of many high-school English classes, was attacked for years because of its vulgarity and irreverence. The same novel has been attacked recently for its lack of "multiculturalism," and the book has disappeared from many schools because it does not present various cultures (Wax, 2001). It can be far too easy to condemn the controlling of Salinger's story as "censorship" when the grounds are moral and to forgive the book's suppression when the grounds are cultural. The effect is much the same.

This PBL experience invites you to think about the matter of censorship *before* you face a challenge to your work or your colleague's work. As Jean Brown and Elaine Stephens write, "A censorship challenge does not happen to just one teacher or one librarian. When a challenge occurs, it happens to everyone in that school, to everyone who uses that library, to everyone in that community" (in Brown, 1994, p. 125). In keeping with what makes PBL effective, work hard to see multiple perspectives, to understand the complexities of various players' positions. We shortchange our learning when we jump quickly to fixed reactions.

PROBLEM CONTEXT AND SOLUTION PARAMETERS

Context

The faculty at Rosa Parks Elementary School, located in a rural community in the Southeast, had barely recovered from the controversy generated by the changing of the school's name. For generations, Calhoun Elementary served its neighborhood "nobly," as one opponent to the name change put it. Still, the shifting demographics and values of the community made school officials receptive to the change, and faculty had gradually adjusted.

On the heels of that controversy, however, a new one arose. The school principal, Mrs. Laura Jones, received a phone call from one angry parent of a third grader. This parent, a local business owner, complained that her daughter was being forced to listen to her teacher read inappropriate material. When asked about the nature of the material, the parent indicated that she had not read the book herself, but that she didn't like the kinds of things her daughter was saying about it. The book was *Harry Potter and the Goblet of Fire,* the fourth in a popular fiction series by J. K. Rowling.

Problem

After reflecting on the issues raised by this parent, Mrs. Jones called in the teacher in question, Ellen Rathsmann. Ms. Rathsmann explained that the book was "an excellent hook" to draw her students into the world of reading. She said she knew the book pushed their comprehension abilities some, but that the best way to work for higher standards in school was to challenge children.

Mrs. Jones asked if Ms. Rathsmann assumed the children had already read the first three books in the series, and Ms. Rathsmann replied that they didn't need to—that the fourth book stood adequately on its own. Mrs. Jones asked if it would be appropriate for some of the children to be excused from the oral reading, and Ms. Rathsmann replied that this would not be workable. After all, what do you do with the students? Send them to the office for Mrs. Jones to deal with?

The conversation ended amicably, with Mrs. Jones simply requesting that Ms. Rathsmann demonstrate sensitivity to the concerns of the parents. But the issue went further. Dissatisfied with the action of the school, the parent contacted one of her business associates who also happened to be a school board member. This school board member complained to the school district superintendent, who informed Mrs. Jones that "until further notice, no *Harry Potter* books will be read in any elementary classrooms." Mrs. Jones gave these instructions to all of her teachers.

Through her local branch of the National Education Association, Ms. Rathsmann filed a formal complaint against her principal, and the matter is once again under consideration by the school board. This time, however, the issue is not to be addressed through networks of individuals, but in a public meeting.

Solution Parameters

As a colleague of Ms. Rathsmann, you have been asked to join with other teachers to present a proposal to the school board to resolve the conflict. You understand that there have been community demands for the firing of Ms. Rathsmann; you also have heard that the American Civil Liberties Union (ACLU) is interested in the case. It seems dramatic, and you wonder what is really at stake here.

Your group will be allowed to make a proposal to the school board, lasting between ten and fifteen minutes. In this proposal, you will need to clarify what the true nature of this problem is, why there is a controversy, and what is the best way for the school board to address this controversy. You can expect that board members will have strong opinions about these issues, and that you will need to cast your proposal in such a way that you can convince this tough audience. Board members will ask questions about your proposal, its justification, and its consequences.

As a follow-up to the presentation, write a one-page memo to Mrs. Jones from your individual perspective. How would you advise the principal to act in this case? What do you see as the most defensible action to take as an educator?

WORK THE PROBLEM →

PROBLEM DOCUMENTS

To assist you in understanding various aspects of this situation, the following documents have been provided to you:

12.1. Mrs. Jones's memo outlining the temporary policy on *Harry Potter* books

12.2 The parent's formal letter of complaint, addressed to the school board

12.3 Note from Ms. Rathsmann to the language arts director, Arlena Simonson, indicating her reasons for using the *Harry Potter* book.

12.4 Ms. Rathsmann's grievance initiation letter to her local NEA officials

12.5 A transcript of comments Ms. Rathsmann made at a roundtable session on censorship at the Fall Conference of the State Education Association (November, 2003), reprinted in association newspaper

12.6. A copy of the current school district policy on selecting instructional materials

12.7 Mrs. Jones's request for volunteers to address the school board

---

PROBLEM DOCUMENT 12.1	*Mrs. Jones's Memo Outlining the Temporary Policy on* **Harry Potter** *Books*

❖ ROSA PARKS ELEMENTARY SCHOOL ❖
A New Beginning—A Bright Start

Memorandum

From: Mrs. Jones

To: All faculty

Date: 10/1/03

RE: Harry Potter in the classroom

I realize a number of you have enjoyed bringing Harry Potter into your classrooms. I'm sure the experience of reading these books has been fun for you and your children. In fact, I'm going to read one of these books one day soon.

However, I'm sure you're aware that the books have sparked some controversy in our community. It's truly unfortunate that our efforts to resolve this situation have not been successful. I believe that compromise and sensitivity are the solutions to most problems.

This problem is now out of my hands—and out of yours, too. We have been informed by the superintendent that there will be a temporary moratorium on the use of any Harry Potter books in the classroom. As I understand this directive, there is no comment made about the books in the library, but to be on the safe side, I've asked Mrs. Wellins to pull the books off the library shelves, too, though children can still request these books if they have a note from their parents.

I know we will give 100 percent cooperation on this matter at RPES. Our school is the place of new starts, not the place of building walls. We have a job to do; let's do it!

An Open Letter to the Elected Board of Education, Ellensburg, South Carolina

Dear Board Members:

I write to you as a dedicated and concerned parent and community member. I have always been a great supporter of our schools, having volunteered my time on many occasions to assist with classroom activities, to raise funds, to enhance the beauty and effectiveness of our whole system. Those who know me know that I am not a rabble-rouser or a person given over to causes. I'm a tax-paying citizen who has created jobs for other members of this community so they can pay taxes, too. Please keep this in mind.

My daughter is a third-grade student at Parks Elementary. She's a good girl, who has never, to my knowledge, caused a disruption or acted in the least bit disrespectfully. She's in school for one thing and one thing only: to get educated. I don't believe the school has any business trying to build her into some kind of an ideal person or modern woman or anything else. Just educate her, and we'll all be happy.

She recently came home to tell me that they were studying about witches in her class. Witches. I seriously doubt that reading about witches is a crucial part of her education! And from what I understand, the source of their information is a book that goes well beyond witches. *Harry Potter and the Goblet of Fire,* I'm told, is a book that will take my daughter into the realm of treachery in school, demons and ghosts, drugs and sex, and violence, even death. At the third grade, mind you!

I tried a reasonable approach with this, talking both to the teacher in question and to the school principal. I requested that some consideration be given to the age and sensitive dispositions of these youngsters. But my pleas went unanswered. My daughter continued to bring home accounts of some aberrant school of witchcraft until the superintendent stepped in and put a stop to the madness. Now I'd like to see some more permanent, stable solution to this ridiculous situation.

I am asking you, as our elected leaders for education, to assert your leadership. This school system is under your care, and you alone can bring some reasonable limits to the situation. Please protect our young ones from exposure to things they simply are not ready to deal with yet, and which they should not have to deal with yet. Please protect my daughter and her young friends from the world of witchcraft and evil. Surely there is no shortage of good books to give our children. Why must we give them trash? Enact a policy that will end the indoctrination of children into an acceptance of what most decent people see as evil.

Note from Ellen Rathsmann to the Language Arts Director

September 4, 2003

Hey, Arlena!

Just a quick note to bring you up to date. I've decided to read the 4th Potter book out loud to my class. I love those books—and I know you do, too. It's been a long time since we've had such a boost to reading. Kids are more interested than I've seen them in years. It must give you goose bumps as the language arts specialist!

Anyway, I thought I'd just tell you what my thinking is. I've been talking to the kids, and there are a few who know nothing about Potter. There are a few who've read the whole set. I decided to try number four this year just to work for the freshness. I figure that in some ways, it's the toughest of the books. So if I read it aloud, that should send the kids back to their own books to catch up. Don't know if it will work, but I'm sure willing to give it a try! I can't see any problems with starting at the fourth, can you?

I'll let you know how it goes. Whatever gets the kids excited about reading is worth trying.

Ellen

Ms. Rathsmann's Grievance Initiation Letter

October 5, 2003

Albert Simmons, President
Ellensburg Education Association

Dear Mr. Simmons:

As you know, the charge we have been given as educators is to open the world to our students. There is no better way to open the world than through the pages of a book. Each book opens its own world, but more importantly, the skill and comfort a child acquires in opening a book really opens limitless other worlds, too.

I have been told to close the world to my students. I have been instructed NOT to read to my children, when what they most need in their young lives is to read and read and read. As a member of the EEA, I appeal to you and my association to stand up for me in this matter. I believe the superintendent has unjustifiably overstepped his authority in commanding that I, and all my colleagues at the elementary level, immediately cease from reading or assigning or even making available any of the *Harry Potter* books. I don't believe the merits of this particular fiction series are at issue in the least. I believe the issue here is a fundamental incursion on the rights of students and teachers to free expression as guaranteed in the U.S. Constitution.

The Board of Education will be reconsidering its position on censorship as a result of my actions. I ask the EEA to formally protest the actions of the superintendent and my principal and to insist on academic freedom in this community.

Ellen Rathsman

Ellen Rathsman

Excerpts from Ellen Rathsmann's Comments at the State NEA Fall Conference

Note: Ms. Rathsmann's appearance in numerous articles and news accounts led to her invitation to address the convention prior to the main speaker. Her presentation was enthusiastically received at the convention, with several interruptions due to laughter and applause.

I appreciate being invited to speak to you all today, because I know we share the same core, the same rock-solid beliefs in freedom. My story could be your story or your story or yours. It's really, in the deepest sense, our story.

For those of you who don't know the details, let me put it in the simplest terms. I have been told I may not read a book to my children. I did not offer them drugs. I did not encourage them to abandon their churches. I did not incite a riot among these third-grade boys and girls. I read to them. Read to them, do you hear? And I've been told I will either stop reading or stop teaching.

I've got news. I won't stop anything!

You know the controversy Ms. Rowling has generated in our state and elsewhere. The gall of that woman, to get so many kids interested in the written page again. What nerve! If something isn't done soon, the kids will start thinking. What a mess we'd have then.

So I stepped into the controversy. I could have side-stepped it, I know. There are lots of good books and lots of fine stories. I could have read them. But I'll let you in on a little secret—among friends. I couldn't wait for someone to take a shot at my reading choice! I couldn't wait because I want something to happen here in our state that should have happened long ago. I want us to finally once and for all say that there is

such a thing as intellectual freedom. I'm sorry if using "intellectual" is in bad taste for my critics, but it's the right word even if it has more than three syllables.

You might ask me why I chose to jump ahead and read the fourth *Harry Potter* book to my children. Another secret. I knew it had witchcraft in it; I knew it had hints of young love; and I knew it had the death of a student. Sorry if I ruined the story for any of you—I won't say more. I knew it had all these things and that's *why* I chose it. I wanted the book banners and the book burners and the thought police to have a big target so there wouldn't be a mild, "now just get along, Ms. Rathsmann" from my superintendent. When you're dealing with the intellectually-hard-of-hearing, sometimes you gotta shout!

I invite the small-minded, self-appointed censors of our society to tell me what I can or can't do in my classroom. Let's clear the air once and for all! And I call on you, my colleagues here and across the state, to step forward in the cause of intellectual freedom. Support the right of teachers everywhere—the right guaranteed by our First Amendment—to be able to read what we feel should be read to our students. Support the right to make thinkers of our children even if that threatens the nonthinkers who somehow intimidate administrators in their stuffy offices.

I've been attacked on TV and in the papers; I've been confronted in the grocery store for what I'm trying to do. I love it. I can't think of a better way to make an impact. But I warn you all. It'll be a lot easier for each of you to make the decisions you want to make if you raise your voices with mine to let the people of this state know that we're not going to be bullied anymore.

Thank you.

Ellensburg School District, No. 42
Policy Manual of the Board of Education

1   Policy #89-304

2

3   Category: Instructional Materials Selection

4   Adoption date: March 17, 1989

5   Revision date(s): NA

6

7   **Purpose:** The purpose of this policy is to establish guidelines for the evaluation and selection of

8   instructionally appropriate materials for use in classroom situations.

9

10   **Summary of policy:** Materials for use in instructional settings shall be selected to enhance the

11   intellectual development of students. The established curricular guidelines of the district shall be

12   the basis for decision-making in material adoption; the local curriculum council shall assist in mate-

13   rials adoption questions. Final responsibility for all decisions rests with the Board of Education.

14

15   **Provision I: Authority for adoption of materials.**

16   1.1   Final authority for all decisions regarding materials use and adoption rests with the Board of

17   Education.

18   1.2   The Board of Education authorizes building principals or their designees to grant tempo-

19   rary approval of materials use, subject to oversight by the Board.

20   1.3   The Board of Education authorizes classroom instructors to select materials designed to

21   enhance the curriculum opportunities as implied by the curriculum guides outlined in Pol-

22   icy Manual section 200–299c (curriculum).

23

24   **Provision II: Guides for appropriate materials.**

25   2.1   Certified and licensed staff shall be expected to make decisions regarding instructional

26   materials on the basis of the established curriculum guidelines, in conjunction with defensi-

27   ble practice, as outlined in 2.2–2.6 below.

28   2.2   Materials drawn from best practice recommendations of professional associations (e.g., IRA,

29   NCTE, NCTM, NSTA) shall be considered appropriate.

30   2.3   Materials subjected to professional review by school- and district-level curriculum commit-

31   tees shall be considered appropriate.

32   2.4   Materials subjected to scientific/research examination and associated with enhanced student

33   performance on standardized assessments shall be considered appropriate.

34   2.5   Materials recommended by joint committees of students, parents, and staff shall be consid-

35   ered appropriate.

36   2.6   Materials deemed to be consistent with the overall purposes and goals of the Ellensburg

37   School District shall be considered appropriate.

38

39   **Provision III: The right to challenge material selection.**

40   3.1   The Board of Education recognizes the right of informed parents to challenge the inclusion

41   of materials in the curriculum when such materials have not been specifically approved by

42   the Board of Education.

43   3.2   A challenge to any curricular material or practice should be initiated at the school level and

44   resolved through the assistance of the designated school authority.

45	3.3 If such resolution (3.2) cannot be achieved, the challenging party must address his or her
46	concerns to the Board in writing for consideration at a future regular meeting.
47	3.4 Challenging parties are permitted to address the Board in person at the designated meeting.
48	3.5 The instructor and/or administrator who stands in defense of the material will be given
49	equal time at the designated meeting.
50	3.6 At its discretion, the Board may appoint a committee of community members and school
51	officials (equal representation) to investigate the material in question and report back to the
52	Board.
53	3.7 Use of challenged materials shall not be restricted before the final disposition of the challenge.

| PROBLEM DOCUMENT 12.7 | *Mrs. Jones's Request for Volunteers to Address the School Board* |

❖ ROSA PARKS ELEMENTARY SCHOOL ❖
A New Beginning—A Bright Start

Memorandum

From: Mrs. Jones

To: Designated Faculty Members

Date: 10/25/03

RE: Volunteers for Board Presentation

As you know, the controversy surrounding our school and the use of certain materials has reached a level where the Ellensburg School Board will be considering whether to revise district policy on the use of materials. I am requesting that you serve on the committee to help resolve this matter. I do not want our school to appear irresponsible, yet I am uncomfortable with some of the decisions I have had to make.

Are we handling this situation correctly? Is there something we could do differently at Rosa Parks Elementary in order to serve our students and remain in the good graces of this community?

As a member of the RPES materials committee, you are being asked to make a reasonable recommendation to our school board and to help us move forward in this situation. Of course, nothing I am asking you to do should be construed as oppositional to the EEA.

••••PROPOSE A SOLUTION ➤

SOLUTION SUMMARY

Before proceeding to the reflection section of this chapter, write a brief summary of your team's solution here:

Our team defined the "real" problem here as _____

_____

_____

_____

_____

_____

_____

_____

_____

The key features of our solution were _____

_____

_____

_____

_____

_____

_____

_____

My personal view of the problem and solution is _____

_____

_____

_____

_____

_____

_____

_____

TIME FOR REFLECTION

To conclude your work with the censorship problem, this section guides you to reflect on a number of issues. What is censorship? It may seem like a simple question to start with, but it's important to give this some careful thought before you face a challenge. This line of thought leads us to consider what it means for teachers to make responsible choices in the selection of materials. Next, the reflection considers school boards and their authority over the curriculum. Finally, the reflections conclude with thoughts about the professional associations of teachers.

What Is Censorship?

People have defined censorship in a variety of ways, and the one thing virtually all definitions have in common is that it is an ugly word. Consequently, almost no one considers his or her actions as acts of censorship, and the language used typically couches such actions in different terms. The parent group that objects to a young adult novel featuring sex will speak of protection, not censorship. The community group protesting a book that features racism will speak of cultural sensitivity, not censorship. Are the results the same, whatever we call it?

Consider, for example, Brinkley's (1999) definition of censorship: "action taken by a person or group of persons who feel able to decide what information or experiences other persons should not have access to" (p. 32). That definition would encompass, for example, the actions of groups that don't want the word "evolution" to appear in any textbooks. But it would also encompass the actions of virtually every teacher. Out of the limitless array of information and experiences available to students, teachers select what they will expose the students to. And those things that are left out become part of what Elliot Eisner (1985) calls the null curriculum, that which we don't teach. Are teachers, then, censors? Was Ms. Rathsmann a censor because she decided not to provide her students access to, say, *Gentle Ben*?

One feature of the debate that seems to come up regularly is the distinction between parents' asserting some control over what their own children experience and citizens' asserting control over what other people's children experience. Most writers concede that parents ought to have significant say over what their own children are exposed to, but that this right should not extend to other people's children. In the classroom, this presents unique challenges. If a teacher honors the wishes of various parents, at what point does the class disintegrate into 25 different classes? And even if the teacher provides alternative experiences for a particular child, this may be a naive solution, especially as children get older, when they become aware of both what the other children are doing and what the other children may be thinking about them. As usual, the complex issue is not easily resolved.

Many teachers are tempted to engage in a form of self-censorship, selecting materials that are likely to be inoffensive, materials that will not be challenged (see Chapters 4 and 12 in Brown, 1994). But of course, those selections may not be the best ones for helping students learn to think or become interested in reading. Moreover, even those materials may be challenged, so self-censorship is not a completely safe avenue.

One of the conversations you ought to promote at your school is a discussion of censorship. Find out what the history of censorship has been in this school; talk to your colleagues about how they handle controversial material. Consider how you can fulfill your obligations to your position and remain faithful to your beliefs about intellectual freedom.

Responsible Choices

One implication of the issues raised in this PBL experience is the obligation of teachers to make responsible choices. What forms the basis for these choices?

Ms. Rathsmann, by her own admission, wanted to provoke controversy. It seems the basis for her decision to read *Harry Potter* was the potential this book had for stirring up controversy. If she had an interest in connecting with her children, that seems to have been a distant second to her interest in making a point to the public at large. Was her decision justifiable? What constitutes an ethical approach to the teaching of controversial materials? Of course, the remarks we read from the state convention do not exactly match her note to the curriculum specialist in charge of language arts. Is it possible that Ms. Rathsmann had another reason for choosing this particular book, but that she, herself, was swept up in the controversy of censorship? Did circumstances move her to fight a symbolic battle beyond what she originally hoped for her children?

At base, decisions about teaching materials ought to derive from the mandate a teacher accepts in becoming a public servant. That is, the state does not hire teachers to provide them with personal soap boxes and captive audiences. In the 1980s, a teacher gained some notoriety in the Canadian province of Alberta through his practice of teaching high school students that the Holocaust was actually a Jewish fabrication intended to discredit the Germans. Did this teacher have the right to express his deeply-held beliefs? Beyond that, did this teacher act responsibly in presenting only one side of a story—especially since the weight of historical evidence and the provincial curriculum mandates were against him? It seems obvious that this teacher was irresponsible. To make such irresponsibility the poster child of anti-censorship thinking would be equally irresponsible.

A starting point for making responsible choices is to acknowledge that most parents want to support their children in a positive learning experience. That is, most parents do not seek conflict with the teachers, and they aren't on the prowl for opportunities to discredit educators. They entrust that which is most valuable to them over to you, and you can do much to win their confidence by demonstrating your own commitment to helping their children succeed.

Given this agreement on purpose, responsible decision making means that the teacher should take into consideration the consequences—intended and unintended—of her or his selections. This means paying careful attention to how your community "reads" the materials you read or have your children read.

Special emphasis should be given to that word, *community*. Teachers form a vital part of the community. You must decide whether actions with a deliberate political motivation, such as appears to be the case with Ms. Rathsmann, serve to disrupt that community. It's not an easy matter to balance your role as public servant and mentor for children with your role as a public conscience or critic. But there is little promise in the kind of polarity that sees all concerned parents as Hitleresque thought police and all teachers as Marxist manipulators.

School Boards and Authority

Many novice teachers are unaware of the importance of the governing body for their school districts. Sometimes it is difficult to wade through the layers of bureaucracy. You may have a lead teacher at a grade level or a team leader; you may have a math coordinator or some similar teacher leader. Your school will undoubtedly have a principal with a good deal of authority. You may have a site council or a parent teacher organization with some decision-making powers. In addition, you may find that your professional association has been empowered to contribute to the decision-making process. At the district level, you will find a superintendent or chief executive officer, usually surrounded by a corps of assistants with individual realms of authority.

Whatever else you find, ultimately, there will be some governing body that has final authority over the educational system. As opposed to the federal government, the states have been empowered to control education. However, most often, states hand over the control of the educational system to local school districts, governed by elected school board members. There are approximately 15,000 school districts in the United States, and though that number is significantly smaller than the 120,000 districts in 1937, that's still a lot of school boards each asserting some local control (Labaree, 2000). The larger the district, the less likely it is that individual teachers will interact with the school board. In smaller districts, the school board may be more closely connected to teachers. My first interview for a teaching job, for example, placed me in a room where I was grilled by the entire school board of a small Montana community.

It is this group of community members, committed enough to give their time, that has the authority to decide what will take place in the school curriculum. That's why it is important for teachers to participate in the process of electing committed board members; that is also why it is important for teachers to understand the role of the board, and where appropriate, to cultivate positive relationships with the board. If all a school board hears is the emotional ravings of a small group of parents—small, but nevertheless able to impact the outcome of elections significantly—what will the board think? On the other hand, if teachers help to educate board members with rational, defensible positions, the board is more capable of making balanced decisions. In short, teachers remain ignorant of the board at their peril. It will serve you well to recognize that you can do much for yourself and the credibility of your profession by maintaining a thoughtful, positive relationship with the school board.

Professional Associations

Ms. Rathsmann found an outlet, and presumably a receptive audience, for her ideas through her association with a branch of the National Education Association (NEA). One of two large teacher associations, the NEA is considered by many to be one of the most powerful lobbying groups in the United States. It is also a member-run institution that offers support for its members in a variety of venues, ranging from legal support to classroom materials.

While the question of union membership has little bearing on the resolution of this PBL experience, you do well to begin thinking about your perspective on unions. In many cases teachers are presented with a choice about union membership when they begin their first job (in some cases, they are required to be a member). What is the relationship between such an organization and its members? Will you, like Ms. Rathsmann, find social support and a unity of purpose with such an organization? Or will it be a matter of finding a force to negotiate your salary and benefits for you? (Only rarely do teachers do such negotiating on their own.)

DISCUSSION QUESTIONS

1. If you found yourself in a school with a teacher like Ms. Rathsmann, what sort of relationship would you seek to develop with her? Does her position strike you as a role model for teachers or a warning? Was she manipulated by the system in any ways?

2. After working with a school board, albeit a "mock" board, what are your reflections on the relationship of teachers to their governing bodies? What dilemmas are created when a group of trained professionals is subject to the authority of a group of interested amateurs? Does a professional association provide some level of protection in such circumstances?

3. What do you see as the appropriate role of a teacher in establishing good public relations with the community you will be serving?

4. How will you determine the acceptability of materials as you work to educate the children entrusted to your care? Should teachers seek to avoid controversy?

5. Considering the PBL process, what did you learn about your interests and strengths as an inquirer through this experience?

FURTHER READING

Brinkley, E. H. (1999). *Caught off guard: Teachers rethinking censorship and controversy.* Boston: Allyn & Bacon.
    Brinkley's book takes the position that teachers must prepare for challenges to their classroom choices rather than being caught off guard. She presents a generally fair perspective on the issues, as opposed to some works on censorship that lack empathy for another's perspective. The first two chapters are especially helpful in getting a broad perspective on

issues of censorship. In addition, her chapter on literature and the final two chapters that focus on creating policies and taking action, are relevant to the issues addressed in this problem and provide excellent resources for future teachers to become familiar with. There are other chapters—on science, writing, religion, moral education, and so on—that provide further information for the teacher in specific situations where censorship may become an issue. Here's a sample of Brinkley's thoughtfulness on the issue of religion in the school curriculum: "Teachers do not pretend to be able to solve all the controversial issues that must be addressed within the larger community and society, but they do need to consider the place of religion in the curriculum. Society as a whole will benefit if students learn at school that religion has played and continues to play a role in history and culture" (p. 180).

Brown, J. E. (Ed.). *Preserving intellectual freedom: Fighting censorship in our schools.* Urbana, IL: National Council of Teachers of English.
This collection of articles provides numerous examples of censorship (from Shakespeare to *The Lorax*) and perspectives on how to deal with it. Of particular interest to the beginning teacher: self-censorship among elementary teachers (Chapter 4), taking a proactive stance (Chapter 12), cautions for novice teachers about censorship and their language arts practices (Chapter 16) and legal issues in censorship (Chapters 20 through 22).

Hydrick, C. J. (1994). Slugging it out: Censorship issues in the third grade. In J. E. Brown (Ed.), *Preserving intellectual freedom: Fighting censorship in our schools* (pp. 198–203). Urbana, IL: National Council of Teachers of English.
One of the chapters in the Brown book, this brief account is worth highlighting for its proactive approach to censorship. Hydrick relates how she was able to make a powerful lesson for her third-graders by examining the picture book, *Slugs*, and the students' reactions. Acknowledging the range of responses, from disgust to enjoyment, Hydrick helped her students see the potential consequences of allowing any one person's list of "books to go" to become the controlling force for all other readers.

WEB SITES

The American Library Association
www.ala.org/alaorg/oif/censorshipintheschools.html
ALA's site for news and information about censorship in the schools.

Banned Books on Line
http://digital.library.upenn.edu/books/banned-books.html
Just like it sounds.

REFERENCES

Brinkley, E. H. (1999). *Caught off guard: Teachers rethinking censorship and controversy.* Boston: Allyn & Bacon.
Brown, J. E. (Ed.). (1994). *Preserving intellectual freedom: Fighting censorship in our schools.* Urbana, IL: National Council of Teachers of English.
Eisner, E. W. (1985). *The educational imagination: On the design and evaluation of school programs* (2nd ed.). New York: Macmillan.
Labaree, D. F. (2000). Resisting educational standards. *Phi Delta Kappan, 82*(1), 28–33.
Wax, E. (2001, January 16). Schools are seeking a multicultural Holden. *Washington Post,* p. A01.

CHAPTER THIRTEEN

REFLECTING ON PROBLEM-BASED LEARNING

At this point you've worked through a number—perhaps a great number—of PBL experiences. You have been forced to take on new roles, to perceive the occupational world of teaching from a host of new perspectives, and to make recommendations about issues that you may not have even realized were a part of the teacher's work. If the experience has helped you to see that the teacher's work goes beyond preparing lessons, gathering materials, helping children to get along, and completing paperwork, then it's been a good addition to your career. Given this base of experience, the challenge now is to incorporate what you have learned into a framework that assists you in becoming successful in the multi-faceted role of an elementary teacher. In the next chapter you will have the opportunity to work through a process to help you design PBL experiences for your future students. This chapter will provide some guided reflection to help you make sense of your experience. The chapter invites you to think about your experience, perhaps to jot some ideas, and at the end to discuss the experience with your peers. The common ground of your experience provides the basis for making sense of what you've learned.

One caution. I realize that you may not have worked through each of the problems here. When I refer to a particular problem as an example, my intention is to draw on the reader's experience. It might be helpful for you to review the types of problems that have been featured in this text (Figure 13.1).

The selection of problems in the text was designed to expose you to the wide variety of issues you might face as a teacher. Of course, you will face more types of problems than these, and you'll face problems that are similar to these, but which will send you in completely different directions for a solution, based on the community and school where you work. So, how can this experience help you in the face of the certainty of new problems? The goal of this chapter is to help you make certain you can grow professionally from what you have experienced.

This chapter is organized around several questions. First, what can you as a learner transfer from your experience with PBL? Second, what does your experience in PBL tell you about yourself as a problem-solver and what does this mean for you as a self-directed learner? Third, what have you learned about working with your peers? Next, what do you take away from your experience related to the

FIGURE 13.1 Summary of Problems Presented in Part II

CHAPTER	TITLE	BRIEF SUMMARY
3 (pp. 27–44)	What Should We Do about Andy?	A child study team cannot come to agreement about what is best for a middle-school student's IEP.
4 (pp. 45–63)	Whose Discipline Problem Is This?	A principal at a combined middle school and high school demands that teachers adopt a uniform policy/procedure for classroom management.
5 (pp. 64–85)	Math Makes Tracks	A middle school committee must respond to charges that the elimination of honors math sections is merely an example of political correctness interfering with best practice.
6 (pp. 86–105)	Multigrades or Migraines?	A group of teachers has protested the decision of their principal to reorganize this elementary school into all-nongraded classrooms.
7 (pp. 106–124)	Raise Those Scores!	Teachers examine a superintendent's call for schools to institute a "test-prep" program in order to enhance the schools' performance on the state standardized test.
8 (pp. 125–143)	Just the Facts, Please!	Teachers at an urban elementary school must respond to their site council's demand that all classes adopt constructivist teaching techniques.
9 (pp. 144–163)	Retention or Pretension?	The retention policy at a small school-within-a-school is challenged by a difficult case.
10 (pp. 164–181)	Hyper Kid, Hyper Mom, Hyper Teacher— Who's Hyper?	Student study team must look into the conflict between a parent and teacher on whether or not to medicate a fifth-grade girl for ADHD.
11 (pp. 182–198)	Bully Troubles or "Boys Will Be Boys"?	A parent objects to the lack of a firm bully policy in a school where his child may be a victim.
12 (pp. 199–213)	Who Says No to a Book?	A teacher's use of reading material is questioned by a parent, and teachers are asked to address a censorship policy to the school board.

specific issues that have provided the focus of the problems? And finally, what does this mean for your development as a teacher?

THE TRANSFER ISSUE

One question that ought to be addressed by all teachers arises from what the educational psychologists term "transfer." Think of it this way. When you learn a particular skill, are you able to apply it in a situation that is similar to the learning situation? If so, then you have "transferred" the skill. For example, you learn the skill of estimating a solution through a series of math activities. Later, in solving a different kind of math problem, you draw on the estimating skill to come to a solution. That's transfer. It would be even more exciting if that estimating skill surfaced when you were dealing with an area other than math, such as purchasing materials for a series of bulletin boards. Woolfolk (1998), citing Salomon and Perkins, calls this "low-road" transfer, which she says involves practicing a skill so often that it becomes automatic. "High-road" transfer, in contrast, is when you apply abstract knowledge to a new situation. Woolfolk's example is the application of what you learn in an anatomy class to a drawing class. When you hear someone arguing that lessons learned in World War I have a message for us in our global politics, you are seeing a conscious effort at transfer.

There is some controversy over how and whether transfer works, though that controversy is beyond the scope of our examination (it suggests a new PBL focus!). In short, most people agree that the closer the new situation is to the learned situation, the more likely transfer will occur. But not always. I recall a situation in a middle school where I was an English teacher. The department had just finished working on creating some learning modules for our students. One of the modules was on "creative problem solving," where we designed an experience to teach the process to our students. A key element of that process was to defer the solving of problems until the students had generated a variety of potential solutions to evaluate. We emphasized over and over again with the students that even if that first solution proves to be the best, it is crucial to generate a pool of possibilities so that creative ideas are not neglected. Even while we were taking our students through the process, a problem arose for the department related to resources. As one of the novices in the department, I was surprised and a little horrified to watch our group jump on the first solution presented without even pausing to consider what some other possibilities might be. This isn't a case of a lazy student—*we were teaching this stuff, and still we could ignore it*! That's anecdotal evidence, I know, but not atypical. It suggests to me that all of us need to consider how we can enhance transfer.

Specifically, from your experience in PBL, the question of transfer asks what you will take with you from your work. Will it be specific content knowledge, such as learning from Andy what an IEP is or learning from the math problem what some of the consequences of tracking might be? Will it be cognitive practices, such as engaging in perspective-taking in order to identify the "real" problem when you are problem solving? Will it be presentation skills, useful in persuading audiences of your view, with a sensitivity to the different kinds of audiences you might face? How did you adjust the presentations to the informal setting of a principal's office (the management problem) versus the formality of a school board (the censorship problem)? Will it be skills of collaboration, such as drawing out a quiet, but crucial, group member or resolving conflict without damaging a person's self-esteem? All these are examples of potential areas where you might transfer your learning to new situations. The likelihood of your transferring what you learn is increased if you consciously consider how you might do so. In a sense, this chapter is a model for you. I'm attempting to help you maximize the chances of transfer, just as you will one day want to maximize such chances for your own students.

And there is cause for a cautionary note here. Experience can lead you to insight, but it can also lead you to erect limitations. Far too often, a student teacher's experience with only one mentor teacher leads that future teacher to view the world in a very restricted manner. It's not uncommon for a student teacher to dismiss a wealth of information and techniques because one "real-world" experience doesn't match what he or she was told. Your mentor doesn't use cooperative learning, so you dismiss the technique altogether. In a similar manner, your PBL experience should not be used to self-impose limitations. You want to be careful that you don't assume too much from your experience with PBL in the situations you face later. For example, your team may have reached a decision to adopt the test-prep program STAR for your hypothetical school system (Chapter 7) based on the evidence you discovered. That doesn't mean that every similar situation would call for the same solution. Having gone through one examination of nongraded schooling through PBL should sensitize you to various issues; the experience should not persuade you that every call for school re-organization must be resolved exactly as your team decided in this case. Your examination of homelessness in the retention problem should not lead you to forming a rule such as "never retain homeless children." Transferring what you have learned in these complex situations always demands that you exercise professional judgment, which should have been stimulated and encouraged through the process of addressing the problems.

HOW DO I SOLVE PROBLEMS?

A second area for contemplation is the area of problem solving. What did you learn about yourself as a problem solver through your PBL experience?

In previous work with students new to PBL, I've found some surprising things. Some students have discovered, for example, that they actually enjoy research. Given an authentic context for discovering information rather than simply acquiring facts without a meaningful purpose, they have learned that this activity motivates and interests them. Research often has a bad reputation with students and—surprisingly—with teachers. Too often we hear comments such as "you can make the research say anything you want" from teachers. Thus, when debating something like the proper way to teach reading, teachers dismiss research findings. By divorcing their practice from a scientific basis, they become vulnerable to the criticism that what they do is arbitrary and ultimately indefensible. For teachers to discover a value to research is a powerful lesson in one part of the problem-solving process.

Consider what you might have learned about your own problem-solving. How do you respond to the ill-structured and complex nature of PBL experiences? Does it bother you that the details are "messy," with extra facts but never enough information? Some students have a definite preference for very clear limitations on the problems and very clear expectations about the solutions. In fact, most problems you will face as a teacher will be similarly complex and messy. There might be a clear "due date" (deadline), but exactly what constitutes an ideal solution will likely be more complicated than "write 500 words explaining why future teachers should study technology." So, if you are a problem solver who is made uncomfortable by the mess, what should you do? Part of the response involves career guidance. The world of teaching is messy and uncertain, and if this generates discomfort, you may want to consider seriously whether teaching is a good fit for you. Should you put yourself in a situation that calls for traits that you don't possess? Even if you love children and you can communicate well to others, the realities of teaching suggest that you need a high degree of tolerance for uncertainty. That is not to say that you cannot develop a higher level of comfort with uncertainty. I indicated in Chapter 2 that medical students who encountered PBL as a learning method often went through an extensive period of "grieving" about this change in their lives. But such a change was important for them, given the nature of medical practice (which is far different from the conditions of a traditional educational system). These students continued to practice PBL, continued to work together to overcome their discomfort. If you found the messiness of PBL to be difficult, you may need to continue more practice with such frameworks. You may also want to discuss with your professors and mentors ways of dealing with the uncertainties of the teaching profession.

Consider, also, where your particular strengths and weaknesses were in the problem-solving process. Were you a leader for the group's attempts to identify the problem? Did you resist looking at the problem from different perspectives? Were you able to encourage divergent viewpoints in generating solutions, or were you frustrated by those who seemed to distract the group from a clear focus? Were you one who encouraged mixing of ideas and discussion of both the nature of the problem and the possibilities of solution and presentation? Were you one who wanted to get to solutions quickly and directly? Did you advocate a strict division of labor or did you see the mixing of roles as worthwhile?

These questions may seem to sit out there without any practical value, but the reality is that you need to consider them for two basic reasons. First, as a member of the community of professionals in schools, you will find yourself involved in problem solving. Patterns you see from your work in PBL are likely to intensify in your professional practice, particularly since it is unlikely anyone will ask you to reflect on your problem-solving practices with detachment. Are you pleased with yourself as a problem-solver? The reality you will see in your occupation is that there will be people who not only do not contribute to solving problems, but who actually block the problem-solving efforts of others. While there is no secret that will make you a great problem solver, your awareness of your own tendencies, abilities, and limitations in this area can help you become better.

Second, you will probably want to teach your own students to be problem solvers. Your awareness both of the general process and your own application of that process will help you to be a more effective teacher. For example, it is unlikely you will convince your own students to consider multiple perspectives if you don't believe—and practice—this principle yourself.

SELF-DIRECTED LEARNERS?

One of the claims of research about PBL is that it encourages people to become self-directed learners (or SDLs). For example, Blumberg's (2000) review of the (limited) research literature indicates that medical students using PBL actively use libraries, utilize study strategies that enhance deep understanding, and see themselves as on a path to continuously improve their SDL skills. As professional educators, you should find the possibility of creating self-directed learners to be a promising idea.

Even if your focus right now is not on what kind of learners you turn out, it's worth your time to consider how you can make your own growth a priority throughout your career. As knowledge workers, we need to keep an ideal of continuing stimulation and growth alive. While the notion of "teacher burnout" is a complex issue in our system, at least a small part of the problem rests with teachers who do not choose to make learning a constant feature of their professional lives.

In her research on what makes effective elementary teachers of mathematics, Ma (1999) compared Chinese and American teachers. Ironically, though the Chinese teachers had far less formal education (and math courses, in particular) than their American counterparts, the Chinese teachers developed a deeper understanding of the math concepts they were teaching. Part of the explanation for this paradox, Ma concludes, rests with the fact that the Chinese teachers saw themselves as active learners, and in addition to careful study, these teachers spent time working with their colleagues to build understanding.

To put it at a personal level, do you see yourself as a self-directed learner? Does the pursuit of understanding motivate you? Is your curiosity alive? Or, in contrast, do you gather information for practical purposes only? Once the assignment is completed, has the curiosity subsided?

Problem-based learning is intended to assist you in becoming more self-directed in your learning, but it is only an environment to encourage such growth. You are the one who must make the decision to embrace lifelong learning. You alone can decide that as a professional educator, you will continue to inquire into what is best practice. Unlike members of most other professions, teachers tend not to read the professional journals in their fields. Far too many teachers end their own education with the last class in their college preparation—and even the courses they are required to take for re-certification tend to be viewed as hoops to jump through. By developing a self-image as a self-directed, lifelong learner, you can provide yourself with the limitless stimulation of a progressing career, and you can do much to enhance the credibility of the profession. There's also something infectious about a person who is passionate about learning—an important role model for the students who come to us.

WORKING TOGETHER—DOES IT WORK IN SCHOOLS?

Among the most thoroughly researched techniques in education, cooperative learning has become well established in the schools. As you may have learned in your professional education, cooperative learning is more than putting kids into groups where they do the same things they used to do individually. Cooperative learning involves changing the environment of the classroom, the goal and reward structure for the students, the structure of tasks, and even the assessment of student work. In light of problem-based learning, are such changes worth making? Does this working together work in schools?

If you've been through a relatively faithful version of PBL, you've had some significant experiences in working with groups. And if you're like most people, you've had a range of quality in your experience. It's likely that you've encountered someone who was *not* cooperative, who actively resisted the spirit of PBL and the efforts of your instructor and classmates to make the groups work. You've probably met a student who talked too much, another who knew too much, and another who had absolutely nothing to say. You may have even met someone who taught you a great deal.

Congratulations. You've met another slice of reality. In fact, in almost any walk of life, there are no perfect groups. Employers frequently complain that their new workers can be trained to do the technical aspects of their work, but that the new workers lack the ability to get along with co-workers. In too many cases, students in K–12 schools have learned what Haberman (1997) calls an ideology of nonwork, where the learners focus on excuses, developing a victim mentality, and living at a low level of expectations. Among other problems, students too often fail to see that they can play an important role in performing tasks as a group.

I have been surprised to find how often students in higher education have similar problems. Indeed, many post-secondary students make it through their educational experiences without any serious need to collaborate with peers. This was a concern among medical educators, and a key reason for the development of PBL in the professional education of physicians. Teachers, like doctors, find themselves frequently in need of collaboration in their working worlds. Even though a classroom may be a private and isolated work world (Lortie, 1975), the school world beyond the classroom door calls for all sorts of collaboration.

And as any teacher could tell you, virtually all the problems you might encounter as a member of a group in college will await you in your future job. There will be people who are late to group meetings, people who don't do their assigned tasks, people who will try to pull rank, people who will make personal attacks. You may find yourself assigned to a teaching team where your colleagues have little training in effective ways of working as a unified group (Kain, 1998). A key difference will be that there is no threat of a grade to pull your groups into focus and no professor with a clear line of authority. You will need to be an effective group member, not only in attending to your own behavior, but also in steering your groups to better performance.

So what have you learned about yourself as a member of a group? Consider both your actions and your colleagues' actions in the PBL experiences you have encountered. Perhaps you recall some of the roles of group members (Chapter 2). Did you find it helpful to establish formal roles? That is, when someone was assigned to be the group leader, did leadership emerge more effectively than when no one was assigned this task? How did you provide leadership for your groups? How did you handle conflict in your groups? Were you able to discuss this openly, or did your groups develop a means of addressing conflict that relied on denial? Were you and your peers consistent in addressing problems directly, or did you find yourself gossiping about other group members as a third party?

These questions are not merely an exercise for your time as a student. The career path you have chosen puts you in a place where effective group skills are central, and flashing a set of *A*'s from your education courses is no substitute for being a positive contributor to the collaborative environment of an institution (Little, 1982). As you reflect on your experience, consider what strengths you can build on and what areas of weaknesses you might have to address. The prompts in Figure 13.2 might help you in this reflection.

FIGURE 13.2   Prompts for Reflection on Group Behavior

1. I was most comfortable in group situations when I took the role of _____

_____

2. I found the most difficult interactions with my peers to be when _____

_____

3. My greatest strength as a group member appeared when I _____

_____

4. If my group members had been fellow teachers in a school, they would probably have perceived

me as _____

_____

5. I think practicing teachers would be different from the group members I worked with in that the

practicing teachers would _____

_____

6. The area I need most to work on in order to be a more effective group member is _____

_____

7. As an honest evaluator of my work in PBL group situations, I would summarize my performance

as follows: _____

_____

ISSUES AS VEHICLES OF LEARNING

One difference between this book and most that you are likely to encounter in professional education is that it deals with a number of issues but brings closure to none. You may have formed some powerful conclusions about issues such as retention, but your peers may have differing views. The perspective I have tried to communicate here is that all of these issues are complex and multi-faceted and need the careful deliberation of ethically-guided and competent professionals.

In the long run, your decision about what to do about Andy or what management system to use or whether Edward is a bullying victim is not the crucial issue. You will face these questions in different forms throughout your career. What you have learned about the "issues" through your experience may not impact your practice as much as the fact that you have learned a professional way to address the issues you will face one day.

LOOKING FORWARD: WHAT'S THE PLACE OF PBL IN MY CLASSROOM?

As you close your reflection on what you have experienced through PBL, a final important question to think about is what role PBL will play in *your* classroom. Is there space for this technique in the array of tools you plan to use with your future students?

I was startled once to read this comment from one of my students, who had completed several PBL units: "I really like PBL, but I don't see how I could use this in my subject—biology." My surprise, of course, arises from the fact that sciences tend to build so much on the inquiry process embedded in PBL that the fit seems natural and effortless. Part of the problem was with this student's understanding of the nature of her subject. To complete a degree in biology without seeing the role of inquiry in the discipline is an amazing (and discouraging) feat. But I also take the student's comment as an indictment of my presentation of PBL. Somehow I had not managed to communicate to this student the value of PBL for her future students. I believe a central factor in this is that I didn't actively call on my students to connect their learning experiences with their future learners through deliberate reflection.

For that reason, the next chapter walks you through the process of building a PBL experience for your students. You will be able to use the chapter to guide the construction of a problem-based unit appropriate to the grade level you hope to teach. However, even before that step, it is valuable for you to consider what kind of classroom you want to create for your future students. The PBL classroom draws on a view of learning as student-centered, collaborative, and centered around inquiry. How does that match your developing conception of what counts for an effective learning environment?

Obviously I have a bias in this, and I believe you serve your students well to move them into greater inquiry and problem-solving. However, what you think is what counts in this matter. Have you given thought to the overall climate that you will create for your students? Have you considered the messages you will give students by the way you organize their learning for them?

And is this a matter of all or nothing—either a student-centered PBL classroom or a traditional approach? Can a teacher be eclectic in pulling together teaching techniques? Is it appropriate for you to mix various models of teaching and learning, even if some of them appear to be contradictory in spirit? (Recall the decisions you made about a school committed to constructivist teaching techniques.) Can you do good lectures and guide your students through PBL experiences?

Such questions as these are important for you to think about as you build the classroom that matches your strengths, goals, and interests with the needs of your students and the communities you serve. It is appropriate as you complete or enhance your professional education to move beyond the learning of techniques and to begin to contemplate the impact on your students of the experiences you provide them.

DISCUSSION QUESTIONS

1. As a student of teaching, what are the three most important observations you have made in your work with PBL? Compare these with your colleagues' ideas. What does your experience tell you about the nature of learning and teaching?

2. What issues in the PBL experience surprised you as you think about the complexities of the teaching career? What areas of concern appear as a result of your encounter with teachers' work? How do these compare to your colleagues' areas?

3. When do you shift from your role as a learner in a teacher-preparation program or graduate school to your role as a lifelong learner? What are the implications of this for how you actually organize your learning?

4. What areas of problem solving do you see as your own strengths and weaknesses? How can you build on your experience to provide a more powerful experience for your future learners?

5. Where can you see connections between the subject or subjects you will be teaching and the PBL technique? Where can you find allies to help in the creation and implementation of inquiry teaching strategies?

6. Given the focus of most of the PBL units on "occupational" issues of teaching, which areas do you think you need further education? How might you enhance your understanding of occupational issues in the teaching career?

FURTHER READING

Levin, B. B. (Ed.). (2001). *Energizing teacher education and professional development with problem-based learning*. Alexandria, VA: Association for Supervision and Curriculum Development.
    This collection addresses a number of issues that might be worthwhile as you reflect on the relationship between PBL and your future classroom. There are some sample PBL units,

some principles for organization, and perhaps most useful to the teacher new to PBL, a final chapter of frequently asked questions.

Woods, Donald R. (1994). *Problem-based learning: How to gain the most from PBL.* Waterdown, ON: Author.

I recommended this book at the end of Chapter 2, but it's worth coming back to at this point. Woods does a wonderful job of focusing on the student's perspective in a PBL environment. His work was useful for preparing to learn; it is just as powerful as you reflect on what your experience has been in the PBL model.

REFERENCES

Blumberg, P. (2000). Evaluating the evidence that problem-based learners are self-directed learners: A review of the literature. In D. H. Evenson & C. E. Hmelo (Eds.), *Problem-based learning: A research perspective on learning interactions* (pp. 199–226). Mahwah, NJ: Lawrence Erlbaum Associates.

Haberman, M. (1997). Unemployment training: The ideology of nonwork learned in urban schools. *Phi Delta Kappan, 78*(7), 499–503.

Kain, D. L. (1998). *Camel-makers: Building effective teacher teams together.* Columbus, OH: National Middle School Association.

Levin, B. B. (Ed.). (2001). *Energizing teacher education and professional development with problem-based learning.* Alexandria, VA: Association for Supervision and Curriculum Development.

Little, J. W. (1982). Norms of collegiality and experimentation: Workplace conditions of school success. *American Educational Research Journal, 19*(3), 325–340.

Lortie, D. C. (1975). *Schoolteacher: A sociological study.* Chicago: University of Chicago.

Ma, L. (1999). *Knowing and teaching elementary mathematics: Teachers' understanding of fundamental mathematics in China and the United States.* Mahwah, NJ: Lawrence Erlbaum Associates.

Woods, D. R. (1994). *Problem-based learning: How to gain the most from PBL.* Waterdown, ON: Author.

Woolfolk, A. E. (1998). *Educational psychology* (7th ed.). Boston: Allyn & Bacon.

CHAPTER FOURTEEN

USING PBL IN YOUR CLASSROOM

Now that you've experienced problem-based learning from the perspective of a learner, it is appropriate to look at the world from the other side of the desk. Indeed, all the problems found in this text have pushed you, as a learner, to see the occupational world of teaching. You have been urged to think like a teacher in a host of situations. The one role you have not been asked to assume is the one most commonly associated with teacher education: preparing lessons. This final chapter asks you to do just that. In this chapter, you will draw on your experience as a learner in PBL situations to assist you in planning PBL experiences for your students.

The process described in this chapter involves a number of steps. First, you must select a problem that is worth developing and that connects in a reasonable manner to your curriculum. Next, you develop the problem situation, including the roles your students will assume (if any) and the parameters of the solution. After this, you must create any problem documents and assemble necessary resources. Although you will have already considered the solution parameters, you must next give further attention to the ways in which students will frame their solutions, including how you will assess the learning that takes place. Throughout this process, it is important to be aware of the role of the instructor, who, having developed the basic problem and documents, steps into a tutorial posture as opposed to a provider of information. Finally, the prospective PBL teacher must consider how to put it all together into a coherent program.

A PBL Option

This chapter is written in a fairly traditional, explanation-based manner. That may be most helpful for some learners, but other learners might profit from a different approach. You can take on this last PBL task in the same manner you took on the others—solving a problem.

Here are your parameters: Select an area of your curriculum that you feel is appropriate to a PBL approach. Design a PBL unit directed at a specific group of learners in a specific place. Create a problem description, the necessary problem documents, an assessment plan (with a rubric), and an evaluation of your work. You may use any of the documents in this text as a model and refer to whatever sections of this chapter you find appropriate.

SELECTING AND CONNECTING GOOD PROBLEMS

Judging the Value of Problems

To use problem-based learning in a way that benefits students, teachers must select and develop worthwhile problems. Barrows (1996) explains the importance of organizing learning experiences around good problems: "The curricular linchpin in PBL—the thing that holds it together and keeps it on track—is the collection of problems in any given course or curriculum with each problem designed to stimulate learning in areas relevant to the curriculum" (p. 8). Before considering what such a "collection" might look like and how the collection relates to the curriculum, think about what makes an effective problem.

Selecting a problem might be an individual task if a teacher intends to develop and implement the problem alone. On the other hand, given the complexities of most "real life" problems, selecting a PBL experience provides a powerful opportunity for teachers to work with one another to create problems. Together, teachers can help colleagues select problems that highlight the important ideas of the subject they teach. In either case, teachers need to have a sense of what constitutes effective problems, and when teachers work together, a common language. The following section provides both a discussion of good problems and a rating scale to use in judging the potential of a problem idea.

The experience of educators in a variety of fields suggests a number of characteristics for effective problems. These characteristics are listed in Figure 14.1.

Delisle (1997) adds that a problem should be developmentally appropriate to the students, curriculum-based, and grounded in student experience (p.18). Torp

---

FIGURE 14.1   Characteristics of Effective Problems

- Problem has relevance (contemporary) to students, touches their interests

- Problem is real versus contrived (students sense it could be or is an actual event)

- Problem has significance

- Problem has contextual details, but not enough to solve without going beyond the problem documents

- Problem is ill-structured (messy), opening the way for multiple solutions

- Problem has important learning targets embedded in it

Source: Adapted from Bridges and Hallinger (1995) and Glasgow (1997).

and Sage (1998) emphasize the importance of student interest and learning characteristics in selecting good problems. The criteria outlined in Figure 14.1 are elaborated below.

Relevance.   If the experiences provided to students seem to be "teacher issues," then PBL becomes nothing more than business as usual. This is not to argue that effective learning experiences must have a novelty to them; clearly, learning can occur in all sorts of situations. However, the unique demands of PBL require student engagement in order for students to take initiative and control their learning. Thus, a problem must not resemble the stereotypical application problems at the end of a chapter ("one train left Boston at 4:00 p. m., traveling west at 60 miles per hour; another train left Chicago . . . "). Instead, an effective problem gives credence to student perspectives. That is, a problem designer must learn to see the world through students' eyes and seek problems that will engage students. The best learning, according to Wiggins and McTighe (1998), is found at the intersection of what is effective practice and what is engaging to students.

Real.   This criterion may be a refinement of relevance. Effective problems have an authenticity to them. That is, effective problems arise from what is actually going on or what could happen. We often cast students in roles to address problems, and these roles may be far from the students' current perspectives. However, whether students assume distant roles (acting as consultants or government researchers, for example) or take on roles that may actually be a part of their lives (acting as the student government or a class committee), the central issue is that a problem could be real to someone somewhere. In other words, the problem does not appear to students as a contrived, school-based exercise.

Compare the following two tasks for their authenticity:

a. Create and present an oral presentation on any topic you like. You will speak for between five and seven minutes, and you must use at least two visual aids.
b. After completing your investigation into the issues related to creating a bike path to the school, present your recommendations to the City Council. The Council allows speakers only seven minutes each, so you will need to organize your presentation carefully. You may find it helpful to reinforce your presentation with visual aids, such as charts and graphs.

In example *a*, students are given clear boundaries for their work, but the task is the stuff of classic school exercises: no sense of audience or purpose or passion. Example *b* has students doing much the same task, but this task is framed as a real-life issue, a situation the students could face one day and a situation the students could witness at City Hall next week. The authenticity motivates students. And, of course, it is important that the situation is directed at the appropriate level for your students. While the bike path problem fits a fifth- or sixth-grader well, a first-grader may be more intrigued with the problem of deer eating the roses around your school.

Significance.   Not all that glitters is gold. The fact that a problem situation seems relevant to children and authentic does not mean it is worth spending the time that PBL (done right) requires. As a problem designer, you should ask yourself and your colleagues if the particular problem you have in mind contains enough significance to devote the time and energy needed to create the PBL experience.

Of course, significance is a range concept (from little to much) rather than a categorical concept (yes or no). And significance, like beauty, is, to some extent, in the eye of the beholder. Still, professionals are always making decisions about what to teach (remember Ms. Thompson's choice about an approach to teaching reading?); they are always making judgments of the value of learning experiences. Every time we choose to do one thing in a classroom, we are choosing *not* to do an infinite array of other things. Given the fact that a teacher cannot do everything, it is important that a teacher chooses significant things to do.

Consider the choices of Mr. Willis. He wants his fifth-graders to learn to be critical thinkers, and he also knows they need to learn something about U.S. history. He has time this term to implement one PBL experience related to U.S. history, a topic large enough to generate thousands of problems. His colleague, Ms. Valenzuela, convinces him that a PBL unit based on transportation would be worthwhile. She suggests that they jointly create an experience that has students design, build, and equip a mock Conestoga wagon—and she has the shell of a wagon to work with. But Mr. Willis has misgivings. Surely such a task would be engaging to his students, but is it something worth the amount of time it requires? On the other hand, he has an idea for a different problem, based on a developing community's dilemma about choosing a rail system or a canal system. Though he lacks the materials for this idea, it strikes him as being more significant in that it raises questions about the role of transportation in developing the country, the role of communication and networking, and so on. How does he decide?

One way to think about this is to ask the following question: What would a "critical friend" say about each unit? Which has greater significance in terms of leading students to think about big ideas, powerful ideas of the discipline? Despite the greater difficulty in designing a PBL experience around systems of transportation, Mr. Willis decides this is more significant than an experience in packing a wagon—though each experience promises to be engaging and to make history come alive.

Contextualization.   One of the issues raised in the previous chapter was the danger of focusing too much on the details of the problem itself instead of the larger learning issue the problem represents. The reason why this even becomes a problem is that a good problem is rich in contextual detail. In selecting a problem, the designer should make certain that the problem provides the potential to generate contextual detail, but that it also sends the students beyond the details provided to find a solution.

Consider the problem of what to do about Andy (focus of an IEP, Chapter 3). This particular problem was supported by documents from teachers, family members, the school psychologist, and official records. Rich details were available, but it's doubtful anyone could find the solution in that mix of documents. For one thing, what does the law actually say about special education? That was nowhere to be found in the documents. What is the difference between a learning disability and limited English proficiency? One has to go beyond the problem documents for such information.

In the same way, when you are designing a problem for your students, consider whether the problem invites the use of artifacts (documents, realia, artwork, and so on) that will give a context for students. However, a prime goal of the PBL process is getting learners to ask questions and seek information. A good problem will not have all the answers right there, because a good problem will generate questions even the designer hasn't anticipated. Here's a good rule of thumb: A good problem will always have more information than is needed to solve it, but never enough to solve it. When you work through the paradox of that statement, you'll have a good sense of the balance of details in a PBL experience.

Ill-Structured.   This descriptive phrase makes it sound as though the problem designer is incautious or haphazard. Clearly, that is not the intention. A problem designer must be very deliberate and cautious, and the goal is to design a problem that has the potential to generate multiple solutions, arising from multiple solution paths.

Perhaps the best way to think about this is to recall some of the science labs you may have experienced as a student. Often such labs are "cookbook" experiences, where the learners follow a prescribed path (the steps are laid out by the instructor), and the teacher crosses her fingers, hoping that the students get the "correct" results (and students often do not!). Atkinson and Delamont (1984) describe this sort of experience as a "mock-up," and they question whether any real learning is going on. Teachers design labs that students dutifully execute, and then teachers are left to explain why the labs didn't work.

In contrast, current thinking about problem solving emphasizes students' selection and justification of a solution path (as recommended by the National Council of Teachers of Mathematics and the National Science Teachers Association). Good problems for PBL experiences are those that do not suggest only one way to go about solving them. Indeed, good problems for PBL experiences call on students to dig around the details before even defining what the problem is, let alone how to solve it. And the teacher must be prepared for different groups to define the problem differently. Thus, "ill-structured" refers not to a lack of care on the part of the designer, but to tremendous care in selecting problems that will permit students to devise varying solution paths. Gallagher (1997) uses the paradoxical phrase "well-constructed, ill-structured problem" (p. 337) to indicate this complexity.

Embedded Targets.   Finally, a good problem for a PBL unit must connect to the curriculum mandate each teacher faces. Teachers should not be arbitrary about selecting learning experiences; each teacher answers to someone for the curricular choices he or she makes. Whether the mandate comes from a district guide, a school or department's "scope and sequence," state standards, or the proclamations of a professional organization, there is a larger community that helps define what students ought to know and be able to do. We ignore this mandate at our peril.

A good problem is one that connects to the mandate by embedding important learning targets in the problem. Generally, connecting to the curricular mandate is not a matter of teaching a particular discrete fact or skill. If the state department of education says you must teach the capitals of all fifty states, that is probably *not* the stuff of problem-based learning. Teach the capitals, but use a more appropriate means. The important embedded target for a good problem is what we might call a big idea, or what Wiggins and McTighe (1998) call an "enduring understanding." For example, if your mandate says something to the effect that students should understand science as an inquiry process (which is roughly what the first science standard the state of Arizona calls for), you can readily design a PBL experience in which students experience science as inquiry rather than science as the memorization of a bunch of facts someone else discovered. A PBL experience in which students look into the alarming increase in mosquito populations (see Torp and Sage, 1998) allows such inquiry, giving the learning process credibility due to embedded targets.

Each of the above characteristics is important for selecting worthwhile problems to develop. True to the nature of problem solving, no problem is likely to be perfect for every characteristic, so the designers must make judgments about the value of specific possibilities. To assist with this, the following rating scale (Figure 14.2) provides systematic attention to each characteristic. The best use of this scale is to have more than one teacher consider and rate a problem before developing all the support documents and resources. After rating the potential problem, teachers join together in a discussion of the potential benefits to students of creating and implementing the problem. There is no magic number or score that determines the worth of a problem, but a rough guide is provided with the scale. Remember that professionals make judgments and justify them according to professional standards and criteria.

Sources of Problems

Where do problems come from? There are several sources available. One can find problems through some of the exemplars published in current texts (Delisle, 1997; Torp & Sage, 1998); there are also online sources, such as the Center for Problem-Based Learning, based in the Illinois Math and Science Academy (www.imsa.edu). Textbooks themselves suggest problems, though it is unlikely any text will actually present material in a PBL format; the creative teacher must see how to transform texts into resources for engaging learning rather than seeing them as repositories of facts that dictate course structure.

Given the importance of relevance to the students' lives, perhaps local issues provide the best source for problems. For example, in the Association for Supervision and Curriculum Development's videotapes on problem-based

FIGURE 14.2   Rating Scale for Potential Problems

Problem Synopsis: _____

_____

_____

Features of Effective Problems	Score						
	Low		**Medium**			**High**	
1. Students will be **interested** in the problem (relevance).	1	2	3	4	5	6	7
2. Students will perceive the problem as like **"real life."**	1	2	3	4	5	6	7
3. Outsiders would see the problem as a **significant** issue, worth spending time on.	1	2	3	4	5	6	7
4. The problem can be **contextualized** through documents, but still provide opportunities for students to **inquire beyond** these documents.	1	2	3	4	5	6	7
5. The problem is **messy** enough to allow multiple solutions and solution paths.	1	2	3	4	5	6	7
6. The problem has important **learning targets (standards)** embedded in it.	1	2	3	4	5	6	7

Score	Reasonable Response
34–42	Looks very promising. Now work together to create the PBL.
22–33	There is potential here, but enough doubt to cause you to reconsider. Could the problem be adapted to improve its potential?
6–21	There is never enough time to teach. You can do better things with your time than this.

learning (1997a; 1997b), high school students pursue problems related to traffic flow and the building of a bridge in their community, while middle school students address a problem of turning a prison facility into a public building in their community. Younger children investigate an issue from their school cafeteria. Every community has issues that bring to life the learning targets of our subject areas—indeed, it is in seeing the usefulness of school subjects for solving life's problems that students find reason to learn. The astute teacher, sensitive to creating powerful learning experiences, is always on the lookout for potential problems that can engage students while accomplishing the goals of instruction. At times teachers will design problems around local issues that "could have been." For example, one team of middle school teachers, recognizing the conflict in their area concerning anthropological digs, devised a "could have been" problem that had students determine the rightful ownership of what may have been a grave site in a farmer's field. And soon after the teachers implemented their unit, there was a news story about the discovery of a 1,000-year-old skeleton in that community. You can imagine how real the situation became for the students. Do the turkey farms in your region create a stench at your school? Potential problem! Is the city thinking about new park facilities or changing the playground equipment? Potential problem!

Teachers can profit from conversations with their peers about potential problems, both as these problems arise from local events and concerns and as the problems emerge from the curriculum in place. Jacobs (1997) describes a curriculum mapping process that can assist teachers in finding common ground in their curriculums to use as the basis for cooperatively developed PBL experiences. In an elementary school, such curriculum mapping can be a terrific way of bringing to light the sort of gaps and duplications that occur when teachers don't talk. After mapping out the curriculum as a school faculty, teachers are much better prepared to identify the "big ideas" that they want their students to encounter. Problem-based learning is ideal for those "big ideas."

Connections among Problems

As you are selecting problems, one of the tacit considerations you will make is how to connect problems to one another and to other aspects of the curriculum (Hmelo, 1998). As indicated in Chapter 1, some courses are organized so that all learning is done through PBL. Other courses are organized along a "post-hole" model (Stepien & Gallagher, 1993), whereby key PBL experiences anchor other learning experiences. This model is the one employed in the Integrated Secondary Teacher Education Program (I-STEP) at Northern Arizona University (Figure 14.3). Typically, the post-hole model allows teachers to use some problem-based learning without completely revising their curricula.

The post-hole model used in I-STEP works as follows. The conceptual framework of I-STEP focuses on five "habits of mind" that future teachers use to examine each issue they encounter in their professional education. Five areas of focus ask students to consider the *learners,* the *context* of the environment, the *curriculum, assessment,* and instructional *methods.* Thus, if the focus issue for the week is the organization of schools, I-STEP students examine each of the five habits of mind in relation to the question of organizations.

Post-hole problems highlight these areas as well. However, the nature of real-life problems is such that there is inevitably overlap among the focal points. The problem of Andy's IEP (Chapter 3, "What Should We Do about Andy?") has special emphasis on considering the learner. Of course, dealing with this problem demands an exploration of instructional methods, curriculum, and assessment to a lesser degree. The preparation of future secondary teachers is enhanced by the post-hole problems that interact with the habits of mind indicated in Figure 14.3.

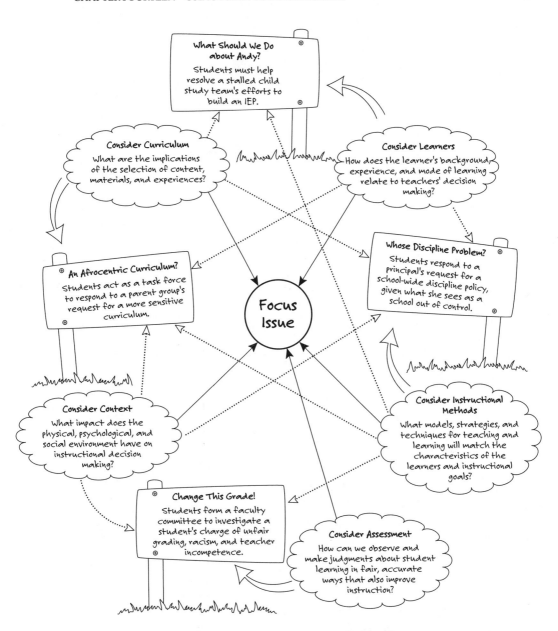

What Should We Do about Andy?
Students must help resolve a stalled child study team's efforts to build an IEP.

Consider Curriculum
What are the implications of the selection of content, materials, and experiences?

Consider Learners
How does the learner's background, experience, and mode of learning relate to teachers' decision making?

An Afrocentric Curriculum?
Students act as a task force to respond to a parent group's request for a more sensitive curriculum.

Focus Issue

Whose Discipline Problem?
Students respond to a principal's request for a school-wide discipline policy, given what she sees as a school out of control.

Consider Context
What impact does the physical, psychological, and social environment have on instructional decision making?

Consider Instructional Methods
What models, strategies, and techniques for teaching and learning will match the characteristics of the learners and instructional goals?

Change This Grade!
Students form a faculty committee to investigate a student's charge of unfair grading, racism, and teacher incompetence.

Consider Assessment
How can we observe and make judgments about student learning in fair, accurate ways that also improve instruction?

FIGURE 14.3   I-STEP Habits of Mind Connected to "Post-Hole" Problems

One approach to making connections among PBL experiences, whether in a single classroom or in an interdisciplinary context, is to develop a concept map of the relationship of PBL experiences to the flow of the course and the "big ideas" of the course. A generic map is provided in Figure 14.4. It is not necessary to have the complete picture to implement a PBL experience. In fact, success with one

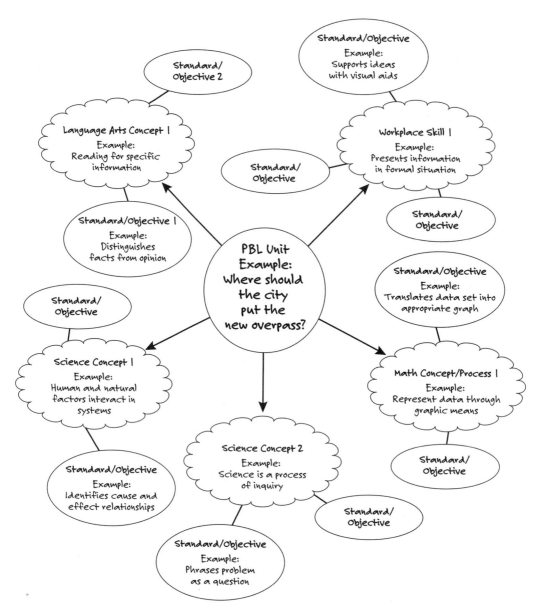

FIGURE 14.4   Concept Map for Course Connections with Examples

experience will often lead teachers to create more PBL units, which then demand attention to the connections among units. A series of fragmented PBL units, though engaging, will not benefit students as much as a carefully designed progression of experiences.

PRESENTING THE PROBLEM SITUATION

You have selected a problem that is worthwhile and now you need to develop it into an experience for your students. One of your early considerations ought to be how you will present the problematic situation.

Even before this, you would do well to recall that for most students, the learning experience in PBL is not like typical school learning. That is, for many students, learning has been a matter of finding out what the teacher wants and then doing some memorization. For students who have been successful in this traditional model, PBL will be uncomfortable. Recall some of the activities from Chapter 2 that helped prepare you for your work as a PBL student. These can be readily adapted to K–12 learners. For example, you would do well to have your students role-play confronting a student who does not do his or her share of the work before that situation actually arises. For many elementary students, such role playing helps children practice under safe conditions the skills that they need for the changing expectations about how to interact with others.

Assuming you prepare your students to be successful in PBL, you still must introduce each problem to them. This step of the process is well worth some extra thought. In their book, *Understanding by Design,* Wiggins and McTighe (1998) present a helpful acronym for judging the quality of a unit of instruction: WHERE. Briefly, the *W* stands for where are we going and why, the *H* stands for a hook to get the students' attention, the *E* stands for engaging instruction that will equip and enable students to perform, the *R* stands for reflection, and the final *E* stands for exhibit and evaluate. For the purposes of presenting the problem situation, the hook is of greatest importance.

Wiggins and McTighe (1998) speak of several types of hooks. A teacher can present students with a puzzling situation that demands explanation; a teacher can present students with a provocative question or an anomaly; the teacher can provide a story or puzzle, a far-out theory, or a role play. In some respects, the hook is similar to what Alfred North Whitehead (1929) referred to as the "romance" stage of instruction (his three stages were romance, precision, and generalization). We need to create a sense of romance and excitement.

Torp and Sage (1998) use the phrase "meet the problem" to describe the students' first encounter in a PBL unit. The personal connection suggested by "meet the problem" is appropriate—a metaphor that reminds us of meeting a new person. It suggests we will just get at the edges of a whole new relationship, and that there is much more to come.

Perhaps your problem could be best introduced by orally reading a brief, engaging passage, such as a news report (actual or simulated) of a controversial event. Teachers sometimes show brief video clips, such as a scene in which nonviolent protestors are confronted by angry and violent police. Do not show the three-hour version of *Gandhi* to hook students into a problem on the role of public protest! Some teachers actually create simulated news reports for videotaped introductions; some teachers use graphics, such as a photograph of a crime scene. You might have a colleague or an older student role-play a company executive to inspire the children. Whatever means you choose, remember your purpose: to hook students by engaging their curiosity. Introducing the problem must create some sense of mystery or urgency, inviting students to dig deeper. The hook must lead to questions, not answers. Figure 14.5 provides a means for planning how you will introduce your problem.

FIGURE 14.5   Planning to Meet the Problem

PROBLEM	INTRODUCTORY ACTIVITY	MATERIALS NEEDED
Example: Whose Bones Are These? (An interdisciplinary examination of competing claims at an archeological dig.)	Read newspaper account of adolescent skate-boarders who discovered ancient skeleton on Flagstaff's east side. After discussion, provide first problem document, the letter from the farmer who discovered the bones while plowing.	Newspaper article (*Arizona Daily Sun*) Problem document: farmer's letter.

"AUTHENTIC" DOCUMENTS AND ARTIFACTS

A crucial element of your PBL unit, both at the introductory stage and for the students' determination of what the problem is and how they will inquire into it, is the set of authentic documents or artifacts that students will access. One of the most important tasks for the designer is to assemble or create these documents.

In order to achieve a comprehensive collection of such artifacts a teacher must plan carefully at the outset of the design process. Creating a list of the needed documents and artifacts at the outset helps organize the efforts of a problem designer; when PBL units are designed collaboratively, such a list allows for a distribution of labor.

The documents needed for the "What Should We Do about Andy?" problem (Chapter 3) are listed in Figure 14.6 as a model for planning. Notice that each document must develop some component of the problem, further student inquiry, or stimulate critical and creative thinking. Following this example, there is a blank planning chart (Figure 14.7).

While all the documents in the student study team problem were simulated, it is conceivable that the problem developer could have used actual documents, such as an actual psychoeducational evaluation (with the identity removed). Obviously, to use actual documents, one must seek permission and preserve the confidentiality of the document's originator. For this reason, it is often more efficient to model documents after existing ones, but to create artifacts that are uniquely suited to the problem situation. Of course, you must be sure to use only artifacts that are appropriate to the developmental stage and skills of your students.

For many problems, documents are not the only appropriate artifacts. In the archeological problem referred to above, students actually visited a dig, which teachers had "salted" with artifacts. Photographs, audiotapes, broken furniture, data tables, polluted water samples, police drawings, and cartoons are just a sample of the limitless array of items that may be useful to engage students and to induce inquiry.

Another consideration in your artifact planning is the timing of the students' encounter with each document or artifact. It is sometimes appropriate for students to receive all the documents they will be provided at the outset. At other times, it is appropriate to provide documents on an as-needed basis. For example, you may want to disrupt patterns of thinking in the student solution groups. If you find that the students are not giving enough attention to a particular issue as they seek solutions, instead of telling them to redirect their inquiry, you might provide them with another problem document that brings this issue to the surface explicitly. You can build into your plans that after a certain amount of time investigating a problem such as transportation in a national park, you will "leak" an internal park document that reveals crucial information designed to have students broaden their search. (You might even consider leaking contradictory documents, where students must make decisions about credibility.) After all, it is often the case in "real life" that new information comes to light in the midst of a problem-solving process.

FIGURE 14.6   Document Planning for "What Should We Do about Andy?" Problem

DOCUMENT/ ARTIFACT	PURPOSE	SPECIAL CONSIDERATIONS	DEVELOPER
Andy's latest Individualized Education Plan (IEP)	Demonstrate form of IEP and include some ambiguities.	Include information from the psycho-educational assessment completed by the school psychologist	dk
Statement from Andy's mother about his placement	Identify mother's perspective and establish questions about home life.	Demonstrate frustration with working in system.	dk
Statement from one of Andy's teachers	Show teacher perspective, including reaction to SST.	Details on behavior should appear.	dk
Statement from Andy's school counselor	Establish contradictory position to teacher, including suggestion that teachers aren't fulfilling their obligations.	Establish sympathy for Andy.	dk
Statement from the assistant principal in charge of discipline	Provide disciplinarian's view of Andy.	Raise questions about wisdom of law, but set limits.	dk
Progress reports filed by Andy's math and social studies teachers.	Show format teachers may be asked to follow; also demonstrate varying perspectives on one child.	Be sure that there is disagreement in the view of Andy.	dk
Andy's grade transcript from 6th and 7th grades	Show progress over time; establish context of performance.	Show a general downward trend.	dk
Copy of the King Middle School daily schedule	Allow for possible variations; shows teachers' "typical" schedule.	Demonstrate flexibility options in schedule (blocks, advisory period)	dk

FIGURE 14.7   Planning Chart for Creating/Selecting Documents and Artifacts

DOCUMENT/ARTIFACT	PURPOSE	SPECIAL CONSIDERATIONS	DEVELOPER

RESOURCES

In planning for a PBL unit, a teacher must be sure to provide students with access to the resources necessary to solve the problem. One of the primary appeals of PBL is that this approach to learning helps students learn to inquire, to research, to seek answers. Especially in the early encounters with PBL, teachers should be certain that there are ample resources available for students to use in their inquiry.

Teachers do well to connect with other professionals in their schools and communities in order to build up a list of resources. The teacher-librarian, for example, is a central resource. Teacher-librarians generally delight in helping their colleagues structure student investigations, and often a teacher-librarian will seek sources even outside the school library and media center to assist in this process. Be sure to present your ideas to this colleague early in the process.

Other staff members will have areas of expertise to help you out, also. For example, you may find a counselor or administrator who has a hobby related to your problem. You do not necessarily need to have this person appear as a guest speaker, but you may encourage students to ask questions of your expert peers.

The Internet and e-mail contacts with other students and professionals are terrific resources for your students. Indeed, in the context of inquiring into a problem, learning Internet skills has a purpose that makes the learning more meaningful. The important question to ask yourself is this: Are there resources available to allow my students to inquire into this problem? If not, you should seriously reconsider developing the unit at this time. However, you may want to request resources to allow you to implement the unit later.

FRAMING THE SOLUTION AND ASSESSMENT

As indicated earlier, you should provide students with the parameters for their solution when you have them meet the problem. However, thinking through the issue of assessment in problem-based learning is a crucial component of creating effective and enduring experiences for your students. In fact, Wiggins and McTighe (1998) make a case that one of the most important shifts a teacher needs to make is to move from *thinking like an activity designer* to *thinking like an assessor*. An activity designer focuses on what students will do; an assessor focuses on what evidence will demonstrate that students have understood the targeted learning.

From the beginning of the design process, then, a teacher must pay careful attention to the final performance or task that will allow students to demonstrate their understanding. This final performance must be both authentic and valid. That is, the performance must fit within the context established by the problem. It would make no sense, for example, to have students work on solving a transportation problem over which the city council has jurisdiction and to write a paper to their teacher. The appropriate and authentic context for their solution is a presentation to a city council. At the same time, the solution must provide opportunities for valid assessment. In the above example, if students are solving a transportation problem that is designed (with embedded targets) to help them learn about city government, data collection and analysis, and presentation skills, the final assessment ought to make judgments about students' achievements in those areas, and not simply whether the students talked to three residents and charted a traffic flow. Both authenticity and validity are important.

Assessing student learning, a topic that goes well beyond the scope of this book, involves developing sensitivity to both intended and unintended outcomes. Thus, it is essential that the problem developer consider what objectives or outcomes a student will achieve through the PBL experience. The notion of embedded targets is crucial here. The problem designer selects and creates problems that are connected to important student learning outcomes. At the same time, given the flexibility of this approach and the importance of student control, assessment in PBL needs to allow for learning outside of the intended outcomes.

A good starting point for thinking about assessment is to return to the connection between a PBL unit and the curricular mandate. If, for example, your rationale for using PBL involves helping children understand "science as inquiry," that is clearly one of the big ideas that you should assess in the course of the unit. The design task is to make certain that any final performance includes opportunities for students to demonstrate how they used science as inquiry and that any rubric used to judge student performance includes this important outcome.

Consider your experience with the problem concerning the organization of an advanced math program at the middle school (Chapter 5). This problem asked your group to become a team of educators, charged with looking into a parent group's opposition to the school's plan to reorganize how math would be delivered at the school. Originally, the charge to reorganize came from the school principal, but since opposition went beyond his authority, the school board became involved. The solution, then, must be delivered in the form of a presentation to this same school board. Compare the intended outcomes and the sample rubric for assessing the team presentations (Figure 14.8). What is left out? How could this rubric be improved?

Clearly the assessment suggested by the rubric in Figure 14.8 does not fully address the outcomes listed there. This implies that the problem designer should either revisit the assessment rubric or expand the assessment to include other perspectives—and this is the preferable solution. Assessment in PBL must be carefully designed so that students have a variety of means to demonstrate their achievement of outcomes. Of course, it is wise to focus your work so that as an assessor, you are not looking for too many outcomes at any one time. Sometimes a final assessment is sufficient, but more often, the problem designer should consider assessment from various perspectives and through various means. For example, one useful means to assess student progress in a PBL experience is to have students respond to a prompt in the solution-generating stage. Your instructor may have asked you to complete such an assessment. An example comes from a PBL experience on teaming directed to secondary teachers. This problem asks learners to operate as part of a consulting firm that is making a recommendation about team organization to a large high school. Midway through the problem,

FIGURE 14.8   Learner Objectives and Sample Assessment Rubric for the Math Makes Tracks Problem

Learning Objectives for the Problem

- Understand theories of curriculum development
- Adapt curriculum according to social, philosophical, political, ethical, and historical contexts
- Select appropriate teaching methods for particular contexts
- Appreciate collaboration with peers
- Demonstrate respect for diversity in schools
- Understand governance of schools and teacher's role
- Demonstrate skills in appropriate communication
- Understand strategies for grouping students

Sample Rubric for Evaluating Oral Presentations

- **4 OUTSTANDING:** All members of the group participated actively in the presentation. The problem was clearly and appropriately defined. Solution presented is supported by three or more "expert" resources, with the research clearly tied to the proposals offered. The solution is realistic and reasonable. Community concerns are addressed, though not necessarily as each interest group would like. "Professionalism" is evident in the group's presentation (through language, supporting documents, presence).

- **3 STRONG:** The presentation may have unequally distributed participation. The problem addressed is clear, if only by implication. Experts are cited in the solution, but may not be explained in a manner appropriate to the audience. The solution is reasonable, though it may not take practical realities (e.g., cost, teacher time) into account. Community concerns are addressed, though not necessarily as each interest group would like. "Professionalism" is inconsistent, with presenters adopting more of a "university classroom" than "practitioner" style.

- **2 ACCEPTABLE:** Participation is not equal, but all group members make some contribution. The problem addressed seems relevant, but it is not clearly identified for the audience. Use of expert resources is vague or superficial. The solution presented has some reasonable elements, but has one or more glaring inconsistencies or unrealistic components. Community concerns may not be adequately addressed (i.e., it may ignore key interest groups). The presentation lacks real-world professionalism, taking on the nature of a course presentation.

- **1 WEAK:** Participation is evidently not equal; some members may dominate while others are uninvolved. The problem is not defined, and it is difficult to connect the solution to a specific problem. The solution presented is unrealistic, inappropriate, or detrimental. Connections to established authorities may be missing or so superficial that the citations do not support the solution. Community concerns may not be addressed. "Professionalism" is lacking in the presentation style, support, and/or interactions of the group.

instructors may provide learners with the following prompt, which is a simulated in-progress evaluation by a supervisor:

> The work of this particular CCI team can be characterized as aimless at best. The team has no means of maintaining member or team accountability. The operating procedures are haphazard and unproductive. I find no evidence of progress toward making a defensible recommendation to the Watertown School Board. Indeed, the very reputation of the company (CCI) is threatened by the quality of "work" produced by this team. I suspect that any single consultant could have progressed to the same extent as this team. Perhaps these questionable results are as much an indictment of the CCI move to a team structure as of the members of this particular team. Recommendation: Disband this team and re-assign the contract before it is too late.

Learners are given an opportunity to respond to the criticism of their team, which invites them to engage in self-assessment of their progress. Such ongoing assessments allow the teacher to make more defensible judgments about student learning as it relates to a variety of outcomes. Thus, PBL designers should think of assessment as ongoing and multiple rather than merely as a final judgment. In your work with younger students, consider how you might provide similar opportunities to assess progress along the way. A planning chart for assessment purposes is provided in Figure 14.9.

FIGURE 14.9   Planning Chart for Assessment Activities

ASSESSMENT MEANS	RELATION TO OUTCOMES	PLACE IN SEQUENCE AND FORMAT
Example: Oral presentation to school board.	Allows students to synthesize understanding of key curriculum concepts and to simulate important format for school decision making.	At the end of the problem; create rubric.

Whatever assessment a problem designer creates should include opportunities for learners to reflect on their experiences. Bridges and Hallinger (1992; 1995) use problem "talk back" sheets to structure student responses to a problem. These talk back forms serve both as a means for the students to process their experiences metacognitively and as a means for the instructor to assess the problem and improve it for future use. Similar to talk back forms, this book has provided questions for reflection that are designed to encourage students to deepen their understanding of the important issues raised in each problem and to consider their own development as professionals. As you design your problem assessments, consider how you will provide students with opportunities to reflect on the problem and problem-solving process.

GUIDING THE PROCESS: TUTOR OR TEACHER?

The challenge teachers face once the design of a PBL unit is completed is to redefine their role. Often accustomed to acting as the dispenser of knowledge, a teacher must rethink this role in order to be effective in the problem-based learning experience. Teachers must see themselves as facilitators of learning, tutors of student groups, rather than as providers of answers (Hmelo & Ferrari, 1997). As Shelagh Gallagher (1997) points out, a move to PBL means a change in curriculum (organizing around problems) *and* instruction (relying more on questioning and discussion). Several moves can help the new teacher in assuming this role.

Process Guide.   With the performance end clearly in mind, a teacher has the advantage of perspective. Whereas students have often been socialized into a mentality that sees school work as plodding from one unconnected thing to another, teachers can see the big picture. With this comprehensive view, the facilitator in PBL sees clearly where the process is headed, and can assist groups of students by reminding them of where they are in the process. Ask your students if they have completed the three-part thinking structure: What do we know? What do we need to know? How are we going to find out? Help the problem-solving teams understand where they are in their process and how they can progress to the next level.

Metacognitive Questioning.   The temptation of teachers is to give answers—and if we can resist giving answers, our next favorite ploy is to ask questions that lead directly to answers. Thus, teachers are used to asking cognitive questions, such as "What are the three branches of government?" Problem-based learning, however, aims at having students themselves learn to ask the right kinds of questions. Teachers need to learn to ask *metacognitive* questions (Gallagher, 1997; Hmelo & Ferrari, 1997) that will permit students to take charge of learning. Instead of asking for the names of the branches of government, a good facilitator will ask, "What questions do we need to ask next? Where can we find answers to these questions?" It takes a great deal of discipline for teachers to stay consistent in keeping the focus on metacognitive questioning, but students profit as they learn to question.

Student Relations.   Managing student interactions is always a challenge to teachers, but this is heightened in problem-based learning. Now, instead of a model of individualistic learning (each student's success is independent from every other student's success), students are placed in a cooperative structure where success depends on each member of the group functioning together. As facilitator, the teacher must lead reflection on effective ways of relating to other group members, successful means of heading off and solving conflict. Teachers should maintain a check on the content of the problem, but just as important, teachers must stay proactive in maintaining the relationships among group members. When student groups are working together, the teacher must maintain an awareness of the progress and difficulties of the various groups. Remind the groups of what they learned through role-playing, and keep them focused on their ultimate outcome: the successful solution of the problem.

Learning Issues.   Throughout the PBL process, but especially at the end, the teacher can enhance student learning by reminding pupils that the issues go beyond the particular problem at hand. The teacher, who has the vantage point that permits a view of the whole curriculum, can help students see the issues that are represented in a given problem in order that the student learning does not become so context-bound that no meaningful connections emerge. The power of PBL is in its relevant context, but there comes a time when you must move beyond that context. After the students have worked out a solution to this particular problem with transportation (or animal populations or urban blight or the lockers in the school), it is important to focus on the general principles that one could learn through the process. Guiding student reflection is one way that facilitators work toward transfer of knowledge (Hmelo & Ferrari, 1997).

TOO MUCH FOR BEGINNING TEACHERS?

A beginning teacher might reasonably argue now that it is too early to learn these complex roles. After all, one might say, I have just figured out how to do an effective lecture, how to build learning centers, and how to conduct an interesting demonstration, why confuse me with another way of teaching? This is a legitimate question. Perhaps the most important response to this concern is a perspective on learning rather than teaching. As a *learner* of teaching practices, should one be presented with a hierarchy of models, each dependent on mastery of the one before it? That is, should a student of teaching master the lecture before proceeding to the demonstration before proceeding to concept attainment and so on? Is this how one learns best?

The best evidence we have now is that learning complex behaviors and concepts does not proceed this way. For example, instead of having young children master the sentence level of writing before going on to the paragraph, and mastering the paragraph before attempting the story, and so on, best practice lets students play with the whole form right from the start. Young writers create stories even before they are certain of what constitutes a sentence, and as they progress through their education, these young writers eventually encounter the components to writing a story.

In a similar way, beginning teachers need an interplay of mastery and experimentation. There is no harm in learning how to organize and deliver an effective explanation; indeed, this would seem like an essential feature of a good teacher. At the same time, the lecture is effective for only certain kinds of learning and in certain contexts, just as direct instruction is effective in some situations, cooperative learning is effective in others, and so on. For a beginning teacher to have the proper perspective on what it means to be a teacher, he or she should have a broad repertoire of teaching techniques. Learning to be a facilitator in the PBL model is on a par with learning to guide a direct instruction lesson; it is not what follows. Consider the paradox expressed in this statement: "less teaching can yield better learning" (Wiggins & McTighe, 1998). If our ultimate goal is student learning, we need to know more about guiding students toward that goal.

PUT IT ALL TOGETHER

You have examined problem-based learning through a variety of lenses by now. In Part I of this book, you received a fairly traditional exposition of the process and how it is being used. In Part II, you experienced the perspective of a learner who encounters PBL as a means to learn important knowledge and skills for a specific purpose—becoming a competent, well-rounded member of an occupational community. In Part III, you reflected on the process and saw how it can be broken into component parts so that you could design PBL experiences for your own teaching.

It is now time to put it together by creating a PBL unit that you could use with your future students. If possible, you may find this experience particularly valuable if you work with a colleague whose expertise complements your own. Whether you do so alone or collaboratively, consider how your unit will address the following questions:

- How does the problem connect to the curriculum and embed important learning targets?
- How do students meet the problem initially?
- What problem documents will you select or create for the students?
- What resources will you make available?
- How will you structure time so that you can facilitate student inquiry and effective group relations?
- What parameters will you place on the solution and how will you assess student work?
- How will you organize reflection on the experience so that students increase their metacognitive skills and you learn about ways of improving your unit?

The most useful format for creating such units at this point is to write up your PBL unit with enough detail that a well-informed peer could use the unit in his or her own classroom. Remember throughout the process that a good PBL unit will function like a framework. That is, you will give a basic shape to your students' experience, but if the PBL unit is a good one, the students will take it in directions you hadn't even anticipated. The bare framework you provide them will become an opportunity for them to build a unique structure of learning.

And once you've completed such a unit, sharing it with colleagues for feedback is the next logical step. By immersing yourself in a variety of PBL units that you and your peers have created, you will have expanded your vision of what can be done through this model.

When you use a PBL unit in your class, you can anticipate that it will be exciting and interesting for the students, but also awkward and a little risky—and resisted by some. Remember that learners take time to feel comfortable in a new format, just as teachers do. Be patient with the adjustment involved, and persist even through this discomfort. The opportunities you can provide for authentic, meaningful learning for your students are virtually unlimited. Given time for you and them to practice, a healthy environment where you can process your experience with peers and mentors, and a willingness to break some molds in the predictable routines of elementary schools, you can create a powerful and memorable learning community. You will inspire learners, and you will be a model learner yourself.

REFERENCES

Association for Supervision and Curriculum Development. (1997a). *Problem-based learning: Designing problems for learning* [Videorecording]. Alexandria, VA: Association for Supervision and Curriculum Development.

Association for Supervision and Curriculum Development. (1997b). *Problem-based learning: Using problems to learn* [Videorecording]. Alexandria, VA: Association for Supervision and Curriculum Development.

Atkinson, P., & Delamont, S. (1984). Mock-ups and cock-ups: The stage-management of guided discovery instruction. In A. Hargreaves & P. Woods (Eds.), *Classrooms & staffrooms: The sociology of teachers & teaching* (pp. 36–47). Milton Keynes, UK: Open University.

Barrows, H. S. (1996). Problem-based learning in medicine and beyond: A brief overview. In L. Wilkerson & W. H. Gijselaers (Eds.), *Bringing problem-based learning to higher education: Theory and practice* (Vol. 68, pp. 3–12). San Francisco: Jossey-Bass.

Bridges, E. M., & Hallinger, P. (1992). *Problem based learning for administrators.* Eugene, OR: ERIC Clearinghouse on Educational Management.

Bridges, E. M., & Hallinger, P. (1995). *Implementing problem based learning in leadership development.* Eugene, OR: ERIC Clearinghouse on Educational Management.

Delisle, R. (1997). *How to use problem-based learning in the classroom.* Alexandria, VA: Association for Supervision and Curriculum Development.

Gallagher, S. A. (1997). Problem-based learning: Where did it come from, what does it do, and where is it going? *Journal for the Education of the Gifted, 20*(4), 332–362.

Glasgow, N. A. (1997). *New curriculum for new times: A guide to student-centered, problem-based learning.* Thousand Oaks, CA: Corwin.

Hmelo, C. E. (1998). Problem-based learning: Effects on the early acquisition of cognitive skill in medicine. *The Journal of the Learning Sciences, 7*(2), 173–208.

Hmelo, C. E., & Ferrari, M. (1997). The problem-based learning tutorial: Cultivating higher order thinking skills. *Journal for the Education of the Gifted, 20*(4), 401–422.

Jacobs, H. H. (1997). *Mapping the big picture: Integrating curriculum & assessment K-12.* Alexandria, VA: Association for Supervision and Curriculum Development.

Stepien, W., & Gallagher, S. (1993). Problem-based learning: As authentic as it gets. *Educational Leadership, 50*(7), 25–28.

Torp, L., & Sage, S. (1998). *Problems as possibilities: Problem-based learning for K-12 education.* Alexandria, VA: Association for Supervision and Curriculum Development.

Whitehead, A. N. (1929). *The aims of education and other essays.* New York: Free Press.

Wiggins, G., & McTighe, J. (1998). *Understanding by design.* Alexandria, VA: Association for Supervision and Curriculum Development.

INDEX